Superbrands®

An insight into some of Britain's strongest brands 2012

Superbrands.uk.com

Chief Executive
Ben Hudson

Managing Editor
Laura Hill

Brand Liaison Directors
Liz Silvester
Daren Thomas

Authors
Jane Bainbridge
Karen Dugdale

Brand Liaison Manager
Heidi Smith

Proofreader
Anna Haynes

Head of Accounts
Will Carnochan

Designer
Paul Lynan

Also available from Superbrands in the UK:
CoolBrands® 2011/12 ISBN: 978-0-9565334-2-5

To order further books, email brands@superbrands.uk.com
or call 020 7079 3310.

Published by
Superbrands (UK) Ltd
22–23 Little Portland Street
London
W1W 8BU

Printed in Italy

ISBN: 978-0-9565334-3-2

CONTENTS

Key   Ⓑ Business Superbrands
      © Consumer Superbrands

Endorsements

John Noble
Director
British Brands Group

The businesses featured in these pages demonstrate the versatility of branding. Building strong emotional and rational connections with end users – whether consumers or businesses – has never been more important; they give stand out, a solid reason for people to purchase, and keep copiers at bay.

Here you will certainly find the usual suspects; brands we have grown up with and love such as Andrex®, Dulux, Fairy and MALTESERS®. But you will also find venues such as ExCeL London and the Royal Albert Hall, professional institutions such as the RIBA, RICS and ICAEW, and academia in the form of Warwick Business School. Building and sustaining a strong reputation is crucial in so many areas of business. It is not just about being competitive, it is also about survival.

Brands are vital to the UK's growth and competitiveness, which is why they are worth fighting for and why we are delighted to support this latest showcase.

Suki Thompson
Chairman
Marketing Society

One of the things that you see demonstrated when reading through this latest edition of Superbrands is the high quality contribution of marketing people, as well as those who work alongside them, in respect of sustaining the value and reputation of a particular brand.

This is no mean achievement in an environment where the odds seem to be stacked against brands – due to prevailing economic conditions and a growing propensity for consumers to 'fight back' against brands by utilising the burgeoning communication tools at their disposal.

I applaud all those who continue to brilliantly deploy their skills to keep the brands between the covers of this annual both famous and, above all, highly relevant in conditions that often seem against all odds.

Andrew Harvey
Chair
The Chartered Institute
of Marketing

The Chartered
Institute of Marketing

As social media continues its inexorable expansion, and in the wake of a year that seems to have been dominated by the start-up, the idea of a brand seems to have taken a beating. Now, more than ever, it's possible to start a company one year and sell it for millions the next. Yet the case studies in this book show us clearly that, in a rapidly changing world, brands still have an emotive power that is beyond question and beyond competition. As The Chartered Institute of Marketing celebrates 100 years as the leading professional body for marketers, it's comforting to know that established brands retain a vital edge over the competition.

If the loyalty, passion and excitement that brands inspire is common across all sectors, the superb range of examples in this book provides an invaluable guide to cutting-edge approaches to brand management, which are inspiring in their innovation and diversity. There is plenty here to learn from, and to aspire to, and the collection is essential reading for anyone working with brands today.

Professor Derek Holder
Founder &
Managing Director
The Institute of Direct
and Digital Marketing

the institute
of direct
and digital
marketing

This year there's a special resonance in the IDM's endorsement of Superbrands – with the Institute having recently undergone a major rebrand itself after 24 years. The new IDM could be viewed as a simple change of livery and a revamped corporate identity, but for us – and our customers – it goes much deeper. As any branding exercise should.

A brand is an essence, a reputation, a representation of a set of standards valued by its advocates. The brands you'll find within the pages of this book have all elevated themselves above others in their market through their uniqueness, their quality and a trust amongst customers and fans that they will deliver, time and again, the experience that's expected of them.

For all of us at the IDM, our brand represents what we are and how we operate. The power of a Superbrand is that, for its customers, that brand often represents what they are too.

About Superbrands

First published in 1995, the Superbrands books investigate some of the strongest consumer and B2B brands in Britain and establish how they have managed to achieve such phenomenal success. The 2012 Annual explores the history, development and achievements of some of these much-loved brands, with each case study providing valuable insights into their branding strategy and resulting work.

Brands do not apply or pay to be considered for Superbrands status. Rather, the accolade is awarded to the country's strongest brands following a rigorous and independent selection process; full details are provided on page 158.

This publication forms part of a wider programme that pays tribute to Britain's strongest brands. The programme is administered by Superbrands (UK) Ltd and also features Superbrands.uk.com, a national newspaper supplement, and editorial features throughout the year. The company also hosts regular events that promote networking amongst senior brand owners.

Superbrands was launched in London in 1995 and is now a global business operating in more than 55 countries worldwide. Further details can be found at Superbrands.uk.com.

The Superbrands Award Stamps

Brands that have been awarded Superbrands status and participate in the programme are licensed to use the Superbrands Award Stamps. These powerful endorsements provide evidence to existing and potential consumers, media, employees and investors of the exceptional standing that these brands have achieved.

Quality

Reliability

Distinction

It's The Little Things

Andrex® has been one of the nation's most loved brands for 70 years. With a strong heritage in care, Andrex® understands that it's the little things that can make a difference and continues to produce high quality toilet tissue with outstanding value. Embodying the brand's core values, the Andrex® Puppy is one of the UK's most recognisable brand icons. Having made his TV debut in 1972, the iconic Puppy is celebrating his 40th birthday in 2012.

Brand History

▶ **1942:** Andrex® toilet roll launches.

▶ **1972:** The first Puppy advert airs on TV.

▶ **1978:** Andrex® is granted a Royal Warrant of Appointment.

▶ **1992:** Andrex® is first to market with moistened toilet tissue.

▶ **2001:** Andrex® Aloe Vera launches as the industry's first premium toilet tissue, followed in 2005 by Quilts, and Shea Butter in 2009.

▶ **2010:** In November Andrex® launches a new communications platform, 'It's The Little Things', along with a 21st century makeover for the Andrex® Puppy.

▶ **2011:** Andrex® Limited Collection is launched, reflecting changing interior design trends.

▶ **2012:** In a double celebration for the brand, Andrex® reaches its 70th year and the Puppy celebrates his 40th birthday.

Market

Toilet tissue is one of the UK's largest grocery categories and is worth more than £1 billion. Continual product innovation and creativity ensure the category remains relevant and interesting.

Kimberly-Clark®, which owns the Andrex® brand, grew both its value and volume share of dry and moist tissue in 2011: most notably, value share increased by 2.5 per cent (Source: Nielsen October 2011).

The market is currently dominated by mainstream white products, which account for 58.9 per cent of volume (Source: Nielsen 2011). The premium sector continues to show strong volume growth at 2.7 per cent year-to-date, driven by luxury quilted and lotioned variants.

Product

Kimberly-Clark® strives to ensure that its products are of the highest quality, best value and relevant to consumers. As such, Andrex® offers the widest range of toilet tissue variants in the market.

Did You Know?

Andrex® is the UK's number one non-food brand (Source: The Grocer 2010).

Andrex® sells 29 rolls of toilet tissue every second. In a day, that equates to enough tissue to run around the earth twice.

Andrex® introduced its first coloured toilet tissue, Magnolia, in 1957.

The brand's white Mainline product remains its most popular, as a soft, strong and long product for the whole family. The range also features three coloured variants: Aqua, Natural Pebble and Pink Blossom.

Puppies On A Roll was launched in 2004 and for the first time the Puppy was embossed onto the sheet to create a playful product for all the family.

In reaction to the growth of premium segments across categories, Andrex® launched its own range in 2001. Toilet tissue enriched with Aloe Vera (later rebranded as Skin Kind) became the brand's first premium product. In 2005 Andrex® Quilts (rebranded as Gorgeous Comfort) launched to meet consumer desire for a toilet tissue with greater cushioning. Andrex® Shea Butter (rebranded as Touch Of Luxury) followed in 2009 and is the brand's most luxurious variant: the textured sheets are enriched with shea butter and the roll has a scented core.

2011 saw a key category launch that tapped into consumer interest in contemporary bathroom styles and interior design. Andrex® Limited Collection consists of two premium and unique variants: Bright & Bold and Subtle & Stylish. Each contains six different printed rolls, a selection of which is included at random within four-roll packs. The designs are updated every six months in line with interior design trends.

Andrex® Washlets, the brand's moistened toilet tissue, continues to drive incremental category growth. The lightly moistened, dermatologically tested and flushable wipes are designed for use after dry tissue for a cleaner feeling.

Achievements

Andrex® has been the toilet tissue market leader since 1961, growing by more than £20 million from 2010 to 2011. With a 33 per cent value share and 27.4 per cent volume share of the dry toilet roll market (Source: Nielsen 2011), its success is echoed in the plethora of product, packaging and advertising awards bestowed on the brand.

Accolades include Household Paper Product of the Year 2009 for Mainline; and Kids' Hygiene Product of the Year 2009 for Andrex® Kids. Shea Butter claimed the 2009 GRAMIA Packaging Award, with its Pour le Pup campaign winning the GRAMIA Best Consumer Press Award in the same year.

The brand's resonance with consumers has been utilised in numerous charity partnerships. CLIC Sargent, Teenage Cancer Trust, Guide Dogs for the Blind, Dogs for the Disabled, National Canine Defence League and Comic Relief have all benefited from the sale of limited edition soft toy Puppies in recent years.

Recent Developments

November 2010 saw Andrex® launch its new communications platform: 'It's The Little Things'. At the heart of everything the brand does, this key message demonstrates to consumers that Andrex® toilet tissue really is one of those little things in today's busy lifestyles that can make a difference.

As part of the campaign, the Puppy received its first makeover since 1972, with computer-generated technology giving consumers an insight into the Puppy's World. Further executions of 'It's The Little Things' and Puppy World were delivered in 2011 – most notably for the launch of Limited Collection – with more plans in place for the Puppy's 40th birthday celebrations in 2012.

Promotion

The brand's promotions evolve to keep pace with consumers' ever-changing needs and new communication channels. The Puppy's page on Facebook, for example, has nearly 300,000 active and engaged fans. As a renowned and much loved brand icon, the Puppy continues to embody the brand's core values and ensure that Andrex® is instantly recognisable.

The launch of Andrex® Limited Collection early in 2011 was supported by a through-the-line marketing campaign, with a television advert featuring the new Puppy in scenes that reflect the product's two variants. Andrex® Limited Collection not only demonstrates the brand's versatility but also allows it to capitalise on contemporary interior design trends.

Brand Values

As an icon, the Andrex® Puppy embodies the core values of the brand, from softness and strength, through to family, trust and care. The Puppy's 40th birthday represents a huge achievement for Andrex® – and is testament to the strength of the brand.

▶ **www.andrexpuppy.co.uk**

Did You Know?

Since 1972 there have been more than 140 TV adverts starring the Andrex® Puppy.

The Andrex® Puppy was voted Britain's favourite advertising icon by Marketing magazine.

One in 10 homes in the UK and Ireland owns an Andrex® Puppy cuddly toy, which equates to six million Puppies.

AUTOGLASS®

Autoglass® is a leading consumer automotive service brand, providing vehicle glass repairs and replacements to 1.5 million motorists every year. With the widest reaching auto glazing network in the UK and Ireland, Autoglass® has more than 100 branches nationwide and 1,300 mobile service units operating 24 hours a day, 365 days a year. Autoglass® is part of the Belron® group, operating in 33 countries and serving over 11 million motorists worldwide.

Market

Over the last 20 years, windscreens have evolved to play an integral role in modern automotive design and today's cars typically use 20 per cent more glass than in the 1980s. Windscreens can also incorporate complex technology such as rain sensors, wire heating, cameras and satellite navigation components. The latest BMW 3-Series, for example, has 10 variations and the current Ford Mondeo has 23. Specialist skill is required to ensure they are repaired and replaced to the highest safety standards and that's where Autoglass® excels. The company is the UK's market-leading auto glazing expert.

Product

Quite simply, Autoglass® fixes broken vehicle glass on any make, model or age of vehicle. The company operates a 'Repair First' philosophy ensuring that wherever possible, its technicians will repair a chipped windscreen rather than replace it so the existing seal doesn't have to be disturbed; a safe solution that saves time, money and is better for the environment.

If the damage is beyond repair, Autoglass® will replace the windscreen. It only uses glass manufactured to original equipment maker (OEM) standards, ensuring that each replacement windscreen is as good as the original and a perfect fit for the vehicle. It also uses one of the quickest drying bonding systems for safety and customer convenience. As part of its commitment to the environment, Autoglass® reprocesses any laminate screens it removes.

Appointments can be made by phone or online and customers can choose to take their vehicle into their local branch or arrange for one of the company's 1,300 mobile technicians to come to a location of their choice.

Did You Know?

Autoglass® doesn't just repair chipped windscreens; it has even repaired a chip on the viewing glass of the tiger compound at Glasgow Zoo.

The jingle used in the brand's Heroes adverts has been translated into 12 different languages and is now used by Belron® subsidiaries in 20 countries.

Achievements

Thanks to its focus on delivering a first-class service, Autoglass® was recognised by the Institute of Transport Management as Automotive Supplier of the Year in 2011. Other accolades include two National Training Awards, a Glass Training Ltd (GTL) Commitment to Training Award and the Insurance Times Training Award. In addition, Autoglass® holds the ISO 9001 standard for quality management and ISO 14001 for environmental management.

Because a windscreen accounts for 30 per cent of a vehicle's structural strength, Autoglass® places considerable emphasis on training its technicians to ensure every screen is fitted safely. It remains the only company in its industry to have achieved accredited status from Thatcham and the Institute of the Motor Industry (IMI) for its National Skills Centre in

Birmingham and its Startline Induction and Repair training programmes. Autoglass® was also the first to introduce the Automotive Technician Accreditation (ATA) scheme. Under the ATA, technicians work towards three accreditation levels dependent on knowledge, skills and experience, ultimately leading to Master Auto Glazing Technician status.

Recent Developments

In recent years Autoglass® has invested in innovative devices to ensure it continues to deliver work of the highest standard. The Ezi-Wire®, for example, helps technicians safely remove the glass from the windscreen and enables them to carry out their job both safely and professionally. New windscreen lifting and positioning devices such as the Lil' Buddy and the new Belron® 1-Tek® have delivered many benefits and encouraged more women to consider a career as an auto glazing technician; Autoglass® now employs 20 female technicians.

Autoglass® has also established a team of 'home workers' to provide greater flexibility for its customer contact centre workforce, enabling it to maintain call quality throughout peak periods of demand.

Promotion

Autoglass® became a household name in the 1990s after becoming the main sponsor of Chelsea Football Club. Since then it has invested in a number of high profile brand campaigns to ensure it remains at the forefront of motorists' minds.

In 2005 the Heroes radio campaign launched, using real Autoglass® technicians to explain the benefits of repairing windscreen chips. The campaign became the most successful in Autoglass® history, helping to boost brand recognition and drive contacts via the call centre and website up by 20 per cent. The campaign took double honours at the 2007

Media Week/GCap Radio Planning Awards, winning the award for Outstanding Campaign Above £250,000 and the Grand Prix for Most Outstanding Radio Planning. In 2008 it went on to win the Effectiveness Award for Campaign with Best Results.

In April 2008 the firm brought the award-winning radio concept to TV with a super heavyweight campaign. The advert showed real-life Autoglass® technician Gavin, the popular voice of the company's radio campaign, explaining the importance of getting windscreen chips repaired and highlighting the quality and safety benefits of the Autoglass® service.

The staff testimonial format of the Heroes campaign has been extended to feature a variety of technicians across radio and TV, including the first female face of the brand, Izzy. The Heroes are also featured on the Autoglass® technician vans, website and Facebook page.

Brand Values

The Autoglass® vision is to be the natural choice through valuing its customers' needs and delivering world-class service. Its brand values are: teamwork, improvement, care, excellence and trust.

▶ **www.autoglass.co.uk**

Did You Know?

During 2010, the Autoglass® 'Repair First' philosophy resulted in savings of around 14,500 tonnes of CO_2 equivalent emissions and more than 5,700 tonnes of waste glass.

Brand History

▶ **1972:** Autoglass Supplies Ltd is launched, providing mobile vehicle glass replacement across Northern England.

▶ **1982:** Autoglass Ltd becomes part of Belron®, the world's largest vehicle glass repair and replacement company, extending its UK service into all five continents.

▶ **1983:** Autoglass Ltd merges with Bedfordshire-based Windshields Ltd and becomes Autoglass Windshields, rebranding to simply Autoglass in 1987.

▶ **1990:** The windscreen repair service is launched.

▶ **1994:** Autoglass® becomes a registered trademark after a seven-year IP registration process.

▶ **2002:** Carglass Ireland rebrands to Autoglass®.

▶ **2005:** Autoglass® launches the Heroes radio campaign.

▶ **2006:** Lil' Buddy is introduced to the Autoglass® workforce.

▶ **2007:** Autoglass® becomes the first windscreen repair and replacement company to offer online booking at autoglass.co.uk.

▶ **2008:** Autoglass® launches its first ever TV adverts.

▶ **2009:** The Heroes campaign is extended to the website and outdoor advertising with the introduction of new van livery. Ezi-wire® is also introduced into the Autoglass® workforce.

▶ **2010:** The first female Autoglass® technician appears in the Heroes TV campaign and the brand sponsors the Sky Sports News bulletin. A Facebook page and Twitter presence also launch.

▶ **2011:** Autoglass® becomes one of the first service brands in the UK to utilise F-Commerce, with appointment booking via Facebook. The Belron® 1-Tek® is also introduced to the Autoglass® workforce.

The BBC is the world's best known broadcasting brand, offering the full range of programming from independent journalism to live music, arts and specialist factual programmes to ambitious drama and comedy, and outstanding children's content. BBC programmes are accessed via 10 UK-wide network television services, 10 national and 47 Nations and Regions radio stations, plus online and interactive services.

Market

Broadcasting is changing rapidly worldwide as technologies and markets converge, and as content and competition become increasingly global. The BBC recognises that it exists in an increasingly global marketplace, but through its partnership strategy aims to support UK public service broadcasting and the wider UK media sector.

Difficult economic and trading conditions continued in 2011, highlighting the opportunities and support that the BBC is able to offer to the media industry through its careful investment of the licence fee. It works with the big players such as ITV and Channel 4, through the digital terrestrial service Freeview – with independent producers on a range of programmes – and with the best of UK on-air and off-air talent across its portfolio.

In October 2010 it was agreed that the licence fee would be frozen until 2017 and that the BBC would take on new funding responsibilities for the World Service, S4C and BBC Monitoring. Under the banner of 'Delivering quality first', the proposals set out how the BBC can fulfill this settlement and deliver the highest quality programmes and services until the end of the Charter in 2017. A savings target of 20 per cent has been set with £145 million released for reinvestment.

Did You Know?

The BBC costs each licensed UK household just under 40 pence per day.

The BBC set up the first dedicated children's programme department more than 60 years ago – and Blue Peter has been a stalwart in its schedules for 54 of them.

Product

The BBC is primarily a creator of high quality content and programming on television, on radio and online, with a varied portfolio of major service brands including BBC One, BBC Two, BBC Three and BBC Four on television, while on radio the main terrestrial services – BBC Radio 1, 2, 3, 4 and 5 live – are complemented by the digital brands BBC Radio 1Xtra, 4 Extra, 5 live sports extra, 6 Music and Asian Network.

The BBC supports much of its output online; for example, ensuring children's shows are further enhanced by websites that encourage learning in a fun space. The bbc.co.uk website is a recognised brand leader in the UK and one of the most popular content sites in the world. It is also home to the popular BBC iPlayer.

Achievements

The BBC continues to claim a host of awards in recognition of its high quality programming. In 2011 these included 39 Royal Television Society Awards, 22 BAFTA Awards, 17 Broadcast Awards and 21 Gold Sony Awards. Since its launch, BBC iPlayer alone has received more than 35 marketing and technology awards.

In addition, the BBC maintained its Platinum ranking for 2010/11 in the Business in the Community Corporate Responsibility Index.

Recent Developments

The BBC has progressed its move to MediaCityUK and by spring 2012 more than 2,300 staff will be working in Salford.

BBC Breakfast, Children's, Sport, Radio 5 live, Learning and Future Media are all relocating, bringing with them some of the BBC's most famous shows, such as Match of the Day and Blue Peter.

Brand History

▶ **1922:** British Broadcasting Company (BBC) is formed by a group of leading wireless manufacturers.

▶ **1927:** The BBC gains its first royal charter, ensuring its independence from government, political and shareholder interference.

▶ **1953:** On 2nd June around 22 million people watch the Queen's coronation live on the BBC – a historic event that changes the course of television history.

▶ **1967:** BBC Two begins transmission of the first regular colour television service in Europe.

▶ **1980:** After 25 years, Children in Need becomes an event with a whole evening of dedicated programming – and raises £1 million for the first time.

▶ **1998:** BBC Choice, the first BBC digital TV channel, launches. It becomes BBC Three in 2003.

▶ **2007:** BBC iPlayer launches at Christmas and transforms media consumption in the UK, with 360 million views in its first three months.

▶ **2008:** The first full digital switchover takes place in Whitehaven, Cumbria.

▶ **2010:** BBC Television Centre, the world's first purpose-built television building, celebates its 50th anniversary.

▶ **2011:** The BBC marks the 75th anniversary of the first regular TV service broadcast from the BBC studios at Alexandra Palace, North London.

The move facilitates the creation of new partnerships with independent producers, cutting-edge digital companies and universities across the North of England.

Promotion

The trademark block letters of the BBC master brand are associated worldwide with values of quality, trust, independence, creativity and distinctiveness.

Subsidiary brand identities – for channels and services, or for specific events – are designed to build on those core values and to help audiences find the content they will enjoy through integrated communications campaigns.

In 2011, BBC Radio 5 live's 'Day in the Live' campaign was created to promote 5 live's positioning of getting 'straight to the heart of things'. A dedicated production team captured the best on-air moments as the day unfolded. A trail then aired the same evening to demonstrate how 5 live broadcasts award-winning news, sport and topical issues to a national audience.

The Teen Awards campaign aimed to take the BBC's key teenage event of the year and give full control to its teen audience. Under the 'You Make It' banner, teenagers were recruited to perform in the TV ad alongside Radio 1 DJs and the superstars from the event's line-up. It was complemented with posters in schools, interactive digital advertising and an extensive social media campaign. Views of the event have increased by more than five times year-on-year.

The BBC aims to tell stories that are unrivalled in terms of quality, depth and truth. The 'Original British Drama' campaign made a powerful statement about the collective of

drama content. The positioning was highly successful, with its emphasis on quality and Britishness a timely reminder that the licence fee is invested in UK creative industries.

Brand Values

The BBC exists to serve the public interest and to inform, educate and entertain audiences with programmes and services of high quality, originality and value. The BBC brand depends on the BBC's reputation to offer original and independent news, formal and informal learning to all age groups, and unique and innovative content not found elsewhere. The BBC is a supporter of, and showcase for, the best of British creativity.

▶ **www.bbc.co.uk**

bp

BP is one of the world's leading international oil and gas companies, providing its customers with fuel for transportation, energy for heat and light, retail services and petrochemicals products. The BP group operates across six continents; its products and services are delivered to customers in more than 70 countries through a range of internationally respected brands. Together, they have made BP the company it is today.

Market

BP's specific areas of business include exploration for and production of crude oil and natural gas; refining and marketing of oil products; manufacturing and marketing of petrochemicals; and integrated supply and trading. BP plays a significant role in defining the future of energy by developing lower carbon alternatives such as advanced biofuels.

Product

BP offers a diverse energy portfolio, producing energy resources for people on the road, at home and for business.

BP service stations provide trusted quality fuels and everyday convenience items, while Wild Bean Cafés provide food and coffee for on-the-go motorists. In addition to its own offering, BP has partnered with Marks & Spencer Simply Food at selected locations across the UK to provide customers with an even greater choice.

In 2010, BP Ultimate was relaunched as an improved fuel product that aims to keep petrol and diesel engines fitter and healthier than ever before. A new communications campaign supported the product refresh and featured a striking heart-shaped engine alongside the message: 'Looking after the heart of your car'.

The 'heart' campaign resonates with BP's wider strategy surrounding its partnership with the London 2012 Olympic and Paralympic Games. The analogy between the fuel athletes need to put into their body and the fuel they need for their car in order to ensure a strong performance is a key way of telling the BP Ultimate story.

Achievements

In 2008, BP won the bid to be the Official Oil and Gas Partner for the London 2012 Olympic and Paralympic Games. BP will play a central role, providing advanced fuels and engine oils for more than 5,000 official vehicles, as well as fuel for generators. BP is also London 2012's Sustainability Partner and the Official Carbon Offset Partner with Target Neutral, through which BP will help ticketed spectators offset their carbon footprint as they travel to the Games. As a Premier Partner of the London 2012 Cultural Olympiad and London 2012 Festival, BP is also working with the London 2012 Organising Committee (LOCOG) and arts and cultural partners to create programmes that will inspire millions of young people.

Did You Know?

BP is investing £200 million with partners to build a world scale bioethanol plant in Hull.

To date, BP has invested around £35 billion in the North Sea.

Recent Developments

BP is showcasing its advanced biofuels during the London 2012 Games on a retail site in Hammersmith, West London. The showcase

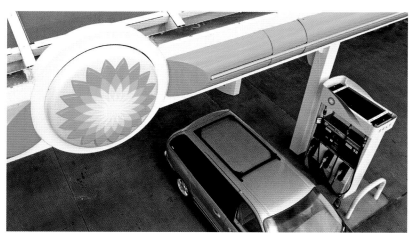

Fuel that takes care of your engine.

Looking after the heart of your car *bp ultimate*

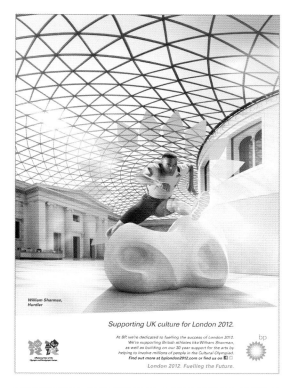

William Sharman,
Hurdler

Supporting UK culture for London 2012.

At BP, we're dedicated to fuelling the success of London 2012. We're supporting British athletes like William Sharman, as well as building on our 30 year support for the arts by helping to involve millions of people in the Cultural Olympiad. Find out more at bplondon2012.com or find us on

London 2012. Fuelling the Future.

Brand History

▶ **1909:** The Anglo-Persian Oil Company (as BP was first known) is formed.

▶ **1940s:** BP's sales, profits, capital expenditure and employment all surge upwards as post-war Europe restructures.

▶ **1954:** BP Visco-Static is introduced – Europe's first multigrade oil.

▶ **1965:** BP finds the West Sole gas field – the first offshore hydrocarbons found in British waters.

▶ **1975:** BP pumps the first oil from the North Sea's UK sector ashore after purchasing the Forties field – financed by a bank loan of £370 million.

▶ **1990s:** BP merges with US giant Amoco, and the acquisitions of ARCO, Burmah Castrol and Veba Oil turn the British oil company into one of the world's largest energy companies.

▶ **2000:** The BP brand is relaunched with the unveiling of a new 'Helios' brand mark.

▶ **2004:** Aral opens the first public hydrogen station in Berlin.

▶ **2005:** BP Alternative Energy is launched, a new business dedicated to the development, wholesale marketing and trading of low-carbon power.

▶ **2008:** BP becomes a Tier One Partner of the London 2012 Olympic and Paralympic Games.

▶ **2009:** BP marks its centenary with events and publications celebrating 100 years of discoveries and achievements.

▶ **2011:** BP sets out priorities for a safer, stronger company.

Providing
lower carbon biofuels
for London 2012.

Stef Reid,
Runner

London 2012.
Fuelling the Future.

will illustrate BP's development of efficient fuels and lubricants through the ages, and show how it aims to be a pioneer in meeting energy challenges over the next 10–15 years.

Promotion

As London plays host to a plethora of spectacular events in 2012, BP is actively communicating its support for the city. Utilising digital, print and broadcast media, it is delivering a communications campaign that focuses on its involvement and commitment to the success of the London 2012 Olympic and Paralympic Games. Social media – such as Facebook, Twitter and YouTube – has played a key role in enabling BP to keep consumers up-to-date on its Games-related cultural, educational and arts programmes, and also provides the latest news on its Athlete Ambassadors from across the globe.

As part of BP's London 2012 sponsorship, BP Target Neutral has been appointed Official Carbon Offset Partner to the Games and is working with other partners to explore ways in which London 2012 can be made as sustainable as possible.

Did You Know?

BP has achieved recognition in the film-making world, winning an Oscar in 1960 for Giuseppina; a BAFTA in 1975 for Sea Area Forties; and a BAFTA in 2011 for The Itch of the Golden Nit – the animated film is part of the London 2012 Cultural Olympiad initiative, Tate Movie Project, and was made with BP's involvement.

BP Target Neutral will aim to offset the carbon emissions from 5,000 official Games vehicles as well as the travel carbon footprint of ticket-holders who sign up to the programme.

The BP Target Neutral partnership is supported by an offline and online campaign, which encompasses a dedicated website and activations such as the British Olympic Ball and Eco Drive, as well as utilising the LOCOG communications channels. BP's Athlete Ambassadors are also playing their part, with BP challenging them to reduce their carbon footprint as they prepare for the Games; their mileage is logged online on the website.

Brand Values

BP's values represent the qualities and actions it wishes to see in itself, as well as those that it already demonstrates when it is at its best. They are a compass to guide the way the company does business and the decisions it makes every day. Above all else comes safety and excellence in operations. Its approach is built on respect, being consistent and having the courage to do the right thing. BP believes success comes from the energy of its people and working as one team.

bp

bp targetneutral

YOU
+ BP TARGET
NEUTRAL
+ LONDON 2012
= HELPING TO SET
A NEW WORLD
RECORD

▶ **www.bp.com**

BRITISH AIRWAYS

During its 90-year history, British Airways, together with its predecessors, has been at the forefront of innovation in aviation. Its pioneering spirit has led to numerous industry and world firsts such as the first commercial scheduled service, the first commercial jet service, the first commercial supersonic service, the first fully flat business class beds, and the only long haul service from London City airport. Today it remains one of the world's most enduring airlines.

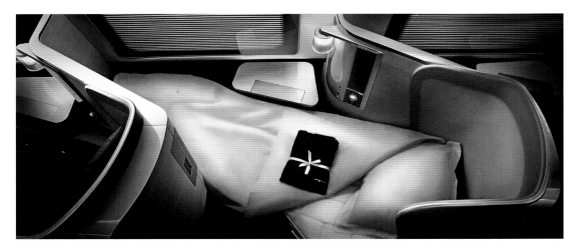

Market

The UK's largest international scheduled airline, British Airways has its principal place of business in London with a significant presence at London Heathrow, London Gatwick and London City. With some 20 million people within commuting distance of the three airports, British Airways operates from one of the world's largest premium travel markets.

British Airways supports the UK economy by providing vital arteries for trade and investment, meeting demand for both business and leisure travel. The airline flies approximately 32 million customers a year to more than 150 cities in 75 countries around the world.

British Airways' cargo business is also extensive, transporting more than 750,000 tonnes of cargo per year.

The airline industry is highly competitive and faces many unique challenges that have forced unprecedented change over the last decade, with the real opportunity for growth now coming through consolidation. British Airways

is a founding member of the oneworld® alliance and in 2010 formed a transatlantic joint business with American Airlines and Iberia. In January 2011 British Airways merged with Iberia to form the parent company International Airlines Group (IAG).

Product

British Airways is a full service airline offering a range of flights to UK domestic, short haul and long haul destinations. Its flagship cabin, First, is designed to be the epitome of understated elegance. A recent £100 million refit took inspiration from the airline's heritage during an era in which luxury travel was pioneered by British Airways' predecessors. British Airways revolutionised business travel with the introduction of flat beds in 2000, and the patented design means that even today British Airways' new Club World remains unique.

British Airways is the only airline to operate a long haul flight from London City airport through its Club World London City service. Launched in 2009, the service to New York JFK consists entirely of business class seating and

offers a range of premium services from fast-track immigration to in-flight SMS and internet access by way of an OnAir communication technology system.

Achievements

In 2010/11 British Airways continued to add accolades to its extensive trophy cabinet. Industry prizes, such as Best Airline Worldwide in the Business Winner Travel Awards, were joined by those voted for by customers, such as Best Airline in the Global Travel Awards.

In recognition of its investment in new technology at London Gatwick, The International Air Transport Association (IATA) recently

Did You Know?

Flying Start, the airline's charity partnership with Comic Relief, has raised in excess of £2 million for projects in the UK and overseas that support vulnerable children and young people. Its Red Nose Day fundraiser in March 2011 set a Guinness World Records title for the highest stand-up comedy gig.

Brand History

▶ **1919:** AT&T operates the first commercial scheduled flight.

▶ **1924:** Imperial Airways is formed as the UK's first nationalised airline to operate UK air services.

▶ **1936:** British Airways Ltd is formed from United Airways, Hillman Airways and Spartan Airlines.

▶ **1940:** BOAC is formed from the merger of Imperial Airways and British Airways Ltd.

▶ **1946:** BEA is formed as the second UK nationalised airline to operate European air services from the UK.

▶ **1952:** The world's first commercial jet service takes off.

▶ **1974:** BOAC and BEA merge to form British Airways.

▶ **1976:** The world's first supersonic service by Concorde takes off.

▶ **1987:** British Airways is privatised.

▶ **1988:** Club World and Club Europe cabins are launched. British Caledonian joins British Airways.

▶ **1995:** A new First class cabin launches.

▶ **1999:** The oneworld® alliance launches with British Airways, American Airlines, Canadian Airlines, Iberia and Qantas as the founding members.

▶ **2000:** The world's first fully flat bed in business class is launched in Club World.

▶ **2008:** British Airways' new home at London Heathrow Airport's Terminal 5 is opened.

▶ **2009:** Club World London City launches – an all business class service with only 32 seats.

▶ **2010:** A redesigned First class cabin is unveiled and a joint business with American Airlines and Iberia launches.

▶ **2011:** British Airways merges with Iberia to form the parent company IAG. British Airways moves into a new £76 million state-of-the-art home at London Gatwick and launches its new brand campaign, 'To Fly. To Serve.'

proud airline partner of the Olympic and Paralympic Games

honoured British Airways with a coveted Gold award; a first for a UK-based airline and only the second time such a distinction has been given to any airline worldwide.

Recent Developments

British Airways launched a £5 billion investment programme in 2011, which will see customers benefit from new aircraft, smarter cabins, elegant lounges, and new technologies to make life more comfortable in the air and on the ground. The new aircraft – 24 Boeing 787s and 12 Airbus A380s – will join the British Airways fleet from 2013.

Its environment programme to accelerate the implementation of biofuels in the aviation sector has made significant progress over the past three years. The latest development is the planned construction of Europe's first biomass-to-liquids biojet plant, to be located in East London. It is anticipated the plant will convert 500,000 tons of waste into 16 million gallons of aviation biofuel each year, meeting all of British Airways' fuel needs at London City airport.

Promotion

British Airways has a reputation for iconic advertising and its 'To Fly. To Serve.' campaign, launched in September 2011, is no exception. The airline's biggest campaign in more than a decade, its objective was to restate what British Airways stands for and to reinforce brand pride and passion among both customers and employees. The campaign ran across a range of TV, press, outdoor and digital channels, and included a launch on Facebook before premiering on ITV the same evening. With more than 3.5 million views on YouTube, the feedback from the campaign was overwhelmingly positive. Indeed, 98 per cent of British Airways employees felt the campaign achieved its aim of making them feel proud to work for British Airways.

Did You Know?

British Airways is the proud airline and tier one sponsor of the London 2012 Olympic and Paralympic Games, and its sponsorship demonstrates the crucial role it plays in the athlete's journey. Its notable 'They Will Fly' campaign featured sponsored athletes such as Jessica Ennis, Louis Smith, Ben Ainslie and Shelly Woods.

Brand Values

British Airways believes in putting the customer first in everything it does, a core value immortalised by its 35-year motto: 'To Fly. To Serve.' In practice this combines three core elements: iconic British style, which runs through everything it does; a thoughtful service that is both intuitive and knowledgeable; and flying know-how. The airline's reputation is built on its heritage of excellence in all areas of flying, and uncompromising standards of safety and security.

▶ **www.ba.com**

BSI is the expert body in the world of standards and since its formation in 1901 has been working hard to help organisations achieve excellence in everything they do. BSI's products and services create value and deliver real business improvement. BSI equips its clients with the necessary means to turn standards into habits of best practice.

Market

Standards impact the lives of everyone. They help businesses to mitigate risk and grow in a sustainable way, while giving consumers the assurance that they are getting products and services of the highest quality. A champion of excellence, BSI has a client base that extends across a myriad of sectors including communications, construction, energy, engineering, electronics, retail, healthcare, agriculture, banking and the public sector.

BSI is a global organisation with clients in 150 countries and plays a key role within the International Organization of Standardization (ISO). As one of its founding members, BSI ensures that British interests are represented during the development of international standards.

Product

BSI has developed more than 30,000 standards in collaboration with over 1,200 panels of industry experts, trade associations and consumers. Topics covered include anti-bribery, business continuity management and energy reduction. Eight of the top 10 most popular management systems standards were originally written by BSI.

As the UK's National Standards Body, BSI also works with multiple stakeholders to identify how standards can cut red tape and encourage self-regulation rather than legislation.

BSI trains its clients' employees to understand standards, tests and checks against them, and provides compliance tools and ongoing training.

All of BSI's testing and certification services ensure that products and services meet safety and performance requirements – from vehicle bodywork repairs to renewable energy products. BSI's Kitemark®, one of the UK's most trusted quality marks, symbolises the company's dedication to delivering comprehensive and robust standards of safety and quality. BSI also provides CE marking for products that need to comply with European Directives.

BSI is one of the largest certification bodies in the world for assessing and certifying management systems. It is the market leader in the UK and North America and has certified 70,000 locations across 150 countries. BSI also supplies comprehensive solutions such as its proprietary Entropy software to help organisations manage their governance, risk and compliance.

The health and medical devices sector is a key part of the BSI business. Its world class health division provides stringent regulatory and quality management reviews as well as being a leading product certification body for medical device manufacturers around the world.

Did You Know?

BSI developed a sustainable events standard (BS 8901) for the London 2012 Olympic and Paralympic Games; the London 2012 Organising Committee (LOCOG) was the first to achieve certification.

Achievements

BSI produces, on average, more than 2,000 standards annually and receives wide recognition from both industry and consumers. These standards also provide real societal benefits to businesses and individuals, from helping businesses to protect customer data to keeping children safe online.

As the world's first National Standards Body, BSI has cemented its position as a leading expert in internationally recognised standards. The quality management systems standard ISO 9001 – conceived by BSI in 1979 as BS 5750 – is now recognised as the world's most successful, having been adopted by more than one million organisations in 178 countries. Furthermore, two BSI standards – business continuity management (BS 25999) and sustainable events (BS 8901) – are being used as the basis for new international standards by ISO.

BSI's Kitemark® has provided public reassurance for more than 100 years. Indeed, in a recent survey of 1,000 UK adults, 72 per cent recognised the BSI Kitemark® and associated it with safe and reliable products and services (Source: GfK NOP December 2010). Building on this success, BSI is expanding the Kitemark® into the sustainability arena.

Understanding Standards - Five steps to describe BSI's business

| Set the Standards | ⋯▶ | Publish the Standards | ⋯▶ | Train how to use the Standards | ⋯▶ | Check & test against the Standards | ⋯▶ | Provide tools to keep the Standards |

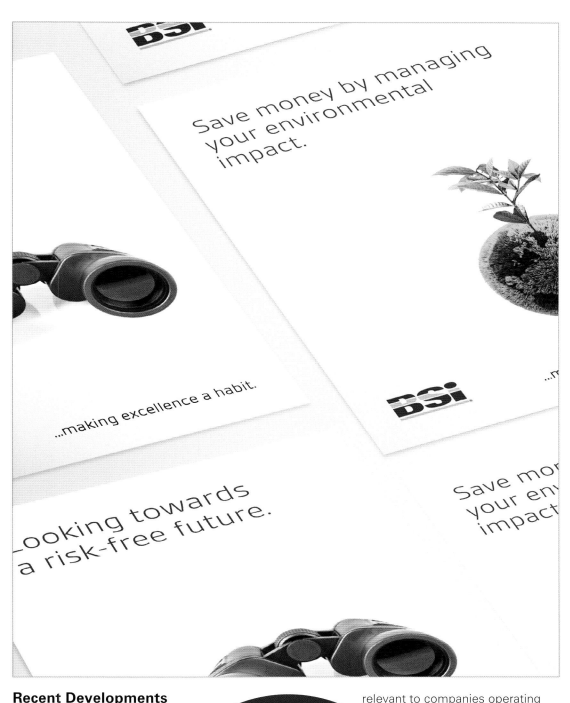

Save money by managing your environmental impact.

...making excellence a habit.

Looking towards a risk-free future.

Save mor your en impact

Brand History

▶ **1901:** BSI Group is founded as the Engineering Standards Committee (ESC).

▶ **1903:** The Kitemark® is first registered as a trademark.

▶ **1929:** The ESC is awarded a Royal Charter and in 1931, the name British Standards Institution (BSI) is adopted.

▶ **1953:** In the post-war era, more demand for consumer standardisation work leads to the introduction of the Kitemark® for domestic products.

▶ **1979:** BS 5750 (later known as ISO 9001) is introduced to help companies build quality and safety into the way they work. The Registered Firm mark is also introduced.

▶ **1992:** BSI publishes the world's first environmental management systems standard, BS 7750 (later renamed as ISO 14001).

▶ **2007:** BSI publishes BS 25999-2 for business continuity management; BS 8901 for sustainable event management; PAS 125, a crash repair standard; and Kitemark® certification for vehicle body repair.

▶ **2011:** BSI publishes BS 10500 for anti-bribery; BS 8901 for sustainability management for the film industry; PAS 200 for crisis management; and Eurocodes PLUS, a revolutionary product that digitises all 15,000 pages of the Eurocodes.

Recent Developments

In June 2011 BSI announced the launch of the first internationally recognised energy management standard (BS ISO 50001), designed to help organisations improve profitability and cut their CO_2 emissions. BSI also revised PAS 2050, the standard widely used to calculate the carbon footprint of goods and services.

Working in conjunction with the Cabinet Office, BSI launched PAS 200 in September 2011. The new crisis management standard helps businesses cope with unexpected emergencies such as civil unrest, employee deaths, corporate espionage and natural disasters.

Furthermore, in December 2011 BSI launched a new standard to help organisations deliver robust anti-bribery policies. Particularly

Did You Know?

Of the companies that have implemented ISO 27000, 87 per cent have reported a positive impact on their business and 47 per cent experienced fewer security incidents (Source: Erasmus University 2011).

Seventy-five per cent of BSI's construction clients certified to ISO 9001 have improved their sales and customer satisfaction levels (Source: BSI Excellerator Report 2011).

relevant to companies operating in countries where corruption is widespread, the standard helps them to independently verify their commitment to good governance.

In 2011 BSI hosted a global conference in London to celebrate 60 years of consumer involvement in standards, and encouraged the British public to 'Get Involved' with the development of new standards. Greater consumer contribution will help to produce standards that more accurately reflect the needs of the entire marketplace.

Promotion

The majority of BSI's marketing activities are delivered electronically, through its website, e-marketing and presence on social networking sites such as LinkedIn and Twitter. Public relations also play an important role

in promoting activities with regular coverage for BSI across national and international print, television and radio, and in key trade publications.

In 2011 BSI worked to build relationships with key industry bodies and trade associations, such as the Institute of Directors, British Chambers of Commerce and the Chartered Quality Institute, to explore ways they can work collectively to demonstrate how standards can drive growth and innovation.

Brand Values

BSI installs the habit of excellence into organisations around the world. Expertise, independence and integrity are key to the BSI offering, as well as a resolute commitment to delivering performance minded solutions. These principles embody how BSI conducts itself in all operations.

Objective in its outlook, BSI is the expert body in the world of standards and is committed to helping businesses achieve excellence every time, time after time.

▶ **www.bsigroup.com**

BT is one of the world's leading providers of communications services and solutions, serving customers in more than 170 countries. It supplies networked IT services to government departments and multinational companies, and is the UK's largest communications service provider to consumer and business markets. BT has four customer-facing lines of business: BT Retail, BT Global Services, Openreach and BT Wholesale.

bt.com/infinity

BT Infinity. Outperforming Sky with four times faster typical broadband speeds

Alistair & Jonathan Brownlee, GB Olympic triathletes

official partner of the
Olympic and Paralympic Games

Market

BT operates in a thriving, multi-trillion pound global industry. In recent years the boundaries between telcos, IT companies, software businesses, hardware manufacturers and broadcasters have become intertwined. The result is a new kind of communications market: one driven by relentlessly evolving technologies and customers' insatiable demand for more ingenious communications solutions.

Product

BT is the leading provider of fixed-line voice and broadband services in the UK. Its fibre-optic broadband product, BT Infinity, offers download speeds of up to 40 Mbps and upload speeds reaching 10 Mbps, providing the capacity and reliability customers need in the online age. Broadband customers also benefit from the UK's largest estate of WiFi hotspots, with access to more than three million across

hotels, coffee shops and travel hubs including Starbucks and Hilton Hotels.

BT Vision, BT's digital TV service, provides customers with the full range of Freeview channels. Viewers can pause, record and rewind live TV, catch up on programmes they have missed, and access extra films, TV shows and sport on demand.

BT's business team builds communications solutions for all types of company; its one million customers encompass businesses of all sizes, from sole traders to start-ups, limited companies to global enterprises.

BT is the only UK supplier for small and medium sized businesses that provides everything from phones and broadband, to hardware, software, support, and professional and managed services. As most owner-managers aren't IT

experts, BT focuses on value and taking away the stress of managing IT. Companies can lose business if their systems let them down, so BT provides its customers with all the service and troubleshooting support they need.

For large customers like Salford's new MediaCityUK, BT designs, implements and manages complex IT solutions. MediaCityUK's private network features more than 20 million metres of optical fibre cable carrying voice, data, high and standard definition video, and wireless communications services.

BT's global services team provides managed networked IT services for 7,000 large corporate and public sector customers. With operations centres all over the world, BT's customers include businesses in financial services, consumer packaged goods, logistics, pharmaceuticals and manufacturing.

BT also operates in key European markets such as Italy, Germany and Spain; conducts business in North America and Latin America; and in 2010, began investing heavily in Asia Pacific.

Achievements

In recent years BT has transformed itself, evolving from being a supplier of telephony services in the UK to becoming a global company selling innovative communications products, services, solutions and entertainment. The UK government, Unilever, Thomson Reuters, Microsoft, Volkswagen, Volvo, BMW, Fiat and the Spanish government are just some of the organisations with which it works. In November 2011, BT Global Services was named Best Global Operator at the World Communications Awards.

As a global company, BT strives to make a positive difference in the countries in which it works. At least one per cent of annual pre-tax profits go into programmes that benefit communities and the environment. In 2010/11, £27.6 million was invested in everything from

Did You Know?

For the London 2012 Olympic and Paralympic Games, BT is delivering 80,000 connections across 94 locations.

During the Games, BT's networks will deliver up to 60 Gb of information each second – the equivalent of 3,000 photographs.

Every official photograph and sports report, as well as millions of calls, emails and texts will be carried over BT's communications networks.

supporting BT volunteers working in schools to helping disadvantaged children in India become part of the digital society.

BT is also supporting educational, community, cultural and sporting activities in its role as a partner to the London 2012 Olympic and Paralympic Games.

In a partnership with Race Online 2012, BT is helping to get 100,000 people online for the first time by the end of the Olympic year. By developing a range of online tools, it is supporting 10,000 Digital Champions as they encourage others in their communities to get online.

Recent Developments

BT is ploughing investment into giving its customers a faster, more entertaining and more useful experience on the web, and it's bringing this super-fast broadband to two-thirds of UK homes and businesses by 2015. The £2.5 billion fund is one of the biggest commercial investments in fibre in the world, and will give customers download speeds of up to 100 Mbps with the potential for speeds of more than 1 Gbps in the future. This will enable them to run multiple bandwidth-hungry applications at the same time;

homes in the near future will see some family members streaming high definition films while others play games, create a photo book or edit videos online.

BT also continues to change its internal systems and processes – so it can create and deliver software-based services to customers at the push of a button, not the turn of a screwdriver.

Promotion

BT is the Official Communications Services Partner for the London 2012 Olympic and Paralympic Games, placing it at the heart of the biggest event the UK will stage in the next decade. BT will be responsible for key communications services for the operational workforce and at Games venues, and has exclusive marketing rights to use the London 2012 brand within its category. BT is also a sustainability partner, and a Premier Partner of the London 2012 Festival.

Brand Values

BT's corporate identity defines the kind of company it is today – and the one it needs to be in the future. Central to that identity is a dedication to helping customers thrive in a changing world. To do that, BT strives to live by its own brand values: trustworthy – doing what it says it will; helpful – working as one team; inspiring – creating new possibilities; straightforward – making things clear; heart – believing in what it does.

▶ **www.bt.com**

BT
Bringing it all together

Accelerating growth in Latin America

For more than three decades Carling has held the enviable title of the UK's best selling beer. Its new brand positioning – 'Refreshingly and Brilliantly British' – underlines Carling's iconic status and sets out its intention to build on this legacy, refreshing its image and re-energising the lager sector along the way.

Market

The UK beer industry has experienced some challenging times of late but within the sector Carling has retained its pole position as a category leader. It has achieved this in part by moving with the times and engaging with consumers to continue market relevance and stimulate category growth. To remain the leading brand, Carling recognises that it must continue to invest within the marketplace, improve brand health and reignite category interest with groundbreaking launches.

Product

When it comes to products, Carling – which is four per cent ABV – remains true to its heritage by using only British-grown barley. The brand's emphasis on local sourcing enables rigorous quality control to ensure that only the best ingredients go into creating Carling products.

Its focus on quality has been recognised through Red Tractor certification, awarded by Assured Food Standards. This independent organisation was established to help make it easier for consumers to choose good quality, ethically and locally produced food and drink products. The Red Tractor logo on Carling is a guarantee that the brand's barley is sourced responsibly from assured UK farmers, and that products meet the highest quality production standards, from the field to the glass.

Carling's substantial brand portfolio is available on draught, and in can and bottle formats – including an innovative new aluminium bottle, which delivers a smooth drinking experience coupled with a stylish look.

The latest addition to the brand's product line-up is Carling Chrome; a crisp, premium lager, precision-brewed for a refined taste at 4.8 per cent ABV.

Achievements

As a brand that's led the UK beer category for more than 30 years, it's unsurprising that Carling has accrued a plethora of industry and creative awards, including a Gold at the Campaign Big Awards.

Brand History

▶ **1840:** Thomas Carling first starts to brew beer.

▶ **1965:** Carling becomes available on draught for the first time.

▶ **1976:** Carling sells its one-millionth barrel of beer.

▶ **1998:** In response to consumers' desire for a snappier 'bar-call', Carling drops 'Black Label' from its name and all merchandising.

▶ **2002:** A new live music initiative launches – Carling Live.

▶ **2003:** Carling sponsors its first season of the Carling Cup.

▶ **2007:** A new campaign – 'You Know Who Your Mates Are' – launches.

▶ **2010:** Carling gains Red Tractor accreditation and launches live TV ads around the Football World Cup.

▶ **2011:** Carling introduces its 'Refreshingly and Brilliantly British' brand positioning, supported by new TV advertising. Carling Chrome also launches.

Many of Carling's award-winning TV advertisements are regarded by the public and the advertising industry as contemporary classics. First aired in 1983, Carling's 'I Bet He Drinks...' commercials are famed for their sharp and acutely topical humour, with more than 41 produced in a 10-year period.

A more recent campaign, 'You Know Who Your Mates Are' launched in November 2007 and uses the same actors in each advert to give the brand familiarity and consistency. In 2010 the brand became the first to air a live ad that detailed the actual scores of the football tournament.

Carling's latest advertising campaign plays on the lager's new 'Brilliantly Refreshing' tagline. It has been directed by award-winning music video director Walter Stern, the creative mind behind iconic 1990s music videos for the likes of Massive Attack, The Verve and Prodigy.

Over the years, Carling has established a strong and unique historical association with both music and football – two of its core customers' favourite things.

Carling has been involved with music events for more than 10 years, conducting various activities to build awareness of, and an affinity with, the Carling brand. The recent focus on summer music festivals fits alongside the brand's social credentials and provides a platform through which to engage with target consumers.

In 1993 Carling signed a £12 million four-year deal with the FA Premier League to create the FA Carling Premiership – Britain's biggest sports sponsorship at the time. Since 2003 it has also sponsored the Carling Cup, taking up the challenge of, and succeeding in, restoring credibility to one of the UK's biggest domestic sporting events.

Recent Developments

Carling's single most important recent development has been the launch of its new brand positioning: 'Refreshingly and Brilliantly British'. The rebrand follows five years of industry research and consumer insight, with the new market look – slick, stylish and sophisticated – reinforced by a prominent new font, creative packaging and a new TV campaign.

Carling's journey to reignite the lager sector follows one man's uniquely British journey to find the ultimate refreshment in a pint of Carling. Set to the music of Wondrous Place by up-and-coming British artist Alice Gold,

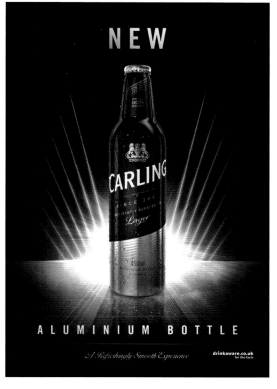

Did You Know?

In the last year, Carling sold approximately 36 pints every second, of every minute, of every hour, of every day, of every week, of every month (Source: Nielsen MAT w/e 29th October 2011).

the campaign supports the brand's new, more sophisticated visual identity and encapsulates the strategic repositioning of Carling, aimed at bringing the brand back to being a confident and proud category leader.

Promotion

From online competitions offering once in a lifetime travel experiences to giving drinkers the opportunity to acquire one of 13 million prizes – including much sought after Isle of Wight Festival and Carling Cup Final tickets – Carling is a brand that takes promotion seriously.

Launched in 2011, the Perfect Pint competition was the brand's most ambitious to date. Run in partnership with 7,500 pubs and bars and 20,000 retail outlets, it was supported by a major marketing campaign and promotional packaging.

Brand Values

Carling is proud to be British. Its aspirational brand values champion the brilliance of modern Britain in many different ways, such as through ingenuity, innovation, creativity and invention. The brand ethos – coming together makes everyday life more enjoyable – is underlined by its celebratory outlook and reflects the quirky and light-hearted side of Carling, while sponsorship is used to build brand health by driving relevance, reinforcing the brand's personality.

▶ **www.carling.com**

CMI Chartered Management Institute

The Chartered Management Institute (CMI) is the only chartered professional body dedicated to raising standards of management and leadership across all sectors of UK commerce and industry. By setting professional management standards – built into its qualifications, membership criteria and learning resources – it recognises individual capability and gives employers confidence in their managers' performance.

Market

The essential skills required to survive and prosper in the modern business environment are constantly changing, having a significant impact on the way in which organisations structure and develop themselves and their managers. Strong business performance and the delivery of public services depend on high quality management and leadership.

The strength of CMI lies in the breadth and depth of its offering. CMI's portfolio encompasses qualifications, training and development, membership, policy development, research and accreditation.

Product

At the heart of CMI's product offering is the desire to raise the standard of professionally qualified managers and leaders – and to increase their numbers.

The tailor-made training programmes and qualifications CMI offers are designed to meet the needs of today's management professionals, and to support its corporate

members in developing and delivering management and leadership excellence across their organisations. CMI is the only body in the UK that awards Chartered Manager status, the hallmark of a professional manager.

Did You Know?

CMI is the only organisation that can award Chartered Manager status – the ultimate recognition of professionalism in management. It signifies to consumers and organisations that utilise the services of a Chartered Manager that they are engaging with those at the top of their profession.

CMI prides itself on being one step ahead when it comes to understanding what might affect managers and leaders tomorrow. It provides up-to-the-minute research on the hottest management issues; information and guidance through its online management centre; and consultancy services and guidance for managers at every level and across every type of organisation. In addition, CMI holds events throughout the year, the highlight of the calendar being the annual National Conference, which focuses on key management and leadership challenges.

Achievements

As one of the UK's leading authorities on management and leadership, CMI challenges policy-makers and opinion formers, ensuring

issues affecting managers and leaders are firmly on the agenda. Its expertise also means it is regularly consulted by other organisations.

Brand History

▶ **1947:** The British Institute of Management (BIM) is formed.

▶ **1951/52:** The UK's first Diploma in Management Studies is introduced by the BIM and the Ministry of Education.

▶ **1987:** The BIM, in conjunction with other bodies, issues two pivotal reports – 'The Making of British Managers' and 'The Making of Managers'.

▶ **1992:** The BIM and the Institution of Industrial Managers (IIM) merge to form the Institute of Management (IM). The transfer of the IM's Awarding Body status to the new Institute is approved by the (former) National Council for Vocational Qualifications, now the Qualifications and Curriculum Authority.

▶ **1995:** The IM publishes 'Test Your Management Skills' – the world's first validated general management aptitude test.

▶ **2000:** The IM accredits its 250th approved centre to deliver IM management qualifications.

▶ **2002:** The IM's management qualifications are recognised as part of the UK's National Qualifications Framework for Higher Education. The IM is granted a Royal Charter and renamed the Chartered Management Institute (CMI).

▶ **2003:** The first Chartered Manager programme launches in September.

▶ **2010:** The CMI names the UK's 1,000th Chartered Manager.

Membership of CMI aims to give managers and organisations an edge over the competition. Indeed, CMI member surveys suggest that its networking events, research reports, training and development opportunities, and information and advice provide members with unrivalled access to the gold standard in terms of management and leadership expertise, support and excellence.

CMI has become the first organisation to provide qualifications at all levels, from school pupils to chief executives and chairpersons, with the introduction of its 'Level 8' qualifications.

Recent Developments

CMI's vision is for all organisations to have first class managers and leaders.

In 2010/11 CMI launched a programme that has the potential to shape the employment landscape for years to come: Campus CMI. The initiative aims to prepare young people, aged between 14 and 21, for the working world. It teaches individuals the management, leadership and workplace skills that CMI knows employers want to see in new recruits. It also aims to give participants the potential to boost their career opportunities.

Reports that focus on the acute skills shortage in the UK are ubiquitous in today's media.

However, the biggest unreported skills shortage in the UK is that of management and leadership. According to the UK Commission for Employment and Skills, an additional 800,000 new managers will be required by 2017 – a figure that doesn't even take into account those who leave the profession. In the current economic climate it is also evident that management skills, and qualified managers in particular, are required. Over the past year, CMI has made a significant contribution to aiding this situation, with its Awarding Body going from strength to strength. A total of 35,500 students chose CMI as their preferred organisation when embarking on a qualification, and 683 approved centres chose to deliver them.

Promotion

Elevating CMI's brand profile is key to its promotional strategy. A full range of marketing and promotional activities are undertaken, from branch events and regional conventions to more targeted PR and marketing activities. Brand marketing focuses on three key areas: opinion forming, influencing and brand building.

Today's generation of managers require both a physical and a virtual presence. Therefore, CMI has invested in social media and its website to allow managers to stay connected with their peers, keep up-to-date with developments that interest them, and access practical resources.

Brand Values

The CMI brand is encapsulated by the phrase: 'Passionate about managers and leaders making an impact.' Everything that CMI does is guided by this principle as it strives to help others achieve management and leadership excellence.

The brand's character can be summed up as: passionate – it believes in what it does and offers; challenging – it believes its members get better answers by constantly questioning the status quo; progressive – it is forward focused; savvy – its knowledge and expertise makes it smart and quick to respond; and professional – in everything it says and does.

▶ **www.managers.org.uk**

Did You Know?

The highest level of CMI membership is the Companion. Involvement is by invitation only, extended to leaders who have demonstrated superior management and leadership achievement in substantial organisations. There are currently around 1,000 Companions.

Clear Channel

Clear Channel's expertise in out-of-home media, gained over 40 years, means it understands how to showcase powerful and effective campaigns for its clients. It enables brands to connect with people by investing in the highest quality sites, new technologies and the latest planning tools. Thanks to strategic partnerships, Clear Channel now has a national network of 60,000 sites, all of which generate word of mouth and help build businesses.

Market

According to the Outdoor Media Centre, the UK outdoor revenues for the period July–September 2011 reached £214.4 million, up 1.1 per cent year-on-year. Six out of the last seven quarters have now recorded positive growth. Digital revenues were up 29 per cent to £30.6 million for the quarter, reflecting new investment in digital and the conversion of traditional sites to digital in various environments.

Product

Clear Channel is the UK's leading provider of 6-sheets in bus shelters and free-standing units, with more than 45,000 panels nationally. In addition, Clear Channel offers point of sale opportunities at some 400 Sainsbury's supermarkets and in more than 85 UK shopping malls.

Clear Channel Billboards is a market leader in quality 96-sheet billboards and provides national, high quality 48-sheet billboards across the UK. The company's Pinnacle division offers premium advertising on more than 200 special high-profile sites such as London's Cromwell Road, Piccadilly Circus and the M4 Towers.

The brand's digital offering in the UK includes a rapidly expanding small format digital network in malls; LD6, the UK's first small format digital roadside network; digital roadside displays in Piccadilly Circus; large format digital roadside sites in London; Socialite, a growing small format digital network in pubs and bars; and small format digital displays in Birmingham Airport.

Achievements

Clear Channel has signed a partnership deal with Curb, a natural media company, to deliver high impact sustainable advertising. The partnership demonstrates Clear Channel's commitment to the environment along with its ongoing drive to provide the latest products for use by creative agencies.

Did You Know?

Clear Channel owns the UK's largest network of digital mall screens.

The Cromwell Road site is the longest advertising face on the busiest road in the UK.

Clear Channel's green credentials are long established, from its commitment to liquefied petroleum gas fuels and greener fleets, which secured the Green Fleet Award 2006 and the Fleet Hero Award 2007, to being named one of the top 60 Best Green Companies by The Sunday Times for the fourth consecutive year in 2011.

Recent Developments

In late 2011 Clear Channel won the outdoor advertising contract for Westfield Regional, which will see more than 100 digital screens installed in top ranking malls in major cities across the UK including Birmingham, Derby and Belfast. This win, along with the retained Meadowhall contract, expands Clear Channel's digital portfolio by 60 per cent.

The new Clear Channel Play division – established in 2011 – will represent Clear Channel's entire digital media portfolio. Clear Channel Play is an engaging way to connect brands with people when they are active and out-of-home, and reflects the company's commitment to drive digital expansion across its UK and international network.

Brand History

▶ **1936:** More O'Ferrall is founded.

▶ **1967:** The Adshel brand is launched.

▶ **1996:** The company is rebranded as the More Group. Two years later the More Group is acquired, Town & City billboard is bought, and the Sainsbury's contract is won.

▶ **2004:** The company wins the malls point of sale (POS) contract.

▶ **2006:** The company is rebranded as Clear Channel Outdoor. It buys Van Wagner in the UK and launches the Pinnacle division.

▶ **2008:** The digital roadside network is formed and the Interact mobile services division launches. Bain Capital Partners LLC and Thomas H Lee Partners LP acquire the company.

▶ **2009:** The digital malls network, national dry-posted billboards and WAVe technology launch. William Eccleshare is appointed president and CEO of Clear Channel International.

▶ **2010:** Clear Channel expands both its digital mall network and its Sainsbury's POS offering. The world's first 'Real 3D' out-of-home campaign also launches, as does 'The Cromination': six consecutive 96-sheets that dominate one of London's prime locations, Cromwell Road. Groundbreaking campaigns include Nike, Emirates, 20th Century Fox, Warner Bros and Tourism Australia.

▶ **2011:** Digital comes to the fore as Socialite launches in pubs and bars across the UK; LD6 digital 6-sheets are unveiled across London; the Westfield Regional contract is won, which will create the UK's largest network of digital mall screens; and Clear Channel Play is established to represent the brand's entire digital media portfolio.

The launch of the new brand will enable Clear Channel to work with partners to open up new possibilities for advertisers to engage with their target audiences and deliver creative, flexible and interactive digital campaigns to build their businesses.

Promotion

Clear Channel not only communicates with its key audiences – advertisers, agencies and other stakeholders – but also promotes the outdoor advertising industry. In partnership with Haymarket Brand Media, Clear Channel launched the Outdoor Planning Awards in 2007, now in their sixth year. Clear Channel also sponsored the Campaign Big Awards in 2009, 2010 and 2011, and sponsored the Outdoor category at the Cannes Lions for the second time in 2011.

Clear Channel's involvement in Bulmers' bespoke digital campaign demonstrates the brand's continued commitment to cutting-edge promotional concepts. In support of the launch of its new variation, Berry & Lime, Bulmers ran a large-scale campaign with the tag line:

'experimenters wanted'. Bulmers wanted to encourage people to interact with the brand via the website and through social media. QR codes on shelter wraps took the consumer straight to the Bulmers website and passers-by were able to interact with Clear Channel touchscreens in bus shelters, creating their own literary masterpiece by dragging fridge letters into place and sharing the result with friends via Facebook.

Did You Know?

Clear Channel has more than 750 digital connection points across multiple environments in the UK, with plans to grow in 2012.

The LD6 network of digital screens in bus shelters delivers 10.8 million views per week.

Brand Values

Clear Channel's vision is to be the outstanding out-of-home media partner. Clear Channel embraces the values of freedom, flexibility, being forward-thinking and fulfilling promises. It inspires the business to focus on services such as the interactive nature of digital outdoor and on the environmental management work and charity support that the company undertakes. The company provides high quality products and services that benefit its clients, partners and communities, and helps to set new standards for the whole sector.

▶ **www.clearchannel.co.uk**

In the wake of an important year for news broadcasting, CNN remains the world's leading global 24-hour news network, delivered across a range of multimedia platforms. The leader in its field since its establishment in 1980, the channel's output comprises a vast range of award-winning programming, including its trademark breaking news, business and sports news, current affairs and analysis, documentary and feature programming.

Market

Since CNN pioneered the genre, the pan-regional news market has expanded to include more than 100 news channels worldwide. CNN has remained at the forefront of this increasingly competitive market, warding off competition with its growing international newsgathering operation and intricate network of regionalised services and affiliates.

Across both online and broadcast television, CNN strives to redefine its cross-platform advertising sales, providing one of the most comprehensive and innovative offerings in the industry. CNN continues to attract a diverse range of high profile advertisers, such as Standard Bank, Rolex and Abu Dhabi Tourism, with its online services the fastest-growing driver of advertising sales.

Product

CNN has evolved into a diverse information hub, boasting 24 branded networks and services, and reaching two billion people worldwide across television, radio, online and mobile.

CNN's global news group comprises nine international networks and services, five international partnerships and joint ventures, and eight US-based services. An expert in breaking news coverage, CNN has transcended the boundaries of traditional news broadcasting and features an eclectic mix of programming.

Did You Know?

CNN dominated one quarter of 2011's top 40 most shared articles on Facebook in the US (Source: Facebook + Media November 2011).

Coverage of the political uprising in Egypt spiked global video usage on CNN.com by 97 per cent, to 6.3 million video views.

Achievements

In what was an especially eventful year in news broadcasting, CNN was frequently recognised in 2011 for its innovative programming and online content. At the Amnesty International Media Awards the network was praised for World's Untold Stories: Locked up and Forgotten, a documentary that highlights the neglect suffered by Kenya's mentally disabled community. CNN International shone at the Royal Television Society Awards, in which it won the Innovative News category for a Twitter tool that enabled web and television viewers to visualise media activity during the 2010 World Cup. CNN International's weekly culture show, Inside Africa, was a finalist in the Best Tourism Feature category at the Diageo Africa Business Reporting Awards.

The year also saw the number of CNN's registered iReporters, contributors to its 'citizen journalism' platform, reach almost one million, as watershed moments such as the Thailand floods and the Occupy Protests prompted considerable increases in traffic.

Recent Developments

CNN continues to invest in intelligent and compelling feature and documentary programming across all digital platforms, forging unique audience connections that truly engage consumers worldwide.

2011 saw the launch of Global Exchange, a daily news show exploring how emerging markets are having an impact on the global financial community, at a time when business is a vital driver of the international news

agenda. This, alongside the network's existing feature and documentary slate, confirms CNN's evolution into much more than a multimedia 24-hour rolling news channel.

Another new launch, Marketplace Europe puts the spotlight on one of the world's most influential and interconnected continents as Europe faces up to the economic challenges and opportunities of the next 10 years. Using CNN's unparalleled access to business leaders and decision-makers, Marketplace Europe delivers intelligent, unmissable features and analysis.

In November 2011, CNN relaunched its iReport site, introducing functions and visuals that more closely resemble social networking sites than standard news sites. Users are now prompted to create a profile and 'follow' other users, while earning awards and 'badges' for accomplishments. Users are also directed to participate in a CNN story by watching on television or online and joining in a discussion about the feature or broadcast.

Did You Know?

CNN iReport has almost one million registered users. With 2.5 million unique users each month, the site has received submissions from every country in the world.

Promotion

Since launch, the CNN logo has been one of the world's most instantly recognised brands, and it continues to be promoted through select marketing opportunities and partnerships.

In 2009, CNN International unveiled a new tagline – 'Go Beyond Borders' – which is an articulation of the network's shared values and commitment to delivering intelligent news in a connected world. CNN International uses this tagline not only as a marketing message but also as a content filter; its news coverage promises to go beyond the expected.

In 2011, CNN International launched a pan-EMEA advertising campaign, which elevated the profiles of its individual news anchors and cemented their relationships with existing viewers. Outdoor posters provided the spine of the campaign – with support from print and digital channels – and featured key anchors alongside the tagline: 'Go beyond borders, wherever you are.'

Brand Values

CNN stands by the news values of accuracy, intelligence, transparency and diversity. The

HALA
"When we know it, you know it.'
Go beyond borders, wherever you are.
"Soyez les premiers à savoir." Avec vous, au-delà des frontières.
CNN

network's commitment to digital integration also ensures that its audiences get access to CNN 'whenever, wherever and however'. CNN is global in its reach and continually aims to break new ground and go beyond expectations.

'Go Beyond Borders' demonstrates that stories and people are not defined or limited by geography, and neither is CNN – it speaks directly to viewers' aspirations and expectations. It also reflects the changing world, as news is consumed across an increasing number of platforms.

Transparency and diversity are crucial to CNN's viewers; they expect their news source to challenge and question, as well as deliver truly international reporting and perspectives.

▶ **www.cnn.com/international**

Did You Know?

The royal wedding in April 2011 increased traffic to CNN.com by 61 per cent and global video usage on the site soared by 379 per cent. CNN's Twitter feed also generated more than 1,600 re-tweets during the wedding's airing.

Brand History

▶ **1980:** CNN launches on 1st June as a single US network; the brainchild of media entrepreneur Ted Turner, it becomes the first round-the-clock news channel.

▶ **1985:** CNN International launches, along with live 24-hour transmission to Europe.

▶ **1995:** CNN.com, the world's first major news website, is launched. This is followed by the all-encompassing international edition.

▶ **1999:** CNN Mobile launches. It is the first mobile telephone news and information service available globally with targeted regional content.

▶ **2008:** iReport.com is born; an online incarnation of iReport, it is CNN's first interactive, user-generated content website.

▶ **2009:** CNN International launches eight new prime time programmes for its European line-up and the 'Go Beyond Borders' tagline replaces 'Be the First to Know'.

▶ **2010:** CNN International launches a new iPhone app, reaching millions of users globally with the latest news and feature content.

▶ **2011:** CNN relaunches its iReport website, creating a social network for news as well as a platform for interactive storytelling and participation.

Coca-Cola

In 2011, The Coca-Cola Company celebrated a momentous landmark: 125 years since Coca-Cola was first sold in the US. Since 1886, Coca-Cola has connected with more people in more places than any other product, and it is now the most universally recognised brand (Source: Company Data). Globally, 1.7 billion servings are made every 24 hours, and in the UK, Coca-Cola and Diet Coke are the two biggest selling soft drinks (Source: Nielsen 2011).

Market

On-going brand and product innovation by Coca-Cola has led to its position as one of the most successful and innovative brands in the world, leading the field in the soft drinks category.

The MyCoke portfolio is worth £1.135 billion in the UK (Source: Nielsen 52 w/e 5th November 2011), having grown in value by seven per cent in the last year. Within this, Coca-Cola is worth nearly £600 million, increasing 6.5 per cent in value year-on-year. Diet Coke is worth £473 million, representing 6.6 per cent value growth, while Coke Zero reached double-digit value growth of 15.7 per cent in 2011, and is now worth £63 million.

Product

The MyCoke trilogy comprises Coca-Cola, Diet Coke and Coke Zero.

Achievements

Throughout its lifetime, Coca-Cola has continued to grow and strengthen its position as the world's leading soft drinks brand. In its 125th year, The Coca-Cola Company set out its 2020 Vision: to double its servings and value to become a US$200 billion brand in the next eight years.

Did You Know?

If all the Coca-Cola ever produced were in eight-ounce contour bottles, and these bottles were laid end to end, they would reach to the moon and back 2,051 times.

Recent Developments

Coca-Cola rolled out its innovative PlantBottle™ packaging in Great Britain in 2011, taking the next step on the company's journey to develop a truly sustainable plastic bottle. Made from up to 22.5 per cent plant-based materials and up to 25 per cent recycled plastic, 200 million Coca-Cola, Diet Coke and Coke Zero PlantBottle™ packs hit UK shelves during 2011, with five billion launching globally. The company's wider ambition is that all its plastic bottles will be made from a combination of plant-based materials and recycled PET plastic by 2020.

Promotion

In its 125th year, Coca-Cola inspired, rewarded and celebrated with consumers across the UK. Working towards the company's 2020 Vision, the brand has a 'liquid and linked' approach at the heart of its marketing campaigns – forging ever-deeper connections with consumers. The strategy places emphasis on dynamic storytelling to engage with people across multiple connection points, creating valuable and shareable content to build brand affection and value.

Inspired by the brand's rich heritage and amplifying its enduring appeal, Coca-Cola embraced its milestone year with an integrated global campaign that celebrated bringing consumers happiness in a bottle for 125 years.

"Thirst asks nothing more"

A new advertisement took fans back in time through a series of montaged retro images, set to the soundtrack from the classic 'Hilltop' ad, which coined the phrase: 'I'd like to teach the world to sing.' Iconic Coca-Cola imagery featured across packaging and the brand's first ever glass bottle, the 1899 Hutchinson, was relaunched.

Spreading festive cheer, Coca-Cola celebrated 80 years since Haddon Sundblom first drew 'Coca-Cola Santa', an image that has since been adopted across the world and to this day remains at the heart of the brand's Christmas campaign.

With a momentous year ahead for Coca-Cola as a Worldwide Partner of the London 2012 Olympic and Paralympic Games, the brand kicked off activity to inspire and reward consumers.

As a Presenting Partner of the London 2012 Olympic Torch Relay, Coca-Cola recognised

Did You Know?

Coca-Cola has been an official partner of the Olympic Games since 1928 – the longest running sports sponsorship in history.

It is documented that Coca-Cola is the second-most widely understood term in the world, after 'okay' (Source: Company Data).

and rewarded the positive contributions of young people, offering the chance to become a Future Flame and carry the Olympic Torch in 2012. The activity was supported by an integrated campaign and partnerships with top music acts including Dizzee Rascal, Eliza Doolittle, You Me At Six and The Wanted.

Inspired by the sounds, spirit and culture of the host city, Coca-Cola also unveiled its global campaign for the London 2012 Olympic Games – 'Move To The Beat'. The activity harnesses teens' passion for music, working with award-winning producer Mark Ronson and chart-topping vocalist Katy B to fuse the sounds of Olympic sports with the beat of London music.

Elsewhere, the brand continued to support The London Organising Committee of the Olympic and Paralympic Games (LOCOG) to ensure London 2012 is a sustainable event with a positive legacy for the UK. Through its 'Live Positively' framework, Coca-Cola is working to promote health and wellness, reduce and compensate for all carbon emissions, and help deliver a zero waste Games.

Diet Coke cemented its fashion credentials in 2011 with a new platform that amplified the brand ethos of 'Love It Light'. The three confident and stylish Diet Coke puppets returned to TV screens while a collaboration with international creative figurehead, Karl Lagerfeld, and fashionable partnerships with brands including ASOS, nails inc. and Model's Own, offered women more moments of uplift and enjoyment.

Coke Zero championed its 'Impossible Made Possible' philosophy through activity that brought to life its unique proposition of 'Great Coke Taste, Zero Sugar'. In the first partnership of its kind, Coke Zero tapped into its audience's passion for gaming through an exclusive promotion with Sony PlayStation and the launch of a Gaming Zone with MSN.

TASTING IS BELIEVING GREAT Coke TASTE zero SUGAR

Brand Values

Since 1886, Coca-Cola has embodied values of happiness, opportunity, authenticity and togetherness, shaping the brand through its 125-year history and spreading optimism to people across the globe.

▶ **www.coca-cola.co.uk**

Brand History

▶ **1886:** Coca-Cola is created by John Pemberton and served at Jacobs' Pharmacy in Atlanta, USA.

▶ **1893:** The Coca-Cola Spencerian script trademark is registered.

▶ **1915:** The contour bottle prototype is designed by Alexander Samuelson and patented. Today, the original glass bottle is the most recognised bottle in the world, and the shape is used for packaging across Coca-Cola products.

▶ **1984:** Diet Coke is launched – the first brand extension of Coca-Cola in Great Britain.

▶ **2006:** Coke Zero becomes the third brand in the Coca-Cola family in Great Britain.

▶ **2009:** The MyCoke portfolio becomes the first brand to top the £1 billion retail sales mark.

▶ **2011:** The Coca-Cola Company celebrates the 125th anniversary of Coca-Cola.

conqueror

Since 1888, Conqueror has been recognised worldwide as a symbol of premium, quality paper for business and creative communications. Conqueror is a pioneer in providing sustainable solutions for impactful communications and in 2010, undertook a complete rejuvenation to showcase the contemporary and dynamic nature of the brand.

Brand History

▶ **1888:** Conqueror paper first rolls off the paper machine at Wiggins Teape. Conqueror Laid is born.

▶ **1945:** Changes in the production of Conqueror take place, and quality control and specialised colour matching are developed.

▶ **1990s:** Arjowiggins Appleton group is formed from the merger of Wiggins Teape with the French paper manufacturer Arjomari and the US manufacturer Appleton Papers.

▶ **2001:** A new contemporary, stylised logo and identity based on the Conqueror name is launched. Innovative iridescent papers are also added into the range.

▶ **2004:** Conqueror Digital Multi Technology is introduced as the only fine paper that is printable on offset and digital presses.

▶ **2007:** Conqueror becomes CarbonNeutral® in the UK, while also using pulp from FSC certified sources across the entire range.

▶ **2008:** Conqueror becomes CarbonNeutral® in Germany.

▶ **2009:** Conqueror launches the first premium 100 per cent recycled paper and becomes CarbonNeutral® in another 10 countries across Europe: Denmark, Norway, Sweden, Finland, Iceland, Austria, Belgium, the Netherlands, Luxembourg and Switzerland.

▶ **2010:** The brand is rejuvenated and its offering is expanded to include the Print Excellence and FSC certified Bamboo ranges, and nine new colours in its Wove and Laid ranges. Conqueror participates in the inaugural One Young World summit.

Market

In today's digital age, the sensory qualities of paper remain a powerful communications tool for companies of any size, playing a pivotal role in conveying their business image. Through their unique visual characteristics and tactile quality, Conqueror products are designed to enrich communications and to ensure messages stand out, while promoting values such as excellence, professionalism, respect and style.

Conqueror is the only premium brand of paper that's available in 120 countries.

Product

Conqueror offers a comprehensive and complementary array of papers, with a portfolio that features 29 colours, 11 grammage variants, 13 finishes, five sheet sizes and seven envelope sizes – as well as papers made from more unusual materials such as bamboo and cotton.

Did You Know?

In 2011 Conqueror participated at the annual One Young World summit for the second time through its Blank Sheet Project. It sponsored seven delegates from different world regions who have initiated projects in fields ranging from environmental sustainability to medical research to cross-cultural education.

In 2010, this diverse and innovative brand added nine contemporary colours to its Wove and Laid ranges; 400g versions of Conqueror's best selling papers; new envelope sizes; and an SRA3 size to appeal to digital printers.

Across its portfolio, the quality and versatility of Conqueror's products guarantee a look and feel of style and expertise combined with impeccable environmental credentials.

Achievements

Since its creation in 1888, Conqueror has been a pioneer in many areas. Today, it's perhaps its unwavering commitment to high quality standards coupled with developing sustainable products that distinguishes the brand.

The Conqueror range offers a complete solution to the growing demand for high quality, yet sustainable papers: all papers are FSC certified; there is a choice of 100 per cent recycled papers, which utilise post-consumer

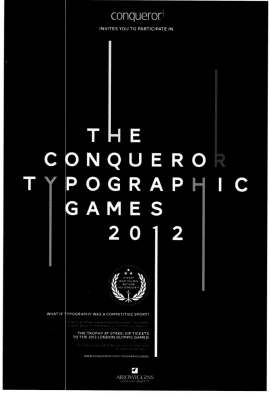

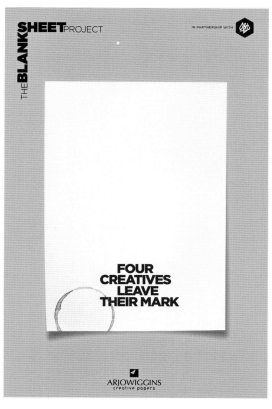

paper pulp from Conqueror's sister company's Greenfield mill in France; and in 12 countries the full range is CarbonNeutral®. In 2010, Conqueror took another sustainable step with the launch of a paper made from bamboo pulp.

For many years Conqueror has pursued a plan of continuous innovation to achieve best-in-category performance and to meet changing market needs. Indeed, Conqueror has embraced digital printing trends by offering papers that are fully compatible with dry-toner machines.

In terms of communications, Conqueror's 2009 Endless Possibilities campaign was a winner at the 2009 Benchmarks Awards, organised by Design Week.

Conqueror also won the prestigious Prix du Design D'édition at the Grand Prix Stratégies du Design in October 2011, as well as at the European Design Awards in May 2011. Both prizes were for the Conqueror Campaign: 'It's not what you say, it's how you say it.'

Recent Developments
Conqueror is proud to be at the cutting edge of the paper industry by investing heavily in product innovation.

The new Bamboo range is its latest eco-sustainable development and offers a unique paper experience. Bamboo provides a fast-growing and renewable source of pulp and the result of working with this unusual and creative

substance is a modern paper with a natural touch and feel. The paper is available in a range of organic colour shades that have been achieved by using natural ochre pigments sourced in the South of France.

Print Excellence uses the latest technology to open up Conqueror to new applications. This new strand of the Conqueror range offers faster drying times, greater uniformity, vivid colours and bolder blacks. The technology will ensure users can be confident that the paper will effectively handle even complicated creative prints and jobs.

Did You Know?

Today, there are some 600 different line items available within Conqueror, with users ranging from royalty to huge corporates to individually-run businesses, the world over.

Arjowiggins has calculated that if all companies switched to using Conqueror paper, UK businesses alone could save more than 23,000 tonnes of CO_2 each year, which is equivalent to the annual emissions of almost 4,200 households.

Promotion
A 'push–pull' marketing strategy has been successfully developed for Conqueror. A strong emphasis is put on brand awareness, including collaborations with well-known designers and illustrators to increase brand awareness within the design community.

In 2010, the comprehensive product rejuvenation was supported by a strong communications campaign based on the theme of 'It's not what you say, it's how you say it.' Conqueror commissioned world-renowned typographer Jean-François Porchez to develop five exclusive typefaces – a Chinese typeface is also available. All are free to download from the updated Conqueror website.

Conqueror has also designed a brochure that showcases how to create a lasting impression through the use of business cards. Building on

one of the brand's existing design partnerships it includes illustrations by Damien Weighill.

To capitalise on the success of the Conqueror typefaces, 2011 saw Conqueror launch its Typographic Games 2012 competition. The concept is for designers to create a typographic poster featuring the phrase: 'It's not how you win, but how you conquer it.' The gold prize includes tickets to the London 2012 Olympic and Paralympic Games, and a jury comprising designers and bloggers, presided over by Jean-François Porchez, will choose the winner.

Brand Values
Conqueror has a rich heritage and shares its key values with the many businesses worldwide that choose its high quality, distinctive and sustainable papers: reliable, high end, contemporary, eco-sustainable, supportive and smart.

▶ **www.conqueror.com**

Passion to Perform

Deutsche Bank is a leading global investment bank with a substantial private clients franchise. A leader in Europe, it continues to grow in North America, Asia and key emerging markets. With more than 100,000 employees in 73 countries, Deutsche Bank offers a vast range of financial services globally. It competes to be the leading global provider of financial solutions, creating lasting value for its clients, shareholders, people and the communities in which it operates.

Market

Deutsche Bank has been a leader, not a follower, throughout the global financial crisis and in its aftermath. While many banks struggled to weather the crisis, Deutsche Bank stood out among its global peers for its greater financial strength, stability and leadership. Corporate, institutional and private clients have recognised Deutsche's strong position among global banks.

Product

Deutsche Bank is one of the most global of banks and offers its clients a broad range of products and services.

The Private Clients and Asset Management division comprises three areas: Private and Business Clients, which provides private clients with an all-round service encompassing daily banking, investment advisory and tailored financial solutions; Private Wealth Management, which caters for high net worth clients, their families and select institutions worldwide; and Asset Management, which combines asset management for institutions and private investors.

The Corporate & Investment Bank (CIB) serves corporates, financial institutions, governments and sovereigns around the world. It comprises three businesses: Corporate Finance, which provides investment banking coverage, as well as mergers and acquisitions advisory; Markets, which partners with clients for sales, trading, structuring and research needs across equities, fixed income, currencies and commodities; and Global Transaction Banking, which offers cash management, trade finance, capital markets sales, and trust and securities services.

Achievements

Deutsche Bank continues to win accolades for its performance across all product disciplines and regions. In the Euromoney Awards for Excellence 2011, Deutsche Bank was named Best Global Bank and received a host of other awards including Best Global Debt House and Best Global Flow House. Deutsche Bank achieved further success in The Banker's Investment Banking Awards 2011 when it was named Most Innovative Investment Bank of the Year.

Recent Developments

In July 2011, Deutsche Bank announced that Jürgen Fitschen and Anshu Jain will become co-chairmen of the Management Board and the Group Executive Committee of the Bank, following the Bank's Annual General Meeting in 2012. Dr Josef Ackermann will step down from his position as chairman after 10 years' service.

Did You Know?

Deutsche Bank has been a collector of contemporary art since 1979 and its acquisitions have evolved into one of the most important corporate art collections in the world.

Deutsche Bank's 'diagonal in the square' logo was developed by Germany's design pioneer Anton Stankowski and first introduced to the public in 1974.

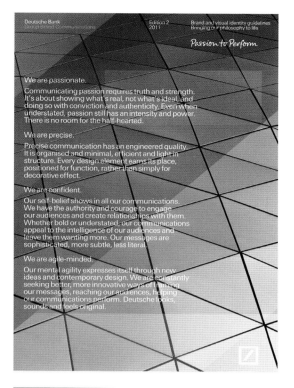

Brand History

▶ **1870:** Deutsche Bank is founded in Berlin to support the internationalisation of business, and to promote and facilitate trade relations between Germany, other European countries and overseas markets.

▶ **1872:** The first international branches open, in Yokohama and Shanghai, and trade relations begin with the Americas. The following year the first London branch opens.

▶ **1926:** Deutsche Bank arranges the merger of Daimler and Benz, takes on advisory roles for BP in a major UK deal, and advises on and finances the £2.6 billion London Underground Financing.

▶ **1970s:** The globalisation of Deutsche Bank continues: Deutsche Bank Luxembourg S.A. is founded and offices open in Moscow, Tokyo, Paris and New York.

▶ **1989:** Deutsche Bank takes over UK merchant bank Morgan Grenfell – a milestone in its presence in the City.

▶ **2001:** On 3rd October, Deutsche Bank lists its shares on the New York Stock Exchange.

▶ **2010:** In November, Deutsche Bank announces successful conclusion of the Deutsche Postbank takeover offer.

▶ **2011:** Deutsche Bank announces that Jürgen Fitschen and Anshu Jain will become co-chairmen of the Management Board and the Group Executive Committee of the Bank when Dr Josef Ackermann steps down in 2012.

With a new management team, Deutsche Bank will remain well placed to continue to seize the new opportunities available.

Promotion

Deutsche Bank's brand and visual identity places its renowned brand icon and the handwritten claim centre-stage. Conceptually, the combination of these two core brand elements has moved Deutsche into the league of modern global super brands. The Bank's recently updated brand strategy has resulted in reduced complexity, increased consistency and efficiency, and the provision of a robust framework to position the firm as a leading global financial institution.

The now globally aligned framework ensures consistent delivery of Deutsche's brand personality across businesses, regions and media channels, and positions it as a confident, premium brand. It provides the basis for a modern way to present and manage the Bank's identity – in terms of content and visual footprint.

In 2011, an identity programme was launched to articulate the key strengths of the Bank to internal and external audiences, with an integrated approach that exhibits the attitude and spirit of Deutsche across people, business, client relationships, shareholders and commitment to society. This narrative has been aligned to a key initiative to actively link Deutsche's DNA and brand identity with the behaviour of its employees, via a joint initiative with its human resources function.

In April 2011, the Bank's brand and visual identity gained external validation and praise from brand valuation specialists Brand Finance: "Over the last couple of years, Deutsche Bank has arguably undertaken the most innovative approach to bank branding in the world. In particular, their decision to focus on building recognition of their logo (decoupling it from their actual name), is unusual given the inherent conservatism of branding in financial services."

In the same month, design magazine Creative Review placed Deutsche Bank's logo at number two in its top 20, which was chosen by the editorial team, the magazine's readers and the wider industry. Deutsche's logo was rated against the likes of Coca-Cola, Chanel, Apple and Pirelli.

The opening of the Bank's BrandSpace at the newly refurbished Deutsche Bank Towers in April 2011 succeeded in transforming the global brand concept directly into a tangible object. It has therefore completed a further stage of Deutsche's brand strategy, in which the experiential spectrum is key.

Deutsche Bank, its foundations, employees and clients play a key role in firmly anchoring its CSR activities around the world. From annual global CSR investments of more than 80 million euros, about 12 per cent is dedicated to the UK. Its activities include the new Impact

Investment Fund, which supports the social finance industry and organisations offering both social and financial returns on investments; Playing Shakespeare with Deutsche Bank, a play specially produced for young people by Shakespeare's Globe Theatre; and more than 20 employee volunteer programmes supporting disadvantaged communities of London. The Bank has more than 40 non-profit partner organisations in the UK and its projects directly benefit hundreds of thousands of people each year.

Brand Values

Deutsche Bank's claim – 'Passion to Perform' – has always been much more than a marketing slogan or advertising strapline: it's the way the Bank does business. Through consistent delivery of the claim and the Deutsche Bank brand personality, the Bank aims to live its brand promise of excellence, relevant client solutions and responsibility to all stakeholders.

▶ **www.db.com**

Manufactured for more than 80 years, Dulux paint has an enviable and established reputation for quality. The brand is instantly recognisable thanks to its iconic Dulux mascot, the familiar Old English Sheepdog that made his debut in a TV advert in 1961. In recent years the brand's remit has expanded to offering not just high quality paint but also inspiration, support and reassurance throughout the decorating process.

Market

Dulux operates within the home DIY market; a busy category in the UK that includes key players such as Crown alongside retailers selling own-label products – such as B&Q and Homebase. Dulux is the leading market brand with 33 per cent volume and 40.9 per cent value share (Source: GfK Total Emulsion MAT November 2011). By going beyond the provision of products, Dulux positions itself within a 'changing spaces' subset of the market – providing the services and guidance necessary to enable people to individually adapt their surroundings and homes to suit.

Product

From primers and paints to applicators and wallpapers, Dulux provides a comprehensive portfolio of home decorating products.

As a leading brand, Dulux stays ahead of competitors not only by keeping pace with industry trends but also by setting them.

The Dulux paint range encompasses formulations to suit any interior and colours for all tastes. Variants include Kitchen+, which guards against permanent staining from grease; Bathroom+, with an anti-mould and moisture-resistant formulation; Endurance™, for hard-wearing colour; Once, which saves consumers time and money by providing a flawless finish in just one coat; and Light & Space™, which reflects twice as much light as ordinary paint and helps to meet the growing demand for brighter and airier living spaces.

Sustainability and the environment are at the forefront of Dulux's agenda and 2012 will see its standard emulsions

Did You Know?

To date, 14 Old English Sheepdogs have filled the role of the Dulux dog, all specially selected from a closely related line of pedigree dogs. Apart from the first dog – Dash – all of the dogs have been breed champions, and five of them have won Best in Show prizes.

A BRAND FROM
AkzoNobel

Willow Tree

MATT for walls and ceilings

A BRAND FROM
AkzoNobel

become even greener. Dulux has also made advances in paint application, launching the groundbreaking PaintPod in 2008. The application system ensures the correct amount of paint is applied to a paint roller via a pump mechanism.

While Dulux is synonymous with paint, its product portfolio also encompasses a range of colour tools and services such as the Dulux Let's Colour Studio app, which helps customers to create coordinating colour schemes, and an in-store colour mixing service that provides more than 1,200 colours.

Achievements

A household name, Dulux has an established and enviable reputation for high quality paints.

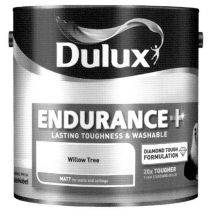

Brand History

▶ **1919:** Naylor Brothers, long-established varnish makers, set up a factory in Slough.

▶ **1926:** Nobel Chemical Finishes acquires Naylor Brothers.

▶ **1932:** Dulux paint is sold to the building trade for the first time.

▶ **1940:** Nobel Chemical Finishes becomes known as ICI (Paints) Ltd.

▶ **1953:** The Dulux brand is introduced to the consumer market for the first time.

▶ **1961:** Dash – the first Dulux dog – makes his debut in a black and white TV advert.

▶ **2004:** The Dulux Easy Living Editions range launches, comprising a palette of 'new neutrals'.

▶ **2006:** The Light & Space™ range launches, introducing a paint that reflects up to twice as much light as existing paints.

▶ **2007:** Dulux unveils a new campaign – We Know the Colours that Go – heralding the start of a new wave of personalisation and colour.

▶ **2008:** The Dulux PaintPod – the biggest innovation in painting since the roller and tray – is launched and AkzoNobel acquires ICI.

▶ **2011:** The Dulux dog, Spud, celebrates his 50th anniversary and the Ecosense paint range is launched.

Over the years it has won recognition both for its products and design services. Recent accolades include a Silver for Ecosense at the House Beautiful Awards 2010, followed by a Silver for its Timeless and Origins paint ranges at the 2011 awards. Timeless and Origins also took top spots at the 2011 DIY Week Awards, while PaintPod and PaintPod Compact have won various awards since their launch.

Recent Developments

Sustainability has been high on the Dulux agenda for many years. The brand remains committed to sustainable development and reducing the environmental impact of its products, services and business while also considering wider issues such as the communities in which it operates.

Dulux balances research into product improvement, such as the reduction of volatile organic compounds (VOCs), with creative projects and long-term commitments. One such commitment is its support of Community RePaint since 1993; in 2010 more than 215,000 litres of surplus and unwanted paint was redistributed to community groups, charities and voluntary organisations.

Launched in 2010, 'Let's Colour' is the brand's global initiative aimed at making a positive difference to people's lives on an international platform, improving living environments for many people in far-reaching parts of the world.

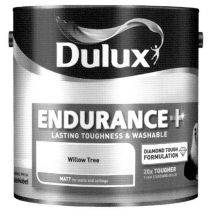

Did You Know?

Digby, the second Dulux dog, starred in his own movie in 1973 alongside Jim Dale and Spike Milligan: Digby – The Biggest Dog in the World.

Promotion

The Dulux dog, an iconic mascot and key advertising tool for the brand, celebrated his 50th anniversary in 2011. To mark the occasion, Dulux launched a host of promotional activities – from a nationwide tour through to a range of homewares featuring the iconic Old English Sheepdog.

The brand has recently revised its promotional strategy to position Dulux as a 'decorating partner'. While product quality remains implicit, the new approach enables the brand to demonstrate that it is there to help consumers at each stage as they transform their home. This widened emphasis is founded on the principle that a fresh coat of paint renews more than walls; it can improve how people feel, their mood and crucially their home life.

The expansion of the Dulux product range to include accessories and wallpapers ties in with the new positioning, while widening its distribution network to include retailers such as Next, Tesco and Wilkinsons also aims to provide a more holistic decorating experience.

Brand Values

Dulux values remain true to its founding principles: inspiring, uplifting, authentic and above all a trusted friend that can be relied on for every occasion.

▶ **www.dulux.co.uk**

Dulux TRADE

Trade & Trusted

Dulux Trade is the UK's leading manufacturer of high performance trade paint systems supporting decorators, specifiers, contractors and merchants. As an expert on environmental sustainability, colour and innovation, Dulux Trade creates solutions that deliver proven performance in the laboratory and in the real world, and sets a benchmark for quality in the coatings industry.

Market

In recent years the paint and coatings industry has experienced significant changes, such as the introduction of strict environmental regulation, company consolidations, and changing consumer expectations and demands. Dulux Trade is the leading brand in the UK trade market, with a 28.5 per cent share and despite the tough economic conditions, continues to perform well (Source: Company Data).

Brand History

▶ **1919:** Naylor Brothers, long-established varnish makers, set up a factory in Slough.

▶ **1926:** Nobel Chemical Finishes acquires Naylor Brothers.

▶ **1932:** Dulux paint is sold to the building trade for the first time.

▶ **1939:** The production of Dulux is suspended due to World War II.

▶ **1940:** Nobel Chemical Finishes becomes known as ICI (Paints) Ltd.

▶ **1948:** Manufacturing resumes and within four years Dulux is the leading paint brand in the trade market, promoted with the slogan: 'Say Dulux to your decorator.'

▶ **1987:** Dulux Trade launches the first automatic in-store tinting system in the UK market.

▶ **2008:** AkzoNobel acquires ICI and the Ecosure range is launched with matt, gloss and undercoat variants – eggshell follows in 2009.

▶ **2010:** AkzoNobel leads the way in implementing the new volatile organic compound (VOC) regulations and introduces the UK's first VOC 2010 compliant solvent-based trim paint for the trade industry.

The brand's success lies in its ability to adapt to market shifts by leading the way in formulation science, and in its commitment to improving the environmental footprint of products.

Product

Dulux Trade's reputation has been built on combining quality, performance, innovation, service and support. It is a recipe that has enabled it to develop a wide range of products and services designed to meet the needs of today's professional tradespeople.

The brand's comprehensive portfolio includes primers, special effects and exterior products in addition to the familiar standard finishes such as vinyl matt, vinyl silk and gloss. In selected outlets, Dulux Trade paints are available in more than 12,000 colours – in a wide range of finishes – via its in-store tinting system.

Dulux Trade remains the market leader by continuously working to improve product performance – such as improving opacity and spreading rates – as well as by offering high levels of service and technical support. Schemes such as Dulux Trade Contract Partnership, for example, help decorating contractors to grow their business by reassuring end customers of the quality of the service they will receive. Membership

Did You Know?

As a firm believer in the emotive properties of colour, Dulux Trade participates in AkzoNobel's 'Let's Colour' initiative. A worldwide project, it transforms grey community spaces – from streets to schools and squares – with colourful paint.

demonstrates that a business operates to a high standard and is committed to providing an outstanding professional service.

Achievements

In 2011, Dulux Trade's manufacturer AkzoNobel was recognised for its commitment to sustainability and minimising its environmental impact. The company was ranked in 100th place in the Carbon Reduction Commitment league table released by the Environment Agency, putting the company in the top five per cent worldwide.

AkzoNobel also picked up two of the three Sustainable Innovation Awards at the British Coatings Federation Awards 2011. The first recognised the development of a new Dulux Trade Vinyl Matt White formula that contains 15 per cent less embodied carbon and uses 20 per cent less water in production than its predecessor. The second was awarded for a rain water harvesting initiative at its Prudhoe factory

in Northumberland, where engineers developed a system to capture up to 1.7 million litres of rain water per year – cutting the factory's annual reliance on mains water by up to half.

The company was also highly commended for sustainable innovations and products that contribute to economic or social aspects of sustainability – such as Dulux Trade Light & Space, which reduces the need for artificial lighting and therefore reduces energy consumption.

Recent Developments

As a world leader in the production of high performance interior and exterior paints and coatings, Dulux Trade works seamlessly to develop new products and services to meet customer needs. In 2008 it introduced Ecosure, an environmentally focused range that balances sustainability and performance,

with matt, gloss and undercoat variants. Ecosure Matt, for instance, uses a unique Dry-Hide technology that enables it to match and in some cases exceed the performance of equivalent matt emulsions, delivering favourable levels of both opacity and coverage compared to ordinary ranges. Ecosure products contain significantly lower levels of VOCs, no added solvents and are low odour. They also contain reduced levels of embodied carbon and 25 per cent of all packaging is recycled. The range was extended in 2009 to include an eggshell variant.

Did You Know?

Dulux Trade runs a paint can recycling scheme across its network of Decorator Centres in England, Scotland and Northern Ireland. Users receive documentation to show that the cans do not go to landfill, and an annual certificate to prove their participation in the scheme. The materials are recycled into items ranging from benches to spanners.

Promotion

With professional contractors, specifiers and decorators making up Dulux Trade's core customer base, promotional activity focuses on the dependability, quality and consistently high performance of the brand. The key message in all promotional activity is that Dulux Trade is the leading UK brand and can be relied upon to get the job done. The two most recent brand straplines are short and pithy to underline this key message: 'Number one and that's a fact' (2010/11) and 'Trade and Trusted' (2012).

The brand bolsters its relationship with trade professionals by providing free-of-charge product guides and tools to help them make informed decisions. Dulux Trade's new Woodcare Product Guide, for example, is a pocket-sized booklet designed to make choosing the appropriate woodcare product quick and simple. The TradeXpress iPhone app, introduced in 2010, goes further by helping professionals research and source a wide range of products on the go.

Brand Values

As a trusted industry authority, Dulux Trade's brand values – integrity, reliability and knowledge – reinforce its uncompromising commitment to quality. Dulux Trade is a dependable brand that professionals know they can rely on for the tools, products, service and insider information they need to do the best possible job.

▶ **www.duluxtrade.co.uk**

DURACELL®

Duracell® has been providing people with power for more than 45 years. The UK's number one selling AA and AAA battery brand (Source: IRI 2011), Duracell® produces a variety of personal power options for consumers' power needs, from traditional batteries through to solutions for power-hungry portable devices. The Duracell® Bunny has become an enduring symbol of the brand; created in 1973, it is now one of the world's most successful brand icons.

Market

Duracell® operates across three power markets: traditional alkaline batteries, rechargeable batteries, and chargers for batteries and portable devices.

In both the total and alkaline battery market Duracell® leads the pack against its nearest rival brand, Energiser. Duracell® is market leader with more than 55 per cent volume share in the total battery market and a 56.7 per cent value share of the £327 million market. In the alkaline market Duracell® has a 66 per cent value share (Source: Information Resources Incorporated (IRI)/Gfk 12 months ending August 2011).

Product

Alkaline batteries make up the greater part of Duracell®'s product line-up, with the two pillars of its portfolio being Duracell® Plus Power and Duracell® Ultra Power. A recent addition is Duracell® Ultra Lithium, the brand's most powerful AA battery ever for long-term performance in medium- and high-drain devices.

Rechargable products also account for a key share, with the range encompassing both family-sized and compact chargers. The Duracell® Speedy Charger has been introduced as part of a refreshed product line-up and is able to recharge AA batteries in as little as one hour. The 15 Minute Charger provides even quicker recharging.

In 2011, the company expanded into portable USB chargers by launching its two Portable models, which work with smartphones and MP3 players. The five-hour charger can charge two devices on the go, while the three-hour offers a slimmer, more lightweight design for charging one device at a time.

Did You Know?

The Duracell® Bunny made its first appearance in a US advert in 1973.

A Duracell® battery appears in the film The Matrix. Laurence Fishburne's character, Morpheus, uses it to illustrate how humans are being used as a power supply.

Duracell® also offers a range of speciality batteries for watches and electronic, security, photo lithium and photo devices.

Achievements

Over the years, Duracell® has received recognition for its portfolio, with consumers voting several products as ones 'which genuinely enhance their lives'. 2011 saw Duracell® Ultra Power win Product of the Year in the General Household category, while Duracell® Ultra won Product of the Year in the Battery category in 2009. Also in 2009 and 2011, independent consumer reviewer Which? awarded Duracell® Ultra AAA and AA with a Best Buy accolade.

Such recognition builds on the success of previous years: Duracell® Mini Charger won Battery Product of the Year in 2008, while PowerPix – a specialist digital camera battery – was chosen as Best Innovation of the Year for 2007 in the Battery category.

Recent Developments

In its ongoing quest to innovate and add value for consumers, Duracell® has upgraded its formulation across all AA and AAA alkaline products as well as improving the functionality, user comfort and design across its product portfolio including cells, rechargeables and torches.

DURACELL®
Rechargeable
15 Minute CHARGER

Ready in **15 Minutes***

DURACELL®

4 AA/AAA NiMH

15 mn* 4x AA/AAA

*Approx. 75% of full charge, when using Duracell 1700 mAh AA or 750 mAh AAA NiMH Batteries

Includes: 2 AA 1700 mAh + 2 AAA 750 mAh NiMH

Brand History

▶ **1920s:** Scientist Samuel Ruben and a manufacturer of tungsten filament wire, Philip Rogers Mallory, join forces to form Duracell® International.

▶ **1950s:** Ruben improves the alkaline manganese battery, making it more compact, durable and longer lasting than anything before it. Eastman Kodak introduces cameras with a built-in flash unit that need the added power provided by alkaline manganese cells but in a new size, AAA – this puts alkaline cells on the map.

▶ **1964:** Duracell® introduces its AAA battery. The consumer market for Duracell® batteries soon rockets.

▶ **2000s:** Duracell® continues to lead the way with product innovation, reflected in the Duracell® Plus and Ultra Power batteries. Duracell® launches its Best Ever Formulation across the AA/AAA alkaline portfolio and a refreshed design of the entire product line-up.

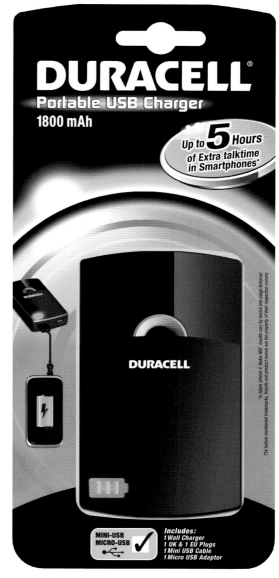

The technology behind Duracell® Ultra Power AA and AAA cells has been improved to make them the longest lasting Duracell® alkaline batteries. Duracell® Ultra Power cells now have a high performance cathode (HPC) with superconductive graphite and a pure and higher level of manganese dioxide (the active ingredient) ensuring the best ever performance from Duracell® alkaline batteries.

Duracell®'s brand extension into gadget chargers has seen the company apply its high product specifications and brand values to a new category with the launch of its two Portable chargers for smartphones and MP3 players.

To meet the desire for more sustainable products, Duracell® is committed to manufacturing batteries and products that minimise the impact on the environment. The company recently completed a lifecycle assessment in partnership with Massachusetts Institute for Technology (MIT) to help understand the opportunities for reducing the impact of single-use and rechargeable batteries.

Promotion

Duracell® continues to invest in the long-term equity of the brand, marketing across multiple touchpoints to support its alkaline, rechargeables and device charger portfolios. TV, print and PR continue to be utilised, while digital spend against display, social media and gaming has been an increasing focus in the past few years.

Brand Values

Duracell® is committed to following consumers' personal power needs, whatever they might be, and this is what drives the brand's innovation. For example, as well as its market-leading alkaline products, Duracell® now also has a range of charging solutions for lithium-ion devices such as phones and MP3 players. As consumers look for convenient power for on-the-go charging, this has become a key focus for research, development and business building.

▶ **www.duracell.co.uk**

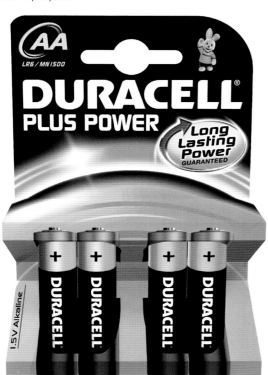

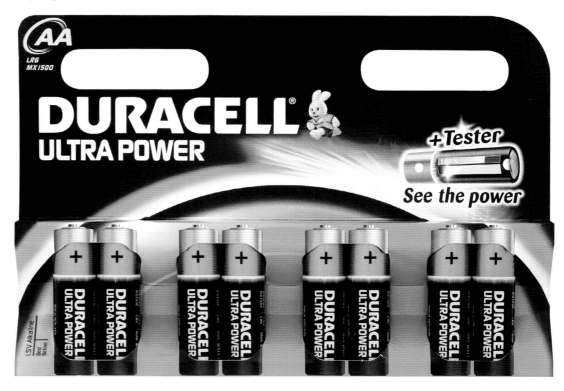

Eddie Stobart

Eddie Stobart is the road haulage element of Stobart Group, a fast-developing public limited company with wide-ranging multimodal transport interests. The UK's best known logistics brand employs more than 5,500 people at over 40 sites, operates around six million sq ft of premium warehousing capacity, has a fleet of 2,280 trucks, and operates two airports and several freight trains.

Market

In the notoriously hard-pressed road haulage sector, the iconic 'Eddie Stobart' name is one of the brand's greatest strengths. Highly competitive pricing and renowned levels of customer service and efficiency, combined with 95 per cent brand recognition throughout the UK, have ensured that Eddie Stobart is not only keeping pace but expanding and increasing in profitability. The UK logistics market remains highly fragmented with Stobart Group having a market share of around two per cent. Group turnover for the year ending 28th February 2011 increased to £500 million with a profit of £34.5 million.

Product

Eddie Stobart is a logistics specialist and as part of Stobart Group, has a full transport service encompassing road, rail, sea and air services as well as strategic warehousing and full distribution logistics offerings.

Achievements

In an ever-more environmentally conscious world, Eddie Stobart has been at the forefront of the road haulage sector's responses to environmental considerations; Stobart Group was one of the first businesses to train drivers in the Safe and Fuel Efficient Driving (SAFED) techniques that can reduce carbon emissions by as much as 10 per cent.

A proactive approach has also been taken to address the traditional haulage problem of 'empty miles'. As a result, Eddie Stobart now has the best fleet utilisation figures in the industry: currently 85 per cent compared to the industry average of 72 per cent. Through incisive planning, shared capacity solutions and more strategic vehicle tracking, Stobart Group is committed to pursuing efficiency even further.

> ### Did You Know?
> **Recent surveys show that when driving on Britain's major roads a Stobart vehicle is passed, on average, every 4.5 minutes.**
>
> **The Stobart fleet travels a distance equivalent to 24 laps of the Earth every day.**

> ### Did You Know?
> **Every Stobart vehicle is individually identified by a girl's name that is unique within the fleet.**
>
> **The Stobart Group has 37,000 tyres in use at any one time.**

Eddie Stobart has also led a campaign to introduce high-volume trailers to UK roads. Its innovative Envirotrailer will deliver up to 20 per cent increased capacity, leading to a reduction in the number of trucks on the roads, and will play a valuable role in cutting waste, carbon emissions and congestion. A government-approved trial of these new trailers begins in 2012.

Recent Developments

In June 2011, Stobart Group agreed a 10-year contract with easyJet, enabling the airline to use the Group's London Southend Airport base. easyJet commences flights to a number of European destinations in April 2012, with around 800,000 passengers expected to pass through the airport each year.

In the second half of 2011, Stobart Rail added more national and international rail freight routes to its portfolio, in partnership with

Stobart Transport & Distribution

Stobart Estates

Stobart Infrastructure & Civils

Stobart Air

Stobart biomass

Stobart biomass — Supplying Renewable Energy

Brand History

▶ **1950s:** Eddie Stobart establishes an agricultural contracting business in the Cumbrian village of Hesket Newmarket.

▶ **1980:** The business relocates to Carlisle. The fleet, numbering just eight vehicles, consists mainly of tippers but rapidly develops to include the more versatile artics.

▶ **1992:** Eddie Stobart is voted Haulier of the Year by the Motor Transport Industry, testimony to its dedication and hard work in revolutionising the sector.

▶ **2001:** Rapid, sustained growth results in a fleet of 900 vehicles and 2,000 staff operating from 27 sites and delivering a turnover of £130 million.

▶ **2004:** The company is acquired by WA Developments International. A major rebrand takes place, from vehicle liveries to clothing, heralding a new era for the business.

▶ **2005:** Eddie Stobart wins its first Tesco Distribution Centre contract.

▶ **2007:** Eddie Stobart merges with Westbury Property Fund in a £138 million deal that sees the formation of the public limited company Stobart Group.

▶ **2008:** The business expands to a total workforce in excess of 5,000 and a fleet numbering around 2,000 vehicles.

▶ **2009:** A groundbreaking Iberian rail freight service is launched.

▶ 2010: Stobart Biomass Products is formed to source and transport sustainable biomass. In addition, a six-part series is broadcast on Channel 5: 'Eddie Stobart: Trucks & Trailers'.

▶ **2011:** In March, Edward Stobart, the early founder of the business, passes away. In the same year, Stobart Group signs a 10-year deal with easyJet, enabling the airline to operate from its London Southend Airport base. The first-ever Stobart Fest attracts thousands of fans as they meet stars of the television documentary.

major retailers. One such key route is the Daventry to Thurrock service. Operating six days a week, it transports groceries for Tesco and will help take 40,000 lorries off the road, saving thousands of tonnes of carbon emissions every year.

Promotion

An observational documentary charting the achievements of Eddie Stobart's transport operations was first broadcast on Channel 5 in September 2010. With each episode attracting around two million viewers, the Eddie Stobart brand was introduced to a whole new audience. A third series is being broadcast in 2012.

The Group operates its own Members' Club with thousands of dedicated followers, and retails a wide variety of branded merchandise. In September 2011 the first-ever Stobart Fest gave fans the chance to see the Eddie Stobart trucks up close and to meet the stars of the

documentary series. More than 6,500 people attended the event.

In 2011 the Group broadened its exposure after a deal with the Professional Jockeys Association saw the Stobart brand emblazoned on the breeches of many of the nation's jockeys as they competed at racecourses across the UK.

Brand Values

Since its inception, the Eddie Stobart brand has built its reputation through a commitment to courteous drivers, its high quality fleet, and exceptional levels of service. Today, adapting to society's changing needs, the Group has added exemplary employment and environmental practices to its core principles and is working to achieve its vision of building a fully multimodal transport offering for its customers.

▶ **www.stobartgroup.com**

eDF ENERGY

EDF Energy is one of the UK's biggest energy companies, the largest producer of low carbon electricity, and energy supplier to more than 5.5 million business and residential customers. With a diverse business customer base including small and medium sized enterprises, public sector organisations and leading high street brands, EDF Energy supplies more power to British businesses than any other energy company.

A range of energy supply contracts means businesses can manage their energy purchasing in a way that fits their in-house skills and appetite for risk.

Streamlined administration simplifies customers' billing arrangements and provides easy access to their account information.

A raft of energy saving measures enables EDF Energy to help businesses reduce costs and meet carbon reduction targets. These range from an award-winning free Energy Efficiency Toolkit, to Energy Performance Contracts with guarantees to reduce clients' energy costs.

Market

There are three key challenges facing the energy industry and its customers. Firstly, price volatility and affordability. The outlook for energy prices remains challenging. At this time of economic uncertainty, managing energy costs is crucial to the survival of many businesses, and energy companies have a duty to care for their most vulnerable customers. EDF Energy consistently offers competitive prices.

Secondly, security of supply. The phasing out of fossil fuels and closure of many existing power stations has produced a growing need for new sources of energy, known as an 'energy gap'. In response, EDF Energy is supporting the government's commitment to develop a diverse energy mix, including low carbon technologies such as nuclear and renewable energy.

Finally, climate change. Carbon reduction through energy efficiency is taking hold as consumers and businesses realise that saving energy is a highly cost effective way to substantially reduce their carbon footprint. Legislation and national targets are bringing this to media attention.

Product

EDF Energy has structured its offering around the four main requirements businesses have of their energy supplier.

Its insight services help businesses to better understand how the energy markets work, the current wholesale energy prices, and relevant regulations.

eNERGY AWARDS 11 WINNER

Achievements

EDF Energy's B2B division earned several accolades in 2011. It was named Supplier of the Year at the 2011 Energy Awards, achieved the ServiceMark standard from the Institute of Customer Services, and was the first large business energy supplier to gain Quality in Credit Management accreditation.

Brand History

▶ **1990:** The UK electricity market undergoes privatisation.

▶ **1998–2002:** London Electricity, SWEB and SeeBoard are merged.

▶ **2003:** The EDF Energy brand launches in the UK.

▶ **2006:** EDF Energy becomes the first UK energy supplier to introduce a social tariff.

▶ **2007:** EDF Energy launches its Climate Commitments, the most significant package of environmental initiatives adopted by any major UK energy company. EDF Energy becomes the first sustainability partner of the London 2012 Olympic and Paralympic Games.

▶ **2008:** EDF Energy launches its Social Commitments, a set of pledges focusing on safety, energy affordability, security of supply, employee development and community investment.

▶ **2009:** EDF Energy merges with British Energy. It also partners with the Eden Project, Global Action Plan and LOCOG to launch Team Green Britain.

▶ **2011:** EDF Energy scores 97 per cent in the Business in the Community Corporate Responsibility Index and is awarded Platinum Plus status. The B2B division is awarded Supplier of the Year at the Energy Awards.

The company has been awarded the Carbon Trust Standard, a mark of excellence given to organisations for measuring, managing and reducing carbon emissions. In addition, its Energy Efficiency Toolkit received a Green Apple Award from The Green Organisation in recognition of its commitment to helping others be more environmentally friendly.

Recent Developments

In 2009 and again in 2011, EDF Energy's approach to sustainability was recognised with Platinum Plus status in the Business in the Community Corporate Responsibility Index. This represents the highest possible standard and recognises EDF Energy as the best in its sector.

Also in 2011, EDF Energy held its third Green Britain Day: a focal point for the Team Green Britain movement, which has been developed in partnership with the Eden Project, Global Action Plan and The London Organising Committee of the Olympic and Paralympic Games (LOCOG). The campaign aims to help people save energy and money,

while having fun in the process. The initiative has hundreds of thousands of members and in 2010 won at the Sabre Awards, the Focal International Awards, the Festival for Media Awards and the Media Week Awards.

Promotion

Energy is a complex and fast changing market for businesses, so much of EDF Energy's promotional activity focuses on education to build credibility and enhance customer engagement.

Did You Know?

In 2011 EDF Energy was awarded the UK's largest ever electricity supply contract by the Government Procurement Service.

EDF Energy is the UK's largest producer of electricity and the biggest generator of low carbon electricity. Carbon emissions from its electricity generation fell from 813 g/kWh in 2006 to 218 g/kWh in 2010.

Did You Know?

EDF Energy is working with ParalympicsGB to make them a green team ahead of London 2012 and make their training camps more sustainable.

Team EDF consists of 20 athletes who are training for the London 2012 Olympic and Paralympic Games. The athletes are all sponsored or employed by the EDF Group.

london 2012
official electricity supplier

In 2011 this centred on challenging existing price-focused energy procurement practices. A new blueprint for energy procurement was also promoted, based on integrating energy supply and demand management to achieve long-term value for money for businesses. The campaign included trade events, public relations and advertising, and

showcased a groundbreaking Energy Performance Contract that guarantees to save Morrisons at least £1 million per year for three years.

EDF Energy's Talk Power conference provides business leaders, policy makers and opinion formers with a platform to discuss key energy issues and share learning. Thanks to a 14-year record, it is widely recognised throughout the industry as the best event of its type and always includes appearances from leading industry speakers, key government figures, and EDF Energy's own supply and trading specialists.

EDF Energy has partnered with publishers of the well-known Dummies® franchise to create 'Carbon Management for Dummies' and 'Electricity Buying for Dummies', providing a step-by-step guide to successfully navigating today's energy market.

Brand Values

EDF Energy's challenge is to lead the decarbonisation of energy in Britain. To achieve this, the company aims to enable everyone to save today for a brighter tomorrow, together.

▶ **www.edfenergy.com/business**

Since 1994 Eurostar has carried more than 100 million people and revolutionised travel between the UK and the Continent. Now the company that heralded the dawn of a new era in train travel is going further with connections to new destinations such as Amsterdam, Cologne and the South of France, but also by enabling customers to get more from their trips through exclusive partnerships and destination offers.

Market

Eurostar operates within the European short haul market. At present, competitors are predominately airline companies that also operate European short haul routes, ranging from Air France and British Airways through to Ryanair and easyJet. The recent liberalisation of the European market for international railway journeys will change this. From 2015 it's expected that on some routes Eurostar will also be in direct competition with other high-speed rail operators as the market becomes more open and competitive.

Product

Eurostar offers daily direct services to Paris, Brussels and Lille. It also offers regular services to Disneyland® Paris (operating daily during school holidays and five days a week at other times), as well as seasonal services to Bourg-St-Maurice in the French Alps in the winter and Avignon during the summer. Thanks to the Railteam alliance with other European high-speed operators, Eurostar also offers easy connections across France, Belgium, the Netherlands, Germany and Switzerland.

There are three classes of service on board: Business Premier for the discerning traveller, offering benefits such as flexible ticketing, 10-minute check-in, access to the Business Premier lounges, generous seating and full catering; Standard Premier, providing spacious surroundings and a light meal; and Standard, which offers excellent value for money.

Achievements

Eurostar's major achievement has been becoming the key transport link between London and the Continent, where airlines were once the default option.

Its dominance in the short haul European market is undeniable, with Eurostar voted the World's Leading Rail Service at the World Travel Awards every year from 2000 to 2009. In addition, it has won a number of marketing distinctions in the UK and Europe including the Grand Prix Effie 2009 in Belgium and the Grand Prix de la Communication Extérieure 2010 in France. In 2011, readers of The Daily Telegraph voted Eurostar their favourite cross-Channel operator.

Since its services began in 1994, Eurostar has regularly held ticket draws for charities and good causes, providing support to local communities particularly around its stations, offices and depot. Eurostar is also a founding member of the King's Cross Business Partnership, which is committed to developing CSR initiatives that help enrich communities for local residents, employees, commuters and travellers, and is a supporter of organisations such as the Young People's Trust for the Environment and the KM Walk to School charity.

Did You Know?

To celebrate the launch of services from St Pancras International, Eurostar commissioned a short film directed by Shane Meadows. Released as a feature length film, Somers Town, in August 2008, it won the Michael Powell Award at the Edinburgh Film Festival and the Best Actor accolade at the Tribeca Film Festival.

Brand History

▶ **1994:** Eurostar launches services between London, Paris, Lille and Brussels.

▶ **1996:** Services begin between London and Disneyland® Paris.

▶ **1997:** A new service launches between London and the French Alps.

▶ **2002:** A route between London and Avignon is launched.

▶ **2006:** Eurostar establishes a partnership with Sony Pictures for the release of the film The Da Vinci Code.

▶ **2007:** Eurostar services launch from the newly reopened St Pancras International, London.

▶ **2010:** Eurostar announces its sponsorship of the London 2012 Olympic and Paralympic Games. To celebrate, a unique Tri-City-Athlon is organised, encompassing three cities in a single day – Paris (swimming), Brussels (cycling) and London (running).

▶ **2011:** A new Eurostar brand identity is unveiled.

Recent Developments

Eurostar has announced the purchase of 10 new Siemens-built trains that are due to come into service in 2014 and expected to be a springboard for services to new European destinations. The company is also undertaking the refurbishment of its existing fleet.

Eurostar recently relaunched its environmental programme, Tread Lightly, furthering its work on sustainable travel. The initiative, first unveiled in 2007, became a hallmark of the Eurostar brand and revolves around three key angles: the Eurostar Ashden Award for Sustainable Travel, which promotes sustainable travel initiatives in the UK, France and Belgium; encouraging more people to switch to train travel for continental trips; and reducing carbon emissions by 25 per cent by 2015.

Promotion

From 1994 to 2007, most Eurostar communications for the UK market focused on Paris, Lille and Brussels (and seasonal services), targeted specifically at London and the South East. Eurostar's move to St Pancras International, however, has made the service more accessible and since 2008 its advertising reach has been extended to regional hubs including Birmingham, Manchester, Leeds, and Bristol. In 2010, Eurostar also started advertising connecting destinations further afield such as the South of France, Cologne and more recently, Amsterdam.

Recent years have seen Eurostar develop bespoke campaigns for overseas markets, with a focus on the US and Australia to encourage visitors to use Eurostar during European trips.

Eurostar has also built on its high profile UK campaigns. For example, an online game was launched as an extension of its partnership with The Da Vinci Code, and during the 2007/08 countdown to the opening of St Pancras International, Eurostar commissioned Somers Town, a film directed by Shane Meadows and set in the local area.

In the autumn of 2011, the brand launched its first pan-European TV collaboration featuring British musician Jarvis Cocker,

Did You Know?

Eurostar set a Guinness World Record for the longest non-stop international train journey in history: in 2006 it carried the cast and film-makers of The Da Vinci Code from London to Cannes, direct.

French film director Michel Gondry, and the Belgian pop star Arno Hintjens.

In 2010, Eurostar announced its newly appointed status as a Provider to the London 2012 Olympic and Paralympic Games through the Tri-City-Athlon, a one-day triathlon across Paris, Brussels and London.

Brand Values

Eurostar is a brand that is always moving forward. Its values are centred on three key areas: being pioneering in spirit, being destination experts and acting responsibly.

▶ **www.eurostar.com**

ExCeL LONDON

An ADNEC Group Company

ExCeL London has staged more than 3,800 events since 2000. More than 12 million people from 200 countries have visited, experiencing everything from sporting events and religious festivals to award ceremonies and conferences. ExCeL London is home to some of the UK's leading exhibitions, including Grand Designs Live and Top Gear Live, and hosts events for blue-chip clients, government organisations and associations.

Market

ExCeL London is one of the UK's premier venues for exhibitions, events and conferences; a market currently worth £20 billion.

The venue operates across the sector and markets itself as able to handle almost any event imaginable. In addition to its two large halls, ExCeL London offers two conference centres, 45 meeting rooms and the UK's largest fully flexible auditorium. The campus also includes more than 40 bars and restaurants, six on-site hotels and a host of additional services.

Product

ExCeL London is a £560 million international venue located on a 100-acre waterside campus in Royal Victoria Dock. It is the largest and most versatile venue in London, boasting 100,000 sq m of available multipurpose space.

It's also home to the capital's first International Convention Centre, ICC London ExCeL, which includes the UK's largest fully flexible auditorium and London's largest banqueting hall: the ICC Capital Hall. A conference suite is also on offer – the ICC Capital Suite – comprising 17 individual meeting rooms with the flexibility to host breakout sessions for 50–1,200 delegates, plus reception and registration areas.

There are six on-site hotels providing 1,400 bedrooms and ranging from budget to four-star, 3,700 car parking spaces, and three on-site DLR stations linking to the Jubilee Underground line. London City Airport, which is five minutes away, offers over 350 flights a day to more than 30 European destinations, as well as New York.

Did You Know?

ExCeL London will be the most complex venue in the history of the Olympic Games, playing host to boxing, wrestling, judo, tae-kwon-do, weight lifting, fencing and table tennis, as well as six Paralympic sports.

Achievements

ExCeL London has received many industry accolades over the years including World's Leading Meetings and Conference Centre at the 2010 World Travel Awards. Recognition in 2011 included Best UK Venue, UK Venue of the Year and Exhibition Venue of the Year at the Event Awards, as well as Best Conference Venue at the Conference Awards.

The venue also has the accolade of being at the forefront of London's Thames Gateway regeneration, playing host to numerous events during the London 2012 Olympic and Paralympic Games.

ExCeL London's green credentials have come to the forefront in the last few years. Developments include an on-site Materials Recycling Facility and colour-coded bins for all events. The venue also has the UK's largest and only commercial wormery, which recycles all types of food waste. In the last four years ExCeL has reduced its gas and electricity consumption by 65 per cent and 28 per cent, respectively, and achieved a 65 per cent reduction in CO_2 emissions. In 2011 ExCeL recycled 89 per cent of its waste.

ExCeL London was ranked 47th in The Sunday Times Best Green Companies 2010 list, while

Brand History

▶ **1855:** The Royal Victoria Dock site, on which ExCeL London will later sit, is opened by Prince Albert as a working dock.

▶ **1960s:** Containerisation and other technological changes, together with a switch in Britain's trade following EEC membership, lead to the Royal Dock's rapid decline.

▶ **1981:** The dock finally closes.

▶ **1988:** The Association of Exhibition Organisers (aeo) approaches architect Ray Moxley to locate and design a new exhibition and conference centre within the M25; the Royal Victoria Dock site is found in 1990.

▶ **1994:** The London Docklands Development Corporation launches an international competition to appoint a preferred developer, which is won by the ExCeL London team.

▶ **2000:** ExCeL London opens in November, as one of Europe's largest regeneration projects.

▶ **2008:** ExCeL London announces its Phase 2 expansion. Event space will be increased by 50 per cent and include a convention centre with a 5,000-seat auditorium.

▶ **2009:** The official identity of Phase 2 – that is, London's first International Convention Centre – is launched and endorsed by the Mayor of London, Boris Johnson, and Visit London.

▶ **2010:** In May, ICC London ExCeL opens – on time and on budget.

▶ **2011:** In November, ExCeL opens its 252-bedroom Starwood Aloft hotel.

additional 'green' accolades include a Diamond Award in the Mayor of London's Green500, a Carbon Saver Gold Standard, and a Gold Award for the National Recycling Stars. Furthermore, in the government's energy performance ratings ExCeL was placed in category C, showing that it was rated as 38 per cent more energy efficient than any other venue of a similar type. ExCeL is also committed to the United Nations Global Compact.

Recent Developments

On October 31st 2011, ExCeL London opened the UK's first Starwood Aloft hotel. Linked to the ICC London ExCeL, the Aloft is influenced by modern urban design, houses 252 bedrooms and aims to deliver a social guest experience – all at an affordable price.

Did You Know?

ExCeL London is the only venue in the UK to span two railway stations.

In summer 2012, ExCeL London will be linked to The O2 by cable car, a first for the city.

Promotion

The marketing team targets two distinct audiences: the exhibitions industry and the conference and events market.

UK exhibition organisers are targeted via a variety of communication channels, including e-bulletins, interactive brochures, PR and the ExCeL London website. The venue also undertakes as much face-to-face marketing as possible, through organiser forums, corporate hospitality, and strategy days.

Unique to the consumer exhibitions campaign is an award-winning marketing and PR support package, tailored for trade and consumer show organisers. 2010 saw the launch of the ExCeL London Supporters Club, which comprises more than 100 businesses in East London, from hotels, bars and restaurants, to airlines and transport providers. Networking events are arranged throughout the year, enabling businesses to discuss ways in which they can help enhance the ExCeL experience for their clients.

The conference and events marketing campaign targets both UK and international event planners and is focused on promoting the venue in the context of London, a key city in Europe. To this end, much of the international activity is executed in conjunction with London & Partners, jointly promoting the destination and the venue.

Brand Values

ExCeL London is more than an events venue. It is an organisation that has made a promise to its clients: ExCeL will continue to grow – through investment, passion, expertise and service delivery – to establish itself as the leading international events venue, while respecting its neighbourhood and the environment. This promise supports the ADNEC Group goals and long-term strategy, and is underpinned by a commitment among staff to deliver the ultimate environment in which events can flourish.

▶ **www.excel-london.co.uk**

FAIRY

Fairy is Britain's number one dish-cleaning brand and has been a trusted household name since it first appeared in 1898 on a bar of soap. Today the brand represents a range of products renowned for their cleaning ability and caring nature, with Fairy consistently bringing effective and innovative new formulas to market. In the last year, 112 million bottles of Fairy Liquid were bought, equating to 61 per cent of the total UK market (Source: IRI October 2011).

Market

The dish-cleaning market contains sink and dishwasher sectors, with Fairy leading the total category in both volume and value sales (Source: Information Resources Incorporated (IRI) October 2011). Fairy has maintained market leadership for more than 50 years thanks to its brand attributes of unbeatable performance and value, lasting up to 50 per cent longer than the next best selling brand (Source: Independent Laboratory Testing).

Product

During the 1950s, most people used powders and crystals to wash dishes and it was Fairy that launched the first liquid product: Fairy Liquid. By the end of its first year, six out of 10 people in the UK had bought it.

Today the Fairy Washing Up Liquid range consists of Fairy Liquid Original and Lemon; the Fairy Aromatics range, with a selection of fresh scents; the Fairy Antibac range, which helps prevent germ growth on sponges for up to 24 hours; the Fairy Clean & Care collection, which comes 'with a touch of Olay softness'; and the new Fairy Platinum range, which delivers the degreasing power of an overnight soak in just 10 minutes.

The Fairy portfolio also encompasses a range of dishwasher detergents and additives, including the revolutionary Fairy Platinum, the first dual action dishwasher tablet that leaves dishes 'sparkling clean' while also maintaining dishwasher cleanliness by helping to prevent the build up of grease on dishwasher parts*.

Did You Know?

One bottle of Fairy Liquid washed 14,763 dirty plates – a world record.

Fairy is recognised by the RSPB as the best product for cleaning birds after oil spills, and Fairy donates products for use during such disasters.

Achievements

Fairy is Britain's number one dish-cleaning brand, and has seen the UK's highest value growth in the dish care sector in the last year, when turnover topped £179 million (Source: IRI 2011). The brand's top cleaning results together with its kindness to skin have seen Fairy certified by the British Skin Foundation.

Industry accolades include Dishwasher Product of the Year for Fairy All-In-One in 2007, Washing Up Product of the Year for Fairy Liquid Fresh Lavender in 2008, Household Cleaning Product of the Year for Fairy Clean & Care in 2009, and a Which? Best Buy award for Fairy Platinum dishwasher tablets in 2010.

Fairy supports a number of charities and has partnered with children's charity Make-A-Wish Foundation for the last eight years, raising more than £650,000 to date.

Recent Developments

The past few years have seen a steady stream of product development from the Fairy brand. 2010 saw Fairy Liquid deliver a wide-ranging innovation programme across the key pillars of its entire portfolio, with formula upgrades in Original and Lemon, and new variants for Antibac and Aromatics. The programme also saw Fairy Clean & Care partner with beauty brand Olay to create a product that is designed to leave hands noticeably softer and smoother – in comparison with Fairy Original – when washing dishes. These breakthrough innovations saw Fairy Liquid reach its highest ever value share in the hand dishwashing market: 72 per cent in December 2010 (Source: IRI 2010).

Fairy continues to bring the most effective and innovative formulas to market to ensure there is a top-performing Fairy product to suit every home and every usage occasion. In August 2011, Fairy introduced its most powerful washing up liquid ever: Fairy Platinum. Since launch it has sold 2.66 million bottles, representing 11.1 per cent of category value in September 2011 (Source: IRI 2011).

Did You Know?

The Fairy baby that has appeared on all of the brand's products since the 1930s is called 'Bizzie'.

Promotion

Fairy Liquid television advertising campaigns first began in the 1950s, instigating a host of celebrity endorsements, including actress Nanette Newman with the much-loved line, "hands that do dishes can feel soft as your face with mild green fairy liquid".

In recent years, Fairy's advertising has seen chefs Ainsley Harriott, Anthony Worrell Thomson and Gary Rhodes front the brand together. Brand communications emphasise unbeatable performance and value due to product mileage. Its FAIRYconomy campaign, for example, highlighted the value benefits of its longer lasting formula to the consumer's pocket and the environment, with fewer bottles required.

In 2010, Fairy Liquid celebrated its 50th anniversary with a limited edition version of the original white bottle and the return of Nanette Newman as the face of the campaign. Within six months of the campaign launch, 3.8 million bottles had been sold (Source: IRI 2010).

In 2011 Fairy launched into the world of social media with its own Facebook page accruing more than 20,000 fans to date.

Brand Values

Fairy is a family-oriented brand with strong links to the kitchen and the role of mealtimes within families. It is also associated with environmental and sustainable organisations such as the RSPB, WWF, Energy Saving Trust, Waterwise and Waste Watch. Its products are concentrated in order to reduce packaging waste, bottles are recyclable, and the dishwasher range is designed to be used in short cycles and at lower temperatures, saving energy. Fairy is part of the Future Friendly programme, a partnership between brands and leading sustainability experts that is aimed at inspiring and enabling people to live more sustainable lives.

▶ **www.facebook.com/fairydish**

Brand History

▶ **1898:** Fairy Soap launches through Thomas Hedley & Sons.

▶ **1930:** Procter & Gamble acquires the brand and Fairy Baby trademark.

▶ **1987:** Lemon-scented Fairy Liquid is introduced alongside Fairy Original. Two years later, a Fairy Non-Biological laundry product launches for sensitive skin.

▶ **1997:** Fairy Liquid with antibacterial action is introduced.

▶ **2000:** The signature white Fairy Liquid bottle is replaced with a transparent version for the first time.

▶ **2003:** Fairy Powerspray launches, for tough, burnt-on stains, adding £9 million to the category.

▶ **2006:** Fairy introduces the first of its Fairy for Dishwashers range, and Fairy sales top £120 million. The following year the Machine Cleaner and Rinse Aid products are launched.

▶ **2008:** Fairy launches Fairy Clean & Care, which provides the dual benefits of helping to keep hands soft and moisturised while leaving dishes 'squeaky clean'.

▶ **2009:** Fairy launches its unique dual action dishwasher tablet, Fairy Platinum. The Fairy Liquid formula is also improved and the bottle is updated with a new ergonomic design.

▶ **2010:** Fairy launches a wide-ranging innovation programme, and Fairy Clean & Care partners with beauty brand Olay.

▶ **2011:** Fairy launches its most powerful washing up liquid to date – Fairy Platinum – and the brand's annual sales top £179 million (Source: IRI October 2011).

*Against limescale, use Fairy dishwasher cleaner.

FedEx is the world's largest express transportation service, driven by a commitment to make every customer experience outstanding. FedEx Express provides fast and reliable delivery to more than 220 countries and territories, by a definite time and date; it delivers more than 3.5 million packages every day. FedEx UK provides road distribution and logistics services for the UK and Ireland, delivering more than 170,000 shipments every day from 66 depots.

Market

During 2011, an improved economy, robust customer demand and decisive actions to grow the business increased volumes and yields across all FedEx transportation segments. Revenues reached nearly US$40 billion, a 13 per cent year-on-year increase, and earnings per share grew more than 20 per cent year-on-year. With its positive momentum, moderate economic growth and diminishing cost head winds, FedEx is well positioned to achieve stronger earnings in 2012.

Product

FedEx Express offers time-definite, door-to-door, customs-cleared international delivery services, using a global air-and-ground network to speed delivery. It can deliver a wide range of time-sensitive shipments, from urgent medical supplies, last-minute gifts and fragile scientific equipment, to bulky freight and dangerous goods. Each shipment sent with FedEx Express is scanned 17 times on average, to ensure that customers can track its precise location by email, on the internet and by telephone 24 hours a day. FedEx Express aims to treat each package as if it is the only one being shipped that day.

In addition to the international product range offered by FedEx Express, FedEx UK now provides customers with a wide range of options for domestic shipping. Within the UK this includes time-definite, next-day and Saturday delivery services. All services are supported by free and easy-to-use automation tools, allowing customers to schedule pick-ups and track their packages online.

Achievements

FedEx Express, which started life in 1973 as the brainchild of its founder and current chairman, president and CEO Frederick Smith, has amassed an impressive list of 'firsts' over the years. FedEx Express originated the overnight letter, was the first express transportation company dedicated to overnight package delivery, and the first to offer next-day delivery by 10.30am. It was also the first express company to offer a time-definite service for freight and the first in the industry to offer money-back guarantees and free proof of delivery. In 1983 Federal Express (as it was then known) made business history as the first US company to reach the US$1 billion revenue landmark inside 10 years of start-up, unaided by mergers or acquisitions.

This illustrious history has resulted in many awards and honours. In 1994 FedEx Express received ISO 9001 certification for all of its worldwide operations, making it the first global express transportation company to

While some dream of success, others are already up working to deliver it.

FedEx

Live to deliver

business.fedex.com/tennis

© Copyright 2011 FedEx

FedEx. OFFICIAL CARRIER | ATP

Brand History

▶ **1971:** Frederick W Smith buys the controlling interest in Arkansas Aviation Sales and identifies the difficulty in getting packages delivered quickly; the idea for Federal Express is born.

▶ **1973:** Federal Express officially begins operations with the launch of 14 small aircraft from Memphis International Airport. It delivers 186 packages to 25 US cities on its first day.

▶ **1977:** Air cargo deregulation allows the use of larger aircraft (such as McDonnell Douglas DC-10s and Boeing 727s), spurring Federal Express' rapid growth.

▶ **1980s:** Intercontinental operations begin with services to Europe and Asia, and the acquisition of the Flying Tigers network sees Federal Express become the world's largest full service, all-cargo airline.

▶ **1994:** Federal Express officially adopts 'FedEx' as its primary brand, taking a cue from its customers who frequently refer to Federal Express by the shortened name.

▶ **2000:** The company is renamed FedEx Express to reflect its position within the overall FedEx Corporation portfolio of services.

▶ **2006:** FedEx Express builds its service capabilities in Europe by acquiring UK domestic express company ANC, rebranded as FedEx UK in 2007.

▶ **2008:** FedEx Express celebrates its 35th year and is now the world's largest express transportation company, operating 650 aircraft and a ground fleet of more than 44,500 vehicles.

▶ **2009:** FedEx Express takes delivery of its first Boeing 777 Freighter, which has significant operational efficiencies and environmental benefits.

▶ **2010:** FedEx Express launches a new connection between Asia and Europe, becoming the first company to offer a next-business-day service from Hong Kong to Europe.

receive simultaneous system-wide certification. In 2008 FedEx Express and FedEx UK were granted the highly regarded and internationally accepted ISO 14001:2004 certification for environmental management systems. In 2011 FedEx ranked eighth in Fortune Magazine's World's Most Admired Companies listing.

Did You Know?

FedEx's UK hub at Stansted Airport in Essex was opened in June 1985 and is the principal sorting and distribution centre for all Express products. The hub sorts around 4,000 pieces an hour. For domestic products, the Central Hub in Newcastle-under-Lyme, Staffordshire, which was built in 1987, operates an automated parcel sortation system (Vanderlande) with a capacity to sort 12,000 packs per hour.

Recent Developments
In 2011 FedEx Express strengthened its position as a healthcare supply chain leader by introducing a suite of new solutions in Europe, the Middle East and Africa.

Designed to help healthcare supply chains manage a range of opportunities linked to globalisation and new outsourcing strategies,

the cutting-edge packaging solutions and advanced distribution models from FedEx will help healthcare companies navigate the complexities of freight management as they expand their operations into new global territories.

Promotion
FedEx and the Association of Tennis Professionals (ATP) have signed a three-year agreement that brings FedEx on board as a new global Platinum Sponsor and Official Carrier of the ATP World Tour. The sponsorship launched in November at the 2010 Barclays ATP World Tour Finals at The O2 arena, London, and extends through 2013.

Reliability of performance is a prevalent theme across all sponsorship activity and is reinforced visually with FedEx branding on court at tournaments across four continents, and on the popular tennis website ATPWorldTour.com.

Brand Values
The FedEx corporate strategy, known to FedEx employees as the 'Purple Promise', is to 'make every FedEx experience outstanding'. The Purple Promise is the long-term strategy for FedEx to further develop loyal relationships

with its customers. The FedEx corporate values are: to value its people and to promote diversity; to provide a service that puts customers at the heart of everything it does; to invent the services and technologies that improve the way people work and live; to manage operations, finances and services with honesty, efficiency and reliability; to champion safe and healthy environments; and to earn the respect and confidence of FedEx people, customers and investors every day.

▶ **www.fedex.com**

Heathrow ⬈

Making every journey better.

Heathrow Airport is the UK's gateway to the world. Each year, around 68 million passengers choose Heathrow as a springboard for travel and adventure, spending time with friends and family, or forging international business links. Along the way, they enjoy some of the best airport shopping in the world. Heathrow helps more passengers travel to where they want to go than any other airport in Europe.

Brand History

▶ **1946:** London Airport opens.

▶ **1966:** The British Airports Authority is created and London Airport is renamed Heathrow Airport.

▶ **1969:** Terminal 1 opens; the existing buildings become Terminals 2 and 3.

▶ **1977:** The London Underground reaches Heathrow.

▶ **1987:** The British Airports Authority is privatised; BAA plc is the new airport operator (later becoming BAA Airports Ltd, part of the Ferrovial consortium).

▶ **1997:** The Terminal 5 public planning inquiry – the longest in UK history – comes to an end.

▶ **1998:** The Heathrow Express rail service begins.

▶ **2006:** The Airbus A380 makes its first UK landing, arriving at a newly built Pier 6 at Terminal 3.

▶ **2008:** Terminal 5 opens and the first commercial A380 flight arrives at Heathrow Airport.

▶ **2010:** Terminal 2 is demolished and work starts on its £1 billion replacement.

Market
In terms of passenger numbers, Heathrow is the world's fourth largest airport. It's also the most international: 62 per cent of passengers are not UK nationals, and eight of the world's 10 busiest intercontinental routes pass through. For 36 per cent of passengers, Heathrow is neither the start nor the end of their journey, but a convenient location for changing flights on the way to somewhere else. That makes Heathrow Europe's most popular hub airport.

Product
At Heathrow, the passenger experience is everything and the airport's product is best defined by its mission: 'making every journey better'. It's all about providing an enjoyable and stress-free transition between home or onward connections and air travel.

Heathrow works to improve every aspect of the airport journey. That includes the ease with which passengers travel to and from the airport, the ease with which they find their way around, the timeliness of their flights, the quality and value of shopping and food, the opportunities for relaxation, the confidence passengers have in safety and security, and the courtesy and attentiveness of staff.

Heathrow is also a generator of wealth. The airport creates employment for 77,000 people at Heathrow and as many again elsewhere in the UK. The business contacts made by people who fly through Heathrow generate international deals worth £590 billion. Those deals contribute more than £150 billion to UK GDP (Source: 'Connecting for growth' Frontier Economics September 2011).

Achievements
The best measure of an airport's success is the Airports Council International's independently rated Airport Service Quality score. Benchmarking passenger experience shows how Heathrow is improving. In 2007, the airport was underperforming compared to the big European hubs; by 2010, it was second best in Europe.

Heathrow often wins praise for its food, retailing, marketing and service, as well as for its sustainable travel projects. In 2011, The Sunday Times Travel magazine named Terminal 5 Best Airport, while Executive Travel (USA) gave Heathrow a Gold award, and Mumsnet bestowed two of its Family Friendly Programme accolades on the airport: a Silver and an Innovation Award.

Heathrow also again scooped the SkyTrax Best Airport Shopping Worldwide award and Business Traveller voted it Best Airport for Tax-Free Shopping for the third year running. The Moodie Report gave Heathrow Best Overall Airport Food in its Airport Food and Beverage Awards.

Did You Know?

The most popular destinations from Heathrow in 2011 were New York (1st), Dubai (2nd), Dublin (3rd), Frankfurt (4th) and Amsterdam (5th).

Heathrow has more than 500 shops and outlets from where passengers can buy almost anything they want – from a newspaper to a £55,000 necklace.

Heathrow's zero-emission travel pods have been nominated as a 'Great' for The Great Exhibition of 2012. The pods carry passengers between Terminal 5 and the business car park.

Recent Developments

Heathrow is a permanent construction site – not that passengers ever notice. The work to improve airport infrastructure involves no disruption to services.

The biggest project is the new Terminal 2, a striking glass-fronted building with a distinctive wavelike roof. When the terminal opens in 2014, it will receive 20 million passengers each year. A new road system will make the journey in and out of the Central Terminal Area easier, and a new 1,300-space car park will take passengers directly to the main terminal entrance.

A project to revitalise airport baggage handling is also underway. The first stage, the boring of a 2.1km tunnel beneath the airport, is complete.

Did You Know?

Heathrow has someone to look after just about everything. The team includes three falconers, four chaplains, six vets and 366 window cleaners.

The tunnel will eventually link all terminals in a single integrated baggage system that will handle 110 million bags per year.

In the summer of 2012, Heathrow will welcome the world as host airport for the London 2012 Olympic and Paralympic Games. Almost 80 per cent of the 'Games family' will pass through one of its terminals. The Games will give Heathrow an opportunity to show the world what it can do, and how it can rise to the logistical challenge of so many bicycles, javelins, vaulting poles and rowing boats. The day after the closing ceremony is likely to be the busiest in the airport's history.

Promotion

With such an international audience, Heathrow takes a multilingual approach to promotion. During the summer of 2011, it ran an advertising campaign in central London in six languages – probably a UK first. A year earlier, Heathrow ran

its first retail advertising campaign: 'Heathrow shopping. The West End for less.'

Heathrow's marketing is earning industry recognition. In the last couple of years, 'Heathrow Commuter', the airport's green commuting campaign, won the London Transport Award for Excellence in Travel Information and Marketing, while Heathrow won twice at The Travel Marketing Awards. An airport parking campaign was the Best Pay Per Click Campaign, while 'A Week at the Airport: A Heathrow Diary' was named Best PR Strategic Campaign. The PR project involved a collaboration with the philosopher and author Alain de Botton, who wrote about his week at Heathrow.

Brand Values

Heathrow puts passengers at the heart of everything it does. By thinking like a passenger instead of an airport operator, it learns how to make every journey better. The challenge is to bring passenger thinking to life in every aspect of airport activity – to present a unified face within which the brand values (internationally minded, stylish and contemporary, efficient, responsible and alert, pace-setting, vibrant) can shine.

▶ **www.heathrow.com**

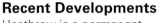

Heinz is one of the most well known and trusted brands on supermarket shelves, a reputation that has grown through generations of enjoyment of Heinz varieties. Founded more than 140 years ago, Heinz products are as relevant today as when they were first sold in London's Fortnum & Mason and have become part of the national diet, offering family mealtime favourites from soups and sauces to beans and pasta.

Market

Heinz has long held number one positions in key grocery categories with its iconic Heinz Beanz, Heinz Cream of Tomato Soup, Heinz Tomato Ketchup and Heinz Salad Cream.

In 2011, Heinz reported record sales of US$10.7 billion, propelled by 12 per cent sales growth in emerging markets as well as growth in its top 15 brands (Source: 2011 HJ Heinz Company Annual Report). Completion of key acquisitions in Brazil and China are set to accelerate Heinz's dynamic growth.

The popularity of Heinz in the UK is illustrated by the fact that 95 per cent of households buy at least one Heinz product every year and the average UK household purchases a Heinz product more than 18 times per year (Source: Kantar Worldpanel 52 w/e 27th November 2011).

Product

Heinz offers a vast range of foods spanning not just sauces, soups, beans and pasta but also frozen and baby products. Its familiar varieties have become household names and include Heinz Classic Soup, Heinz Beanz, Heinz Tomato Ketchup, HP Sauce, Heinz Salad Cream, Heinz Mayonnaise, Heinz Spaghetti, Lea & Perrins, Heinz Big Soup and Farmers' Market Soup.

Achievements

Heinz products enjoy a market leading position in more than 50 countries worldwide. Its top 15 power brands account for more than two-thirds of annual sales; indeed, more than 650 million bottles of Heinz Tomato Ketchup are sold worldwide each year, with annual sales in excess of US$1.5 billion.

It's not only consumers who endorse Heinz varieties. Recent industry accolades include Launch of the Year 2011 from The Grocer for

Did You Know?

Heinz Tomato Ketchup pours from the iconic glass bottle at 0.028 mph unaided.

Since launching Heinz Cream of Tomato Soup in 1910, enough cans have been sold to stretch to the moon and back.

Heinz Tomato Ketchup with Balsamic Vinegar and Heinz Squeeze & Stir Soup, as well as a Gold at The Grocer's Food & Drink Awards for the Heinz Beanz Fridge Pack. Triumphs in the advertising arena include Top Advertising Campaign of the Year from The Grocer for Heinz Soup 'Whistles', while 'IT HAS TO BE HEINZ' took Best Use of Radio to Drive Sales at the RAB's Radio Advertising Awards as well as a Silver at the IPA Effectiveness Awards.

Recent Developments

Thanks to close consumer understanding, Heinz continues to launch new and innovative products, introducing them to loyal fans in original ways.

In 2011, Heinz introduced a new variety of Heinz Tomato Ketchup, launching its first ever limited edition of the much loved sauce: Heinz Tomato Ketchup with Balsamic Vinegar. An initial run of 3,000 bottles was sold exclusively through Facebook, making it the first branded food product in the UK to be sold on the social networking site.

Heinz has also looked at new ways to prepare and package its products with the arrival of the Squeeze & Stir Soup range, the Heinz Beanz Fridge Pack, Heinz Beanz Snap Pots and the new Heinz Pasta Pouches.

Promotion

First launched in 2009, the 'IT HAS TO BE HEINZ' advertising and promotional campaign demonstrates Heinz's understanding of real life moments and its place among them. It creates an engaging context for demonstrating the occasions in which Heinz has become embedded into the fabric of many consumers' lives.

Did You Know?

A staggering 1.5 million cans of Heinz Beanz are sold every day in the UK.

The famous 'Beanz Meanz Heinz' slogan was first introduced in 1967.

Heinz has also been at the forefront of social media activity, becoming the first food brand in the UK to use 'social coupons' on its Facebook page. The campaign allowed consumers to download coupons for the new Heinz Tomato Ketchup with Chilli; if the coupon was shared with friends, the value of the coupon increased.

Other social media campaigns have included launching a barbecue app on Facebook with Heinz Tomato Ketchup and a 'Get Well' soup initiative for Heinz Classic Soup.

Brand Values

The words of its founder, Henry J Heinz, still ring true at the company to this day: "To do a common thing uncommonly well brings success."

Heinz is among the few international companies built on a singular eponymous brand and the values that define it – trust, premium quality, great taste and wholesome nutrition – are central to this success. Heinz is proud to enjoy a special place in the hearts and minds of consumers and to be synonymous with family mealtimes.

▶ **www.heinz.co.uk**

IT HAS TO BE

Brand History

▶ **1876:** Henry J Heinz launches Heinz Tomato Ketchup in the US.

▶ **1886:** Henry launches his business in the UK, selling his first products through London's famous Fortnum & Mason store.

▶ **1896:** The '57 Varieties' slogan is born – although his company is manufacturing more than 60 products at the time, Henry believes 57 is a lucky number.

▶ **1910:** Heinz Cream of Tomato Soup is imported into the UK for the first time.

▶ **1920s:** The UK production of Heinz Baked Beans, Heinz Spaghetti and Heinz Tomato Ketchup begins.

▶ **1931:** Ready-to-serve soups and baby food are added to the Heinz range.

▶ **1951:** Heinz is granted the Royal Warrant, and again in 1954, as Purveyors of Heinz Products to Her Majesty Queen Elizabeth II.

▶ **1955:** The first Heinz television advert airs on the new ITV channel.

▶ **1967:** Heinz's most famous slogan, 'Beanz Meanz Heinz' is born.

▶ **1987:** The first squeezy bottle of Heinz Tomato Ketchup is introduced.

▶ **1998:** Heinz Baked Beans is chosen as one of 12 brands that people think best represent the final decade of the millennium.

▶ **2000:** Heinz launches organic variants of its Tomato Ketchup, Beans and Soup.

▶ **2004:** 'Beans' becomes 'Beanz' and a reduced sugar and salt variety launches.

▶ **2005:** A first for the brand, Heinz introduces a range of flavoured Baked Beanz. Lea & Perrins Worcestershire Sauce and HP Sauce also join the Heinz family.

▶ **2007:** Heinz unveils a new format, the Snap Pot, for its market-leading Baked Beans and Spaghetti Hoops.

▶ **2008:** Heinz Baked Beans is renamed Heinz Beanz.

▶ **2009:** A new campaign – 'IT HAS TO BE HEINZ' – launches. The 50th anniversary of the official opening of the Heinz Beanz factory in Kitt Green is marked by a visit from Her Majesty The Queen.

▶ **2010:** Heinz continues to lead the way in packaging innovation, with the launch of the Heinz Beanz Fridge Pack.

▶ **2011:** The Heinz Squeeze & Stir Soup range launches. Heinz now produces more than 5,700 products around the world.

After more than 30 successful years, Highland Spring remains the leading British brand of bottled water (Source: Zenith Bottled Water Report 2011) and the only major bottled water brand to have its catchment area certified organic by the Soil Association. Highland Spring protects its land in the Ochil Hills, Perthshire, Scotland to ensure its water – drawn from protected underground springs – is as pure as can be.

Full of the joys

Market

Around half of all UK households purchase bottled water every year and the Highland Spring brand is bought by more households than any other bottled water brand (Source: Kantar Worldpanel 52 w/e 4th September 2011). Furthermore, shoppers are buying Highland Spring more often than in 2010 and in larger volumes.

Product

Highland Spring's status as 'the water from organic land' is unique among major bottled water brands. The 1,000-hectare catchment area from which the water is drawn has been carefully protected for more than 30 years, earning it organic status as certified by the Soil Association. This 'untouched' approach reflects the company's overall commitment to minimising its environmental impact.

In March 2010 new PET bottle designs were launched for the 1.5 L and 500 ml sparkling products – at that time the lightest branded sparkling water bottles on the market, using nine per cent less plastic and 39 per cent less paper than their predecessors.

Highland Spring remains the only bottled water brand recognised by the Eco-Management and Audit Scheme, not only meeting the standard but going far beyond what is required to demonstrate commitment towards protection of the environment.

Achievements

Highland Spring is the number one UK-produced water brand and the number two brand in the UK market overall. The brand grew 3.1 per cent on the previous year and now stands at 180 million litres, a 10 per cent volume share of the total market (Source: Zenith w/e 29th October 2011).

2011 was a strong year for Highland Spring's still range, increasing 3.5 per cent to 137 million litres annually. Still water now accounts for 78 per cent of Highland Spring's total volume.

Highland Spring also dominates in the valuable sparkling market segment, producing 40 million litres annually – more than double the volume of its nearest sparkling water competitor (Source: Zenith Bottled Water Report 2011).

In 2011 Highland Spring was recognised for the seventh consecutive year by The Good Shopping Guide as the leading ethical bottled water brand, scoring 100 per cent. The business is extremely proud of this achievement, and features The Good Shopping Guide logo across its packaging.

In addition to retail, the foodservice and on-premise routes to market continue to grow for the brand, with the recent Gold Medal from the Publican Licencees' Choice Awards testament to the brand's popularity in this channel.

Perceived as the 'purest', 'freshest' and 'most trusted' bottled water brand in the UK, Highland Spring is in a strong position for continuing growth (Source: GfK NOP July 2011).

Recent Developments

Highland Spring Group is a privately owned business, headquartered in the UK. In 2009 the Group acquired the Speyside Glenlivet brand, followed by the bottled water business

of Greencore Group plc in 2010, to become the leading producer and supplier of naturally sourced bottled water in the UK market. Highland Spring Group's brand portfolio includes Highland Spring, Speyside Glenlivet, Hydr8 and a range of retailer own-labels and flavoured waters. The Group consists of five rural catchment areas and manages water abstraction rights for 2.2 billion litres per annum. In 2011 the business supplied 379 million litres of bottled water, with a turnover of £81.5 million.

Promotion

2012 sees exciting changes for Highland Spring, as the brand reveals a new positioning, vibrant new packaging and a TV campaign. The sense of well-being that comes from drinking Highland Spring is captured in the phrase: 'Full of the joys of Highland Spring.' A high-profile TV campaign, breaking in March 2012, features various creatures native to the Ochil Hills and a joyful, bottle-playing mole. 'Full of the joys' will feature across a full range of media including press, PR, trade, in-store and online.

> ### Did You Know?
>
> **In 2001 Highland Spring became the first British brand of bottled water to have the land from which it is drawn certified organic by the Soil Association.**
>
> **Highland Spring is a founder member of the Natural Hydration Council, which is dedicated to communicating the facts about natural bottled water.**

2012 also sees a major enhancement of Highland Spring branding with a vibrant new design and colourway guaranteeing improved shelf stand-out across the range.

As advocates of active, healthy lifestyles, Highland Spring is proud to continue its tradition of sports sponsorship. Extending its partnership with the Lawn Tennis Association into 2012, Highland Spring is now the sponsor of Mini Tennis, a programme that aims to attract 3–10 year-olds to the game.

The brand continues its association with Olympic gold medalist Sir Chris Hoy to inspire and motivate British children to get involved in sport and adopt better hydration habits.

The company is also the official bottled water supplier to numerous cycling events and rugby teams including six English premier rugby clubs, 18 Scottish rugby union teams as well as the Scottish national team.

2011 saw the brand invite consumers to collect and redeem codes against a selection of high quality branded sports balls, via its 'New Balls for Britain' integrated promotion.

Brand Values

Highland Spring is an iconic Scottish brand and is committed to protecting the wider environment and developing its business in a sustainable and eco-friendly way.

As the guardian of its land, the company goes to great lengths to protect its source, and to extend its ethical approach to production, packaging, recycling and transport – values which resonate with its consumers.

▶ **www.highland-spring.com**

Brand History

▶ **1979:** Highland Spring Ltd is formed.

▶ **1993:** Highland Spring displaces Perrier from the top spot in the sparkling water market and secures the contract to supply bottled water to British Airways worldwide.

▶ **1998:** Highland Spring becomes the official water supplier to the World Snooker Association.

▶ **2001:** The brand continues to innovate, pioneering the 'kids' bottled water market.

▶ **2006:** The first national TV advertising campaign is rolled out.

▶ **2007:** Highland Spring is revealed as the exclusive drinks sponsor to British tennis star Andy Murray and his brother, former Wimbledon doubles champion, Jamie Murray.

▶ **2008:** Highland Spring signs a major sponsorship partnership with Sir Chris Hoy, multi-gold medal winner at the Beijing Olympics.

▶ **2009:** A refreshed brand identity is introduced across packaging and classic Hollywood stars are used to promote 'the water from organic land'.

▶ **2010:** A new sparkling PET range is launched and wins a prestigious industry award. Highland Spring Group is formed following the acquisition of Greencore Group plc bottled water division, making it the UK's leading producer and supplier of naturally sourced bottled water.

▶ **2012:** A new brand positioning – 'Full of the joys of Highland Spring' – is launched in March.

Founded by Frank Hornby, who made his first train set for the British toy market in 1920, Hornby has a vision to be the most successful model, hobby and collectable toy company in the world. Hornby products, originally intended for children, have fostered lifelong enthusiasm, creating a unique brand that transcends all ages and delivers to an exceptionally passionate audience.

Market

From its headquarters in Margate, Kent, Hornby and its associated brands are market leaders in model railways (Hornby), slot car racing sets (Scalextric), plastic model kits (Airfix), modelling materials (Humbrol), and die-cast collectable vehicles (Corgi). Its products are sold in 60 countries across the globe.

A rapid acquisition programme over the past decade has bolstered sales, with Hornby now owning the leading European model railways brands: Lima (Italy), Jouef (France), Electrotren (Spain), Arnold (Germany) and Rivarossi (Italy). Total sales, including those of the five European subsidiaries, exceeded £60 million for the year ending March 2011.

Hornby's sales are driven by an avid fan base of children who grow up with the company, cherishing the products that offer hours of engagement and no limitations on how much they can build.

Product

From steam and diesel engines to aircraft and vehicles, Hornby products are engineered to replicate real life vehicles on a miniature scale. The brand's 00 scale – which represents a size ratio of 1:76 – enables intricate details to be reproduced precisely, adding to the desirability of the products.

Such miniature masterpieces require considerable time to develop; each new product takes up to 18 months to perfect through a process that emulates the experience of its original engineers. More than 35 in-house designers work in product development, with the exact process for each new model determined by the age of the subject. To recreate a modern car, for example, designers refer to the vehicle's original computer aided design (CAD) drawings. A historical subject, however – such as a steam locomotive that is no longer in existence – sees the development team relying on the original draftsman's drawings alongside any historical illustrations and early photographs.

Brand History

▶ **1972:** The Hornby Railways company is established.

▶ **2001:** Hogwarts Express, the Harry Potter licensed locomotive, launches to great sales success.

▶ **2003:** Hornby launches Live Steam – a working miniature steam locomotive.

▶ **2004:** Hornby acquires Lima and Electrotren, which leads to the formation of Hornby Italia and Spain.

▶ **2006:** Hornby acquires Airfix and Humbrol.

▶ **2008:** Hornby acquires Corgi Classics.

▶ **2009:** The most anticipated model kit for a decade, 1:24 Mosquito from Airfix launches.

▶ **2010:** The Hornby Visitor Centre opens in Margate, Kent; it goes on to welcome 50,000 visitors in its first 18 months.

▶ **2011:** Hornby introduces a major marketing campaign, 'A passion for every generation and the next'.

▶ **2012:** The Hornby Railways company celebrates its 40th year, and Hornby marks the London 2012 Olympic and Paralympic Games with a limited edition range of official merchandise.

THE FLYING SCOTSMAN

The LNER Class A1 4-6-2 locomotive and classic teak coaches in this set is a stylised representation of the Flying Scotsman train as it ran non-stop from London to Edinburgh in the summer seasons of the 1930s. The prototype locomotive had a corridor link through the tender to the coaches to allow crews to switch over without stopping the train. This set contains the Starter Oval track plus extension Track Pack A providing a layout with a siding, but you can also add extra Track Packs when you are ready to enlarge the circuit.

00 GAUGE TRAIN SET

Achievements

Hornby sells more than 165,000 locomotives, 290,000 coaches and wagons, and approximately 3,000 scale kilometres of track every year. In addition, the company sells more than 1,400,000 Airfix model kits, and over 850,000 cars through its Scalextric and Corgi brands. Such consistently high sales are achieved by a continuous focus on consumer demands and interests.

Hornby's dedication to its product range, and to its customers, is recognised regularly by awards from a range of consumer publications and has resulted in a decade of growth for the company. From sales of £24.6 million in 2001, Hornby has experienced growth of 158 per cent to reach £63.4 million in 2011.

Recent Developments

In 2012 Hornby will unveil the latest product developments across its portfolio. New products will include a limited edition locomotive, Evening Star, to celebrate the 40th year of the Hornby Railways company, while Corgi will see a range of small pocket-money vehicles added to its line-up for the first time in almost 30 years.

As a licensee of the London 2012 Olympic and Paralympic Games, Hornby will also introduce a range of official Games merchandise that

encompasses limited edition train packs, a Scalextric Velodrome, and a selection of die-cast vehicles, key rings and figurines. Thanks to its established reputation as a collectable brand – indeed, many of its products appreciate in value over time – Hornby brings significant added value to the London 2012 merchandise.

Promotion

Hornby has utilised a plethora of promotional methods over its lifetime, from TV and print to product placement and social media. Notable adverts in the brand's earlier years include the humour-led billboard campaign of the mid 1970s and the miniaturised Bernard Cribbins TV ad towards the end of the decade, while the 1980s saw Hornby take on a starring role in a Yellow Pages TV slot.

In 2011 Hornby launched a major new campaign: 'A passion for every generation and the next.' The campaign highlights the enduring enjoyment of its products and for the first time, focuses on the family of brands under the Hornby name. The campaign began on TV, running across Sky Sports and ESPN to target men of all ages, before airing in cinemas before key family films in the run-up to Christmas.

Hornby's biggest promotional channel, however, is its passionate customer base. More than 100,000 people subscribe to

Did You Know?

Over the past 40 years Hornby has produced at least 24 variants of the Flying Scotsman locomotive.

More than 25 million Scalextric models have been sold since 1957 and over five million kilometres of track have been produced since its inception – enough to circle the world 125 times.

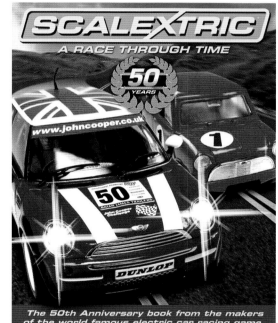

SCALEXTRIC
A RACE THROUGH TIME

www.johncooper.co.uk

The 50th Anniversary book from the makers of the world famous electric car racing game

Hornby's online newsletters and its consumer shows achieved record attendance across the UK in 2011. Thousands keep in touch with the brand via Facebook and Twitter, while rumours of Hornby's product development are often hotly debated on forums and at model clubs across the world.

Brand Values

Founded by Frank Hornby, the inventor of Meccano and Dinky toys, the Hornby brand has a proud heritage – and like its founder, is guided by a belief in quality, passion and a commitment to the detail of the subject. Without the passion of its consumers, however, as well as the dedication of its employees, the Hornby brand would not be what it is today.

▶ **www.hornby.com**

CORGI

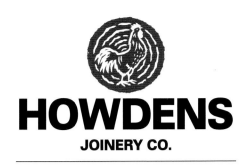

HOWDENS
JOINERY CO.

MAKING SPACE MORE VALUABLE

Howdens Joinery was founded in 1995 in order to serve the needs of small builders undertaking routine joinery and kitchen installation work. It is now one of the UK's leading suppliers of kitchens and joinery products to the trade. Howdens has achieved this by creating a strong entrepreneurial culture within its depots, a close relationship with its customers, and a range of kitchens specifically designed to meet the needs of modern living.

Market

Howdens Joinery operates within the trade or 'done for you' kitchen market, its core customer base comprising local builders and skilled professionals. The company believes that project management by local builders is the best solution for installing a kitchen. The constantly growing sophistication of products, services and end-users' expectations, combined with the need to keep abreast of legislation governing every aspect of materials and installation, has driven dramatic growth in this market.

Howdens helps builders to manage their businesses by guaranteeing product availability from local stock with rigid cabinets that are ready to install, saving builders time and money as well as allowing them to plan effectively. Its versatile supply chain ensures its depots, and in turn its customers, receive a high level of service. Specifically within the trade sector, key competitors are Jewson, Travis Perkins, Magnet Trade and Benchmarx.

Product

Howdens sells kitchens – encompassing appliances, accessories, handles, worktops, sinks and taps – and joinery, such as doors, flooring, stairs and hardware.

The company has the UK's largest kitchen range available from stock and ensures its portfolio remains informed by new product development. As all depots hold stock locally they are also able to offer local delivery to site when required. A free survey and state-of-the-art computer-aided design (CAD) service, which includes a site visit, is also available.

Howdens has developed an exclusive appliance, sink and tap brand, Lamona, and in 2011 launched a two-year guarantee on all appliances.

Achievements

Since it was established in 1995, with just 14 depots, Howdens has demonstrated strong growth and 2011 saw the opening of its 500th depot. Group turnover for 2010 exceeded £780 million and Howdens was named among the Top 25 Big Companies in The Sunday Times 100 Best Companies to Work For 2010 listing.

Each year Howdens supplies around 400,000 complete kitchens to over 260,000 building trade professionals, as well as more than 350 local authorities and housing associations.

Since 2005 Howdens has had a strong partnership with Leonard Cheshire Disability, a relationship recognised with the award for Best Corporate Partnership at the Third Sector Excellence Awards in 2007. Howdens works with Leonard Cheshire Disability services across the UK to develop affordable, attractive

and practical kitchen facilities for people with physical disabilities. It offers a highly accessible kitchen collection called 'Inclusive Kitchens', which is sold through its depots.

Recent Developments

Product development remains key to the company's focus on continued growth. In 2010, Howdens developed the concept of kitchen 'families', which allowed it to maximise the potential of best-selling styles in best-selling finishes. The families were an immediate success, and Howdens now offers more than 35 different kitchen ranges and seven families.

The company has been awarded FSC and PEFC chain of custody certificates for a number of its joinery products, worktops and kitchen ranges, and it continues to strive for additional certification. In 2011, the number of its appliances awarded the Energy Saving Trust Recommended Certification Mark increased, while all of its manufacturing and warehouse sites achieved ISO 14001 for environmental standards in 2010. It also remains certified

Did You Know?

Each year, Howdens sells **400,000 complete kitchens, 500,000 appliances, and two million doors.**

Howdens Joinery's 500th depot opened in September 2011 in Gosport, Hampshire.

under the Carbon Trust's prestigious Energy Efficiency Accreditation Scheme, an accolade that it has held for more than 10 years.

Promotion

Howdens puts the relationship between local depots and builders at the heart of its promotional strategy. As such its kitchen, joinery and appliance brochures, alongside other literature, are specifically designed to help builders in discussion with their own customers. Local marketing is critical and each depot tailors its promotional activity to meet customer needs. Howdens runs a fleet of more than 400 branded delivery trailers and in 2011, continued to make use of promotional items including builders' notebooks and diaries to further develop the brand. Howdens has also continued to develop its website to showcase the company and its complete range of products, and raise brand awareness among builders and end-users.

A partnership between Lamona and John Topham, head chef and owner of The General Tarleton Inn in Yorkshire, began in May 2011 with the launch of the first Lamona Cookbook: Great Food Made Simple. The book features recipes cooked by John using Lamona appliances, and the venture has continued with a Christmas edition.

Since 2009 Howdens has published 10 'Truly Local' books to tell the stories behind individual customer relationships and to illustrate some of the ways in which a Howdens depot is an integral part of its local community. Many depots choose to make donations to local charities and community projects, including sponsorship of grassroots football and rugby teams.

Brand History

▶ **1995:** Howdens Joinery starts trading in October with 14 depots supplying trade professionals with joinery, hardware, kitchen ranges, accessories and appliances from stock.

▶ **1999:** Howdens opens its 100th depot.

▶ **2004:** Howdens sets the standard in the trade kitchen market with its new format high quality Kitchen Brochure.

▶ **2006:** Howdens launches a market-leading Joinery Brochure featuring doors, joinery and flooring.

▶ **2007:** The Howdens website launches in April and the 400th depot opens.

▶ **2008:** The first Howdens-branded delivery trailers go on the road, and the first consumer and trade advertising campaign launches.

▶ **2009:** The Lamona appliance, sink and tap brand, exclusive to Howdens, is launched.

▶ **2010:** Howdens launches a new Appliance, Sink and Tap Brochure. The Kitchen range families are introduced.

▶ **2011:** Howdens opens its 500th depot. The Lamona appliance two-year guarantee is introduced and the partnership between Lamona and John Topham begins.

Brand Values

Howdens is guided by the aim of providing small builders with robust, well-designed and well-made kitchen and joinery products at the best local price and from local stock. The company attributes its success to the strength of the depots' relationships with their customers and the breadth of the market they serve; the quality and range of Howdens products; the ability to service customers from local stock all the time; and the opportunity to streamline the business around supplying one customer, the small builder.

▶ **www.howdens.com**

Created by Accor co-founders, Paul Dubrule and Gérard Pélisson, ibis was launched in 1974 and pioneered the modern budget hotel concept. With a goal to guarantee consistent accommodation and service quality, and at prices 30 per cent cheaper than the local market average, this revolutionary concept was an immediate hit. ibis is now the European market leader in budget hotels, with more than 900 hotels and 107,000 rooms in 48 countries.

Market

As the market leader in Europe and the fourth largest chain in its category worldwide, ibis has earned its global reputation for excellence at competitive prices thanks to its worldwide standard of offering all the major services of a modern hotel at the best local market value.

In 2007 ibis launched the biggest expansion plan in its history, intensifying its growth in emerging markets, particularly Asia and Latin America. Today ibis continues to strengthen its leading position across the world, expanding its network by about 70 hotels per year.

ibis is part of the budget hotel brand portfolio of Accor, one of the world's leading hotel operators (Source: STR Global 2008). Present in 90 countries with 4,200 hotels and more than 500,000 rooms, Accor's broad range of hotel brands provides an extensive offering from luxury to budget.

Did You Know?

ibis opens, on average, one hotel each week worldwide.

Today, 82 per cent of ibis hotels are located in Europe.

Product

ibis stands on the strength of its worldwide standards – a global guarantee to all customers – and provides conveniently located hotels set in easy-access destinations across the globe.

ibis aims to provide a warm welcome, at any time of day or night, from efficient reservations management and a fast check-in process through to clean, peaceful and comfortable rooms with bathrooms maintained to high standards of hygiene. It is this contemporary hospitality, combined with 24/7 dining, that makes the ibis brand.

The brand concept also encompasses a modern hotel design, new restaurant formats (more than 20 around the world), multi-skilled employees, and services such as the 'early bird' and 'late riser' breakfast choices.

In adapting to meet the demands of local markets by providing the best value for money, the ibis standard allows the full-service budget hotel chain to satisfy the needs of its national and international clients.

Achievements

As a pioneer in its commitment to the environment, ibis has achieved significant industry 'firsts'. In 1997 it became the first budget chain to receive the international quality management systems standard ISO 9001, which is recognised in more than 150 countries. Then in 2004, ibis became the first hotel chain in the world to secure the ISO 14001 environmental certification. This global certification validates corporate management policies regarding waste reduction and water and energy consumption. One-third of ibis hotels have already been certified ISO 14001 and it is being rolled out worldwide.

ibis received the Best Advertising Campaign award for its TENor15 'Rock Star' campaign at

the 2010 Worldwide Hospitality Awards held in Paris. The promotion was showcased via a groundbreaking 360°, pan-European campaign conceived and executed by Y&R Paris, who worked in partnership with Wunderman for the viral communication. It played out across television spots, press inserts, online, events, internal communications, point of sale and social media.

Recent Developments

A first from ibis is the 15-Minute Satisfaction Guarantee: a unique contractual agreement between ibis and its guests, whereby every guest is invited to report any issue that may arise. If the hotel is responsible and the issue takes more than 15 minutes to resolve, that service is free of charge to the guest for the night.

Brand History

▶ **1974:** The first ibis hotel opens in Bordeaux, France.

▶ **1976:** ibis opens in Paris. In the same year, the chain expands to Amsterdam.

▶ **1983:** The 100th ibis opens.

▶ **1985:** The first ibis hotel in the UK opens, at London Heathrow. Hotels also open in Austria and Belgium.

▶ **1987:** The 200th ibis opens and the chain expands to Switzerland.

▶ **1990s:** The chain expands to Eastern Europe and Asia. In 1997 ibis commits to the ISO 9001 quality certification.

▶ **2004:** ibis commits to the ISO 14001 environmental certification and opens the first ibis in China.

▶ **2007:** The new ibis room concept is launched.

▶ **2008:** ibis opens its 800th hotel.

▶ **2009:** The chain's 100,000th room opens, in Munich, Germany.

▶ **2010:** ibis wins at the Worldwide Hospitality Awards for its TENor15 fully integrated 'Rock Star' campaign.

▶ **2011:** The 900th ibis hotel opens, in Tangier; ibis now has a presence worldwide and continues its rapid expansion in emerging countries such as China and India.

▶ **2012:** Accor rolls out an overhaul of its economy brands, with ibis becoming a 'mega brand' encompassing ibis, ibis styles and ibis budget.

As part of its development, ibis is investing in its network by establishing new hotels and refurbishing older properties to reflect a new look and feel. At the heart of the hotel, the ibis bedroom has been redesigned to ensure maximum comfort and therefore a good night's sleep. All new rooms feature layouts designed to maximise space, make use of natural colours and materials – such as wooden floors – and include an LCD television.

Further upgrades include the roll-out of ibis Web Corners to all hotels by 2012, allowing guests free access to the internet in public areas.

Did You Know?

ibis was the first budget hotel chain to be certified ISO 9001 for quality globally, and the first to secure ISO 14001 environmental certification.

ibis is one of the rare budget hotel brands to reward its guests via a loyalty programme. Members of Accor's A|Club earn points at more than 2,300 hotels worldwide and can redeem them for reward vouchers or airline miles.

Promotion

The ibis brand successfully communicates to its global audience via a standard creative platform, as evidenced by its 2010 win at the Worldwide Hospitality Awards.

ibis communications focus on being a caring, friendly and welcoming brand with staff at its heart. One of the brand's objectives is to drive direct sales to ibishotel.com through integrated campaigns, communicated in national press and online. In addition, ibis has developed its social networking and rich media presence. Belief in the brand is promoted further by its 15-Minute Satisfaction Guarantee.

Brand Values

ibis is a well-known budget brand worldwide, thanks to its simple-to-understand values, personality and value-for-money offering. The brand is operated according to global standards, giving the frequent traveller reassurance on guaranteed quality. The brand leads the way in offering full-service budget accommodation, in a modern environment, at great-value prices. Above all, the ibis brand sets out to combine creativity, quality and product with a passion for hospitality worldwide.

▶ **www.ibishotel.com**

ICAEW is a professional membership organisation, supporting more than 138,000 chartered accountants around the world. It provides qualifications, professional standards and technical expertise that help shape the global accountancy and finance profession. Having completed the rigorous and globally respected ACA qualification, its members provide high quality personal and business advice to individuals, businesses and organisations.

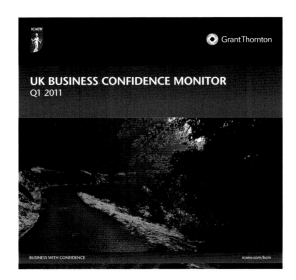

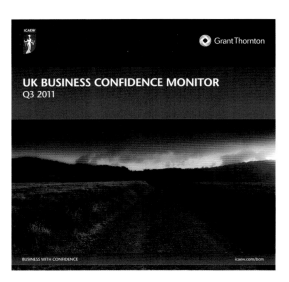

Market

In the changing global economic environment, ICAEW works hard to develop the knowledge and skills of finance professionals, providing them with the experience they need to progress to leadership positions in organisations of any size, across all industry sectors. ICAEW Chartered Accountants play a critical role in helping businesses and markets deliver long-term economic growth through sustainability: using their expertise in business, practice and the public sector to drive efficiencies and promote sustainable business practices.

ICAEW helps to shape the world's accountancy and finance profession, and influence the global business environment. In the UK, ICAEW constantly engages with the government to ensure the policy and regulatory climate supports a business-led recovery, economic growth and competitiveness.

Product

The internationally recognised ACA qualification provides a broad scope and depth of accountancy, finance and business skills, technical excellence and best practice, which is relevant across all industry sectors. ICAEW offers ACA training through more than 2,700 authorised training employers around the world,

from the UK to Malaysia, Pakistan, Russia, China, Cyprus and the United Arab Emirates.

ICAEW also offers a suite of qualifications and programmes designed to support individuals at all stages of their career progression. From the Diploma in Charity Accounting to the Financial Talent Executive Network (FTEN), certificates in International Financial Reporting Standards (IFRS) and the Forensic Accreditation Scheme, it offers a range of specialist financial subjects and skills. In addition, faculties and special interest groups offer a range of resources to support continuing professional development for business and finance professionals worldwide, including technical updates, practical guidance, magazines, events, advice and support.

ICAEW conducts regular research to provide insight and clarity into economic issues. The ICAEW/Grant Thornton UK Business Confidence Monitor tracks a wide range of key economic indicators, providing

a strong steer of the overall direction of the UK economy. Economic Insight, produced in partnership with Cebr for the UK, Middle East and South East Asia, provides critical analysis on current economic issues.

Achievements

At a time when growth is key to the economic recovery, dealing with HM Revenue & Customs (HMRC) has proved a burden to businesses of all sizes. ICAEW called for immediate action, resulting in the Treasury Select Committee hearing evidence on some of the difficulties ICAEW members face on a daily basis when interacting with HMRC. As a result ICAEW is working with HMRC's chairman to help improve customer service.

ICAEW's findings from its series of reports into business debt financing and the ability of SMEs to access bank finance revealed that UK businesses are moving to a more sustainable model of financial management and learning to survive with less debt. The research and the

Did You Know?

Many of the founding fathers of the 'Big Four' accountancy firms were ICAEW early presidents – such as Arthur Cooper, William Welch Deloitte, Edwin Waterhouse and Sir William Peat.

ICAEW is the only international professional body to be invited to join the World Economic Forum in Davos.

ARE YOU TRAINING AN ACCOUNTANT WHOSE EYES ARE ON THE CLOCK,

OR YOUR BUSINESS?

THE CHARTERED ACCOUNTANT. NO ONE'S BETTER QUALIFIED.

84% of FTSE 100 companies have an ICAEW Chartered Accountant on their board.
Now you know who to consider for your next business investment.

It's time to train a chartered accountant. Visit icaew.com/betterqualified

A WORLD LEADER OF THE ACCOUNTANCY AND FINANCE PROFESSION

accompanying policy recommendations to the UK government offered suggestions that would contribute to an improvement in SME access to finance – a prerequisite for a thriving UK private sector recovery – and helped keep this issue in the forefront of politicians' interests.

The 2010/11 student recruitment campaign, launched in September 2010, achieved significant success. The graduate brochure, the campaign's lead component, placed second in the Best Graduate Recruitment Brochure category of the Times Graduate Recruitment Awards 2011. ICAEW is the first and only professional body to have been shortlisted in the category. The campaign also contributed to ICAEW achieving its highest number of new ACA students in 19 years.

Recent Developments
Following a redraft of International Standards on Auditing (ISAs), ICAEW launched a new flexible online learning and assessment package in July 2011 for clarified ISAs. It enables users to familiarise themselves with the principles of clarified ISAs using theory, real life examples and practical illustrations.

Following the success of the IFRS Learning and Assessment Programme over the past few years, and the increase in the global adoption of IFRS, ICAEW launched a specialist Diploma in IFRSs in August 2011.

With SME growth so crucial to the UK's economic success, ICAEW launched the

Business Advice Service in October 2011, which promotes the offer of one free initial consultation with a qualified ICAEW Chartered Accountant. It aims to help small companies and start-ups with business and financial advice to help growth at a time of fragile recovery and limits on public spending.

While the future of UK GAAP is being determined, the reporting requirements of small UK businesses still need technical guidance. In November 2011 ICAEW launched a learning and assessment programme on the Financial Reporting Standard for Small Entities.

Promotion
In September 2011, ICAEW launched a new corporate advertising campaign to promote the skills and expertise of ICAEW Chartered Accountants as leaders of accounting, finance and business.

The advertisements targeting businesses reinforced the idea that training an ICAEW Chartered Accountant makes business sense, while those aimed at students encouraged them to think about their career choices and how becoming 'chartered' can enhance their career prospects. The campaign was broadcast through various outdoor, online and social media channels in the UK and key international markets.

Brand Values
ICAEW believes in acting responsibly, in the best interests of its members and the general public. It acts with integrity, creating

Did You Know?

Economia, the lady featured in ICAEW's coat of arms and logo, was first illustrated in Cesare Ripa's Iconologia in 1603. As the symbol of the highest professional standards, she has been the ICAEW icon since 1880.

effective partnerships with organisations and communities worldwide to ensure the highest professional, technical and ethical standards.

▶ **www.icaew.com**

Brand History

▶ **1880:** A new professional body, The Institute of Chartered Accountants in England and Wales (ICAEW) is created by Royal Charter.

▶ **1893:** Chartered Accountants' Hall, in the City of London, is completed and opened by ICAEW's president Edwin Waterhouse. It goes on to become a Grade II listed building.

▶ **1919:** Mary Harris Smith is admitted to ICAEW, becoming the first female chartered accountant in the world.

▶ **2005:** ICAEW becomes a founding member of the Global Accounting Alliance.

▶ **2006:** ICAEW is appointed by the European Commission to study the implementation of International Financial Reporting Standards (IFRS) throughout the EU.

▶ **2007:** ICAEW wins a £1 million tender from the World Bank to raise standards across the accountancy profession in Bangladesh.

▶ **2011:** ICAEW is awarded the Carbon Trust Standard, becoming the first professional accountancy body to achieve the certification.

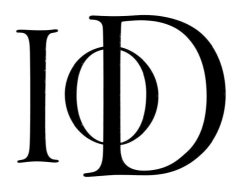

The Institute of Directors (IoD) has long been recognised as an influential and respected membership organisation in the UK. With more than 100 years' success, it is measured by its members who are some of the most skilled and experienced business leaders in the country, representing the full business spectrum – from start-up entrepreneurs to directors in the public sector and CEOs of multinational organisations.

Market

The IoD's most powerful component is the quality of its members; 70 per cent are business leaders from small and medium sized enterprises, and 68 per cent of the FTSE 100 companies are represented. The diversity of professional backgrounds encourages entrepreneurship among the IoD business community, with members sharing business skills and knowledge with each other while also benefiting from the IoD's support.

Product

IoD membership aims to offer a real return on investment, improving cost efficiency while increasing long-term productivity. The portfolio of benefits includes tangible, measurable business resources that support both individual and operational performance.

The IoD provides its members with opportunities to meet and connect, with high-profile occasions such as the Director of the Year Awards – featuring guest speaker Lord Sugar in

2010 – and the Annual Convention, which hosts more than 2,000 business leaders and attracts prestigious speakers such as Dame Fiona Reynolds, David Cameron and Vince Cable. A recent decision to relocate the event from the Royal Albert Hall to The O2 was driven by a desire to improve the delegate experience by offering greater networking space.

Smaller, more regular events are held regionally, with local breakfast briefings and seminars. Members also have free access to workspace in 12 prestigious city premises across the UK.

The IoD is a reputable source for relevant and accurate information on all aspects of business, and the quality of service is taken seriously. The last year has proved a testing time for many businesses and individuals, underlining the importance of support – which sits at the core of the IoD's benefits and services. Its Information and Advisory team handles in excess of 30,000 enquiries annually

while Directors' Law Express – its legal helpline that celebrated its 10th anniversary in January 2011 – has dealt with almost 43,000 calls from 16,000 individual members since its inception.

IoD launched Office Solutions in 2010 to provide members with a unique portfolio of flexible working packages, ranging from an address and virtual offices to full time desk space. Its popularity meant that after just one year the office space, which is located in the IoD's 116 Pall Mall headquarters, underwent an expansion. At the end of 2011 there were more than 200 members using the service.

Achievements

The IoD is recognised for offering creative and flexible training opportunities that can make a significant difference to performance and productivity.

Its exclusive and industry-recognised qualification, Chartered Director, is supported by many major influential bodies and more than 1,000 individuals are now qualified. Through

Brand History

▶ **1903:** WA Addinsell, the head of a family-run accountancy firm, becomes the founding pioneer of the IoD. A group of senior directors meet to form the Council of the IoD, responding to concerns about the creation of new company legislation in 1900/01.

▶ **1921:** The forerunner to Director magazine, Advance, is launched.

▶ **1950:** The IoD holds its first Annual Convention.

▶ **1976:** The IoD moves to its current headquarters, 116 Pall Mall, London.

▶ **1987:** Margaret Thatcher addresses the IoD Annual Convention.

▶ **1999:** The world's first independently accredited qualification for directors, Chartered Director, is launched.

▶ **2001:** The Business Leaders Summits are introduced and iod.com goes live. In addition, Tony Blair opens the IoD's new venue, IoD 123.

▶ **2003:** The IoD's commitment to business excellence expands globally with the launch of IoD International.

▶ **2008:** The IoD launches a private online networking forum for members.

▶ **2011:** The Annual Convention relocates to a new home at The O2.

IoD International, director training is available in countries as diverse as Japan, India and China.

The IoD's authoritative and highly regarded business journal, Director, was redesigned in 2011 as a contemporary title. In November it won its first award since the relaunch, picking up Business Travel Features Journalist of the Year at the Business Travel Journalism Awards 2011.

In recent years the IoD has been involved in initiatives aimed at supporting future business leaders and encouraging entrepreneurs. The IoD is aiming to generate support for global entrepreneurialism and in 2011, led a delegation of three successful UK entrepreneurs to the G20 Young Entrepreneur Summit and started a new initiative aimed at helping start-up companies.

Recent Developments
Increasing networking remains high on the IoD's agenda, more so in the current economic climate when retaining and gaining new business is vital. The LinkedIn IoD member group has continued to grow since its launch and now facilitates an average of 280 monthly member discussions, involving more than 7,000 members, ranging from business advice to the mutual sharing of ideas for business leaders.

In response to the UK Corporate Governance Code's recommendation that FTSE 350 companies regularly undertake an externally facilitated board evaluation, the IoD set up a FTSE Board Evaluation Service in November 2011. The new service rejects the conventional 'tick box' approach in favour of an expert team to tailor evaluations to each organisation.

Of late, the IoD's training and development service has been exceptionally busy as members try to stay ahead of the competition. Initiatives include the Board Evaluation Toolkit, launched in 2010, and new courses created to meet growing demand, such as Coaching for Directors and Women as Highly Effective Directors.

Did You Know?

The IoD's premises have been used for scenes in The Dark Knight, Ghandi, The Apprentice and MasterChef.

Simon Walker, director general of the IoD, previously held the role of communications secretary to Her Majesty The Queen.

Additional brand developments include a new concierge service at the IoD's 116 Pall Mall headquarters, enabling the 400 plus daily members to access time saving services such as organising couriers, deliveries or dry cleaning while working.

Promotion
Recent promotion has placed renewed focus on members and the IoD has launched a range of events that give them regular access to its new director general, Simon Walker. An accompanying promotional strategy features member testimonials and photography on and offline.

A new Director app was launched in September 2011 to accompany and promote the revamp of Director magazine. Exclusively for members, the app offers enhanced content in addition to interviews with leading figures from the UK business world, opinions, debate, news and lifestyle.

Brand Values
The IoD's brand mark represents the essence of the organisation – the 'D' takes precedence over the 'I', illustrating the simple approach that 'Directors come before the Institute'. The elegant, yet commanding design also reflects the IoD's values: professional, inclusive, commercial, enterprising, open and honest.

The IoD attributes its success to the treatment of each member as an individual and to its brand offering of knowledgeable staff, responsive, engaging communication and confident, trustworthy support.

▶ **www.iod.com**

The brand's rich history of sporting saloons and cutting-edge models dates back 90 years with classics such as the SS100, the E-Type and the XJ saloon continually pushing boundaries – an approach that lives on in the current range. Jaguar is a forward thinking, innovative and environmentally conscious brand that is committed to producing beautiful, fast cars.

Market

In the highly competitive UK market Jaguar products perform strongly, with the flagship XJ, the XK sports coupé, and the XF saloon all tangible evidence of a design and technology revolution at the brand. Updated versions of the three models made their debut in April 2011 before launching in September. The XJ leads its market sector, the XK range has accelerated ahead of its competition in the sports car segment, and the XF has grown its market share by 12 per cent in one of the most competitive sectors of the market (Source: Company Data October 2011).

Product

Jaguar's in-house designers and engineers continuously strive to keep the brand ahead of competitors by creating beautifully designed, innovative cars that stand apart from mainstream premium offerings.

The new 2012 range not only embodies Jaguar's brand ideals – innovation, bold design and effortless high performance – but also includes substantial changes and improvements that enhance product performance, refinement and economy, while design modifications strengthen contemporary appeal.

For the luxury Jaguar XJ saloon, a suite of enhancements to the interior and options list includes a new rear seat comfort package that reinforces the ultimate executive limousine experience.

The new XK range builds on the car's award-winning reputation as a high-performance sporting GT. A new range-topping variant,

Did You Know?

Jaguar's original straight-six engine was first developed by engineers on night-time fire watch at the Jaguar plant during World War II. The XK version, introduced in 1949, went on to power Jaguar cars for more than four decades.

the XKR-S, creates a performance flagship for Jaguar by becoming the brand's most powerful production car, capable of achieving 0–60 mph in 4.2 seconds. Design modifications to the front and rear of the entire XK range have enhanced its visual appeal and special order upgrades enable the discerning driver to further emphasise either its luxury or performance features.

The XF showcases major technical advances, including an all-new, state-of-the-art 2.2 litre four-cylinder turbodiesel engine that comes with a fuel- and emissions-saving intelligent Stop/Start system – a first for Jaguar. This model stands out as the most fuel-efficient Jaguar ever made.

Achievements

Over the years Jaguar has accrued many accolades for design and technology, receiving

with the ability to travel at speeds of up to 50 mph under electric power alone, and CO_2 emissions of just 165 g/km, the C-X16 sets a high standard for the next generation of sustainable sports cars.

As a mark of Jaguar's commitment to innovation, it will be investing £1.5 billion in new product development every year for the next five years – which, as a proportion of revenue, is the largest in the premium sector.

Promotion

In early 2011 Jaguar founded in-house creative agency Spark44 to spearhead a new creative strategy across all of its brand communications.

The prestigious and dynamic nature of its product, however, means experiential activities are the cornerstone of its promotions strategy. Hundreds of events are hosted each year – from track experiences to the Goodwood Festival of Speed – that aim to encourage people to get behind the wheel of a Jaguar. The brand also teams up with high-profile partners such as British Airways, The Savoy, Coutts Bank, Stoke Park and Caprice Holdings for additional events and promotions.

As official vehicle provider to the England Cricket Team, Team Sky and the Lawn Tennis Association, Jaguar's sporting credentials are firmly established. The brand has extended its sporting association further by supporting a selection of other clubs, venues and charitable causes. The Jaguar Academy of Sport, in particular, demonstrates its long-term commitment to recognise, celebrate and inspire the next generation of British sporting heroes.

Brand Values

Jaguar's brand values are symbiotic with its product range, combining pace with elegance, quality, value, efficiency and performance.

▶ **www.jaguar.co.uk**

Brand History

▶ **1922:** Jaguar's forerunner, The Swallow Sidecar Company, is founded by William Lyons and William Warmsley in Blackpool, UK.

▶ **1935:** The first car to bear the Jaguar name, the SS Jaguar 2.5 litre saloon, costing £385, is unveiled at London's Mayfair Hotel.

▶ **1949:** The XK120, designed by William Lyons, causes a sensation when it launches at the British Motor Show.

▶ **1961:** The iconic Jaguar E-Type launches at the Geneva Motor Show and is described by Enzo Ferrari as "the most beautiful car ever built".

▶ **1968:** The XJ6 saloon becomes the last car designed by Sir William Lyons and his most enduring creation, with more than 400,000 sales in the following 24 years.

▶ **1972:** Jaguar introduces the 5.4 litre V12 engine for the XJ6, making it the fastest production car in the world at the time, capable of 140 mph.

▶ **1988:** The XJR-9 wins six of the 11 races at the World Sports Car Championship, taking both the driver and team trophies.

▶ **1996:** Jaguar's design team creates a new car for the company's first V8 engine, the XK8. It goes on to become the fastest-selling sports car in Jaguar's history.

▶ **2008:** The XK, the first new Jaguar of the millennium, launches.

▶ **2010:** The launch of the latest XJ marks a clean break with previous models. It becomes a global sales success.

more than 80 awards for the XF alone. One of its most recent is the prestigious Auto Express Car of the Decade award, voted for by more than 300,000 readers. In the What Car? Green Awards 2010, the XJ was voted Best Luxury Car and at the Scottish Car of the Year Awards 2011, journalists from the Association of Scottish Motoring Writers named the XKR-S Best Sports Car 2011.

Recent Developments

Unveiled at Geneva in September 2011, the C-X16 concept marks a new chapter for Jaguar. The two-seater hybrid combines the heritage of the brand's award-winning design with groundbreaking performance to create the most compact and responsive Jaguar in a generation.

Its supercharged V6 petrol engine produces 380 PS (280 kW) and 332 lb ft (450 Nm) of torque. The performance of the C-X16 is further supplemented by a Formula 1-inspired hybrid boost system with a steering-wheel mounted button for on-demand acceleration. Combined

Did You Know?

The XJ-S completed the 3,000-mile coast-to-coast Cannonball Run in the US in 1975, in just 32 hours and 51 minutes – a record that stood for four years.

The XJ220 was developed by a group of Jaguar employees known as the Saturday Club, who worked on special projects in their spare time. Only 300 were made and in the early 1990s it was the world's fastest production car.

John Lewis

Renowned for its high quality products and customer service, delivered by friendly experts who are actually Partners in the business, John Lewis is Britain's favourite retailer (Source: Verdict Research 2011). It is driven by a desire to be the UK's most trusted retailer and a place where customers love to shop, whether in one of its 35 shops or through its award-winning online and multichannel services.

Market

John Lewis is a department store, which means its assortment includes homewares, fashion, beauty and electricals. John Lewis has 29 full line shops and six atHome shops that focus on homewares and electricals. Online sales are growing fast and the brand's leading retail website, johnlewis.com, already accounts for more than 20 per cent of total sales.

The brand's main competitors are Marks & Spencer, national department stores including House of Fraser and Debenhams, and some more exclusive fashion-oriented shops such as Harvey Nichols and Selfridges. John Lewis is the market leader in homewares and a growing challenger in fashion (Source: 'UK Homewares Retailers 2012' Verdict Research 2011, and Kantar Worldpanel 2011).

Did You Know?

John Lewis is the first UK department store to offer customers free WiFi access in its shops.

John Lewis carries more lines than any other department store in the UK.

Product

Carrying over 350,000 different lines – more than any other department store in the UK – John Lewis offers a unique retail assortment, which is accompanied by a simple but powerful brand philosophy: to be Never Knowingly Undersold, on quality, price and service. This longstanding principle ensures that John Lewis matches its high street competitors' in-store and online prices, reinforcing its commitment to value.

Above all, however, John Lewis is renowned for the level of customer service it offers. As a partnership, John Lewis is unique among British retailers; its Partners own the company. As a result, Partners are truly motivated to deliver expert and impartial advice and service. Quite simply: at John Lewis, a customer's happiness is everyone's business.

Achievements

John Lewis is a multi-award-winning business and brand, and was named Britain's Favourite Retailer for the fourth consecutive year in 2011 by Verdict Research. Additional accolades in recent years include Best Online Retailer 2010 from Which?; the Marketing Society's Brand of the Year in both 2010 and 2011 – a particular honour as it is the only brand to have won for two successive years; and Multichannel Retailer of the Year at the eCommerce Awards 2011.

Recent Developments

John Lewis has implemented a series of strategies that will help the business to continue its growth, build its brand, and lead the way in online retailing.

The opening of six atHome shops, with more planned for the future, represents a significant push out-of-town for John Lewis. It gives the brand greater opportunities to showcase its homewares and electricals offering, and to

reach new audiences that visit regional centres when setting up their first homes.

Building on the success of johnlewis.com, a strong focus is being placed on the brand's multichannel retail offering. As one of the UK's leading retailer websites, it carries more than 200,000 products and is growing by a rate of almost 30 per cent year-on-year. A mobile-optimised site was launched in 2010 to cater for the increasingly popular mobile channel and in 2011, multichannel was enhanced further by the launch of a smartphone app. John Lewis is also growing its click-and-collect service, enabling customers to shop online and then pick up the products from their local John Lewis or selected Waitrose, with more collection points on the way.

The launch of its Bringing Quality to Life strategy in 2010 marks the brand's increased commitment to responsible sourcing, and its aim to perform a powerful role as a CSR leader in UK retailing. Allied to this, John Lewis has been at the forefront of a push to 'buy British' in 2011 by sourcing as much as it can from the UK and making clear to customers which products come from these shores.

Promotion

Over the past three years John Lewis has set out to build a strong emotional connection with its core, established audience. Marketing has aimed to build both love and trust in the brand to make John Lewis the place where customers enjoy shopping.

John Lewis has become known for advertising and marketing campaigns that have a strong emotional impact. The Always a Woman TV ad first brought the nation to tears in spring 2010 and quickly became an online sensation; it was shared and commented upon by newspaper websites and social networks, from Facebook to Mumsnet. The Your Song execution for the Christmas 2010 TV ad, which featured Ellie Goulding, stirred up further emotion.

The Long Wait TV ad, aired during the Christmas 2011 season, eclipsed even the success of the previous year. Launched on Facebook to John Lewis fans the day before it aired on TV, the story of a little boy waiting for Christmas proved so popular it was trending on Twitter in the UK and globally within five hours of being posted online. It has gone on to be viewed more than 3.5 million times on YouTube, spoofed by TV channels and the public, and proclaimed 'the best advert ever' by The Telegraph. Unsurprisingly, The Long Wait was named Campaign of the Year 2011 by Campaign magazine.

Brand Values

John Lewis aims to be the most trusted retailer and a place where customers love to shop.

Did You Know?

Ellie Goulding's cover of 'Your Song', which featured in the 2010 John Lewis Christmas campaign, was chosen for the first dance at the royal wedding in 2011.

For decades the brand has captured shoppers' hearts and minds through its enduring proposition: Never Knowingly Undersold. This drives everything John Lewis does, in its shops, and as an online and mobile retailer. Every product is of high quality and competitively priced. But it is the unique customer service that most sets John Lewis apart. Every Partner serves a customer as if they own the business, because they do.

▶ **www.johnlewis.com**

Brand History

▶ **1864:** John Lewis opens a drapery shop on London's Oxford Street – it will become the brand's flagship store.

▶ **1905:** Lewis acquires a second shop, Peter Jones in Sloane Square, London.

▶ **1920:** Lewis' son founds the John Lewis Partnership, making employees Partners and giving each a share of the business. He coins the phrase, 'Never Knowingly Undersold' – an unusual collection of words that stand apart on the high street as an enduring commitment to real value and service.

▶ **2012:** The brand is now a leading multichannel retailer with 35 John Lewis shops across the UK. The core values of its founders remain, however, as does the unique partnership business model.

SINCE 1857
JOHN WEST

In 1857 John West's goal was to bring back the very best tasting fish for the world to enjoy. Today, cans of John West are found in kitchen cupboards across the UK. The brand is synonymous with high quality and taste, traits that have earned it its place as brand leader in the UK, Holland and Ireland. John West trades in 38 markets throughout Europe and the rest of the world.

Brand History

▶ **1857:** John West begins salting salmon in Oregon in the US, packing them into barrels and shipping them to California and England.

▶ **1868:** West helps pioneer a new way of bringing high quality wild fish onto consumers' tables; canned salmon is introduced.

▶ **1874:** John West's dedication to quality is recognised by the Oregon State Agricultural Society when he is awarded the Gold Medal for his canned salmon.

▶ **1882:** As word spreads of John West's high quality canned salmon, he buys a 118 ft propeller-driven steamer – The John West – to meet demand.

▶ **1952:** Canned tuna hits the shelves for the first time.

▶ **1958:** The first John West TV advert airs, promoting canned salmon.

▶ **1966:** A new advertising tagline is born – 'It's the fish that John West reject, that makes John West the Best.' The slogan runs for two decades and becomes synonymous with the brand.

▶ **1993:** On January 11th, the Earth Island Institute grants use of the Dolphin Safe symbol to John West in recognition of its fishing practices.

▶ **2009:** John West introduces a world first to its range, No Drain Tuna, which uses patented technology.

▶ **2011:** An MSC-certified range of salmon, mackerel and sardine products launches, and John West unveils a plan to source 100 per cent of its tuna for UK sale through a combination of pole-and-line or purse seine FAD-free methods by 2016.

Market

The canned fish market is worth more than £475 million in the UK. Of this, John West has a 30 per cent market share (Source: Symphony IR 52 w/e 26th November 2011).

Of the 27 sectors in the canned fish market, John West operates in 23. Tuna is the largest of the sectors, making up 64 per cent of overall canned fish sales. It is followed by red salmon, which has an 11.6 per cent share; pink salmon, which has a 2.9 per cent share; and mackerel, which has a 7.4 per cent share (Source: Symphony 2011).

Overall, John West sells more products across more of the canned fish sectors than any other producer in the UK.

Product

One hundred and fifty years of fishing knowledge means John West is able to find and bring back high quality fish, from Atlantic sardines to tuna from the Indian Ocean. John West believes that carrying out its own fishing is the best way to ensure the best quality, and therefore runs its own fleet of fishing boats.

The John West product offering includes tuna, salmon, mackerel, sardines, speciality fish and seafood, brisling and slid, herrings and kippers, and pate – canned in a variety of formats, from oils and sauces to brine, spring water and 'no drain'. Weight Watchers and Light Lunch products are also available.

VOTED PRODUCT OF THE YEAR 2010
Winner General Food Category. Survey of 10,041 people by TNS

WHERE OTHERS SAID "CAN'T"

WE SAID "CAN"

A No Drain canned tuna was thought impossible. Impossible that is to everyone but us.

Thanks to our can-do philosophy at John West, we've not only created the world's first No Drain canned tuna, we've created one of our biggest ever success stories and won Product of the Year 2010!

It's been such a success that we are launching even more products this year to extend the No Drain range with new No Drain Chunks in Brine and Sunflower Oil; and for ultimate convenience new No Drain Chunks in two individual servings; and Tuna Steaks in Olive Oil and Spring Water. Enjoy.

OUR MONEY'S ON THE BEAR.

We're bringing the famous John West 'Bear' out of hibernation this summer with full national television advertising support. It'll beat the competition. No contest.

Achievements

John West remains true to its founder's pioneering spirit to this day, with the brand claiming a first for the canned fish category by introducing No Drain Tuna in 2009. The patented technology enables canned tuna to be kept moist and succulent without the need for excess liquid. In 2010, John West's No Drain Tuna was named General Food Product of the Year.

John West has also made waves outside of the product arena. Its innovative 'Bear' canned salmon TV campaign – released in November 2000 – was an internet hit, quickly becoming the most forwarded TV advert. The clip of a fisherman and a bear appearing to fight over fresh salmon accrued an estimated 300 million views worldwide by 2006, and the campaign won multiple industry awards.

Recent Developments

The introduction of No Drain Tuna has been at the forefront of recent change at John West. Since its successful launch in 2009, No Drain Tuna has been purchased by 5.5 million households (Source: Kantar Worldpanel 52 w/e 26th November 2011). The range now consists of 130 g No Drain Tuna Steaks in Oil, Brine, Olive Oil and Spring Water as well as 3 x 60g Steaks in Oil and Brine.

NO DRAIN tuna from JOHN WEST

Elsewhere in the product line-up, Steam Cooked Mackerel has been introduced for a fresher, more natural flavour. The mackerel is also sold in larger packs to accommodate full size fillets that are suitable as a whole meal rather than just as a snack. The sardine offering has also been rejuvenated by the introduction of a new preparation, Grilled Sardines, with an authentic straight-from-the-barbecue flavour.

Underlying John West's products is its ongoing commitment to sustainable fishing. In 2010, the company was certified by the Marine Stewardship Council (MSC) for its use of well-managed and sustainable fisheries. A range of MSC-certified salmon, mackerel and sardines was introduced to supermarkets nationwide the following year. 2011 also saw the launch of a pole-and-line-caught tuna range.

Promotion

In October 2011, John West launched a nationwide TV campaign to herald an initiative that allows consumers to trace the origins of their can of John West tuna.

Did You Know?

If you lined up all the cans of John West fish sold in the UK in the past year, they would reach from Liverpool to Bangkok.

A groundbreaking first for the industry, the six-week campaign formed part of a £6 million marketing campaign to reinforce the brand's 150 years of fishing expertise and its commitment to traceability – an important element in sustainability.

The 'Story Behind Every Can' TV commercials feature a weathered old fisherman aboard a trawler recalling humorous stories about tuna fishing trips. He invites viewers to discover the story behind every can of John West tuna – including the name of the boat it was caught on – by inputting a can's unique code into the John West website.

The next 12 months will see the initiative rolled out across the rest of John West's product portfolio. The 360-degree campaign includes TV, digital and below-the-line marketing activity including PR.

Brand Values

Fishing expertise is at the heart of the John West brand and its values spring from life aboard a fishing boat. The company values a strong crew mentality, the bravery to strive for the very best even in the most adverse conditions, and respect for others and the oceans in which we fish.

▶ **www.john-west.co.uk**

SINCE 1857
JOHN WEST
NO DRAIN LESS MESS
TUNA STEAK
With a little BRINE

SINCE 1857
JOHN WEST
TUNA STEAK
NO DRAIN LESS MESS

Kall Kwik offers a range of design, print and e-communications services to help businesses communicate more effectively with their customers, employees, investors and suppliers. With a nationwide network of Centres, Kall Kwik's design and production teams can help with everything from brand design, logos and advertisements, to sales promotions, e-marketing campaigns, exhibition and display materials, signage, business forms and stationery.

business image   operational print   promotional print   exhibitions and events

Market

In the UK, the total print market is worth £12 billion and is forecast to keep growing. The 'on demand' sector of the UK market is valued at £1 billion per annum and has traditionally been served by thousands of small, independent printers. However, the level of design expertise, the quality of printed product and the commitment to customer service can vary considerably from supplier to supplier – which introduces risk for business customers.

In addition, as many independent printers are unable to cover a wide range of print requirements and often have little expertise in implementing e-communications campaigns, their business customers can be faced with the inefficiency of having to work with and manage multiple suppliers.

By contrast, Kall Kwik's network of design and print Centres offers business customers all of the benefits of a local supplier, together with the resources, investment and skills expected from a nationwide operation. In addition,

Kall Kwik's commitment to evaluating and introducing new design and print technologies helps to ensure that its Centres can offer their clients more innovative and eye-catching methods to promote their businesses.

Product

By delivering consistently high customer service, creative design skills and high quality print across all of its Centres, Kall Kwik helps to de-risk the supplier selection process for business customers. Furthermore, as Kall Kwik can cover virtually any design and print requirement, customers only have to brief one team on their needs.

Kall Kwik's products and services address four key areas for business customers: business image, operational print, promotional print, and exhibitions and events.

In order to help its clients manage their business image, Kall Kwik offers design services for corporate identity, brands and logos, corporate brochures and advertisements.

Kall Kwik can support day-to-day business operations, by delivering carefully designed print items that help to streamline key processes, including business forms, carbonless stationery, training manuals and large format plan printing.

To help its clients achieve more from their promotional activities, Kall Kwik designs and produces brochures and catalogues, proposals, tenders and pitches, direct mail and email campaigns, and point of sale materials.

Kall Kwik designs and delivers items that can make exhibitions and events more productive, from pop-up stands, exhibition displays and banners, to personalised invitations for events and branded gifts.

Did You Know?

Kall Kwik has achieved Business Superbrand status for nine consecutive years.

Kall Kwik is a full member of the British Franchise Association.

Achievements

Kall Kwik has received many accolades for its franchise model, including the prestigious title of Franchisor of the Year from the British Franchise Association in 2005.

Having identified the emerging demand for print suppliers that can offer in-house design and e-communications capabilities, Kall Kwik has successfully extended the range of services that its Centres offer. Today, Kall Kwik provides much more than print; Kall Kwik is increasingly recognised as a centre of excellence that businesses can turn to for expert advice on a wide variety of business communications issues.

Recent Developments

In recent years, as the brand has evolved to offer a vastly extended range of products and services, Kall Kwik's central office team

has worked closely with each of its franchisees to help ensure a consistent customer experience across the entire network of local Centres.

The introduction of new capabilities is set to continue, with Kall Kwik investing in the latest technologies and embracing innovation in order to offer customers new ways of ensuring that their business communications and marketing materials stand out from the crowd.

Promotion

In the latter half of 2011, Kall Kwik significantly increased its investment in marketing activities. The brand has already started to roll out its accelerated marketing programme of campaigns to help individual Kall Kwik Centres raise awareness of the new, wider range of services that they offer. Promotional activities are helping Kall Kwik franchisees to win new clients, and sell additional products and services to existing customers.

This increased investment in marketing will continue throughout 2012. An additional campaign is also set for launch, aimed at expanding the Kall Kwik network by recruiting and training new franchisees so that even more business customers will benefit from having a Kall Kwik Centre 'on their doorstep'.

Brand Values

The Kall Kwik brand is synonymous with hassle-free design, print and e-communications services. Each Centre proactively builds on its status as the local, friendly, approachable team of experts that helps to demystify design, print and marketing. In doing so, Kall Kwik helps businesses to achieve more from their communications and marketing budgets.

Brand History

▶ **1979:** The first Kall Kwik Centre opens its doors in Pall Mall, London.

▶ **2005:** Kall Kwik UK is awarded Franchisor of the Year by the British Franchise Association. In addition, the first kdesigngroup studio is opened.

▶ **2008:** kdesigngroup achieves 20 per cent growth, underlining the growing demand for dependable, creative studios.

▶ **2010:** Kall Kwik Studio is launched, providing a web-to-print service that helps customers to realise efficiency gains and cost reductions.

▶ **2011:** Kall Kwik unveils an accelerated marketing programme to help franchisees raise awareness of the breadth of products and services that they offer.

Each Kall Kwik team adopts a consultative approach in order to gain a detailed understanding of the client's business and its objectives. Only then can the team suggest creative design options and products that match each business client's specific aims.

The same creative design skills, print expertise and e-communications know-how are available to all Kall Kwik customers – from large public sector organisations and corporate customers, through to small retailers and local tradespeople.

▶ **www.kallkwik.co.uk**

Thirty years of care and craft have gone into the authentic taste of KETTLE® Chips. What began as a quest for a tasty snack made the natural way has become the UK's number one hand-cooked crisp brand (Source: Nielsen November 2011). Remaining true to its roots, Kettle Foods continues to make KETTLE® Chips in small batches with top-quality potatoes, sunflower oil, and seasonings that have been created from real ingredients by its head chef.

The hand cooked chip.

The hand cooked chip.

The hand cooked chip.

Market

Since the brand's launch, KETTLE® Chips has grown to become a £90 million brand in the UK crisps and snacks market, gaining a reputation for driving category value growth. Its introduction to the UK market created the premium sharing sector, which is now worth £577 million (Source: Nielsen November 2011). Competition has intensified with numerous product launches from brands large and small but KETTLE® continues to grow and thrive year-on-year. Today almost one in four homes in the UK buys KETTLE® Chips (Source: Nielsen 2011), with more than 100 million packs sold in 2011.

Product

The KETTLE® Chips philosophy has always been that the simple approach to good food is always best; so it doesn't add any MSG or artificial colours, flavourings or preservatives.

Did You Know?

KETTLE® launched the first ever beer flavoured chip in 2006 – Mature Cheddar with Adnams Broadside Beer.

KETTLE® Chips appeared on BBC One's hit comedy series Absolutely Fabulous in the 1990s.

The simple hand-cooked process remains the same today as when Kettle Foods produced its first chips. Grown especially for KETTLE®, the potatoes are hand-inspected on arrival so only the best ones go on to become KETTLE® Chips. After being thickly sliced with their skin on, the potatoes are cooked in small batches using sunflower oil – high in polyunsaturates and low in saturated fat – that lets the flavour of the potato shine through. The slices are tended by experienced chip fryers who turn them by hand, using a tool inspired by a garden rake, until they are golden and crunchy all over. The chips are then flavoured with carefully blended seasonings.

Finally, the chips are packaged in the brand's distinctive coloured airtight bags, ensuring the flavour remains as fresh as the moment they were cooked.

Achievements

In 1988 the KETTLE® brand introduced hand-cooked chips to the UK consumer and in doing so, created a whole new category of premium crisps for sharing. Today KETTLE® remains the UK's number one hand-cooked crisp brand, the number one premium crisp brand and the number one sharing crisp brand (Source: Nielsen 2011).

Since its launch in 2005 the KETTLE® Chips 40g format has significantly increased the availability of the brand outside grocery retail. In the last three years alone, KETTLE® Chips 40g has delivered value sales growth in impulse channels of more than 30 per cent (Source: Nielsen 2011).

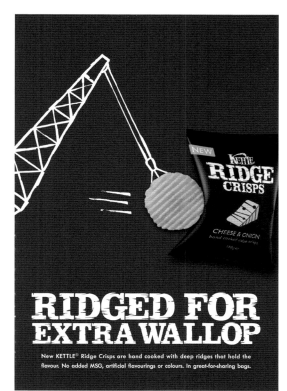

Recent Developments

In 2010 KETTLE® introduced a new range of crisps with simple bold flavours designed for a younger audience enjoying a night in. KETTLE® Ridge Crisps are hand-cooked but with deep ridges to hold the flavour for a bigger bolder taste. A new advertising and PR campaign, with the strapline 'Ridged for Extra Wallop', supported the launch.

Since entering the market in 2007, KETTLE® Chips in multipacks have grown in popularity and have added a premium sector to the multipack category. In 2011 the range was expanded to include a multipack for the Mature Cheddar & Red Onion seasoning, which joined the Lightly Salted, Sea Salt & Balsamic Vinegar and assorted packs already available.

In 2010 Kettle Foods was acquired by Diamond Foods, which recognised the growth potential of the brand and respected its approach to business. In joining Diamond Foods, KETTLE® Chips sits alongside a stable of brands including Emerald Nuts and popcorn brand Pop Secret.

Promotion

To reinforce the KETTLE® brand's status as 'The' hand-cooked chip, a striking new press advertising campaign was unveiled in 2011. Featuring ingredients illustrated with handprints, the ads ran across national premium press.

Did You Know?

A KETTLE® Chip takes six times longer to cook than an ordinary crisp.

All KETTLE® seasonings are created by the brand's head chef, Chris Barnard, who worked as a commis chef under Anton Mossiman at the Grosvenor Square Hotel, London.

An innovative partnership with Lovefilm.com also ran throughout the year to promote KETTLE® Ridge Crisps as the perfect snack for a movie night in. A series of branded mail-outs to two million homes was supported by an online movie competition on Lovefilm.com, which also created a stir on Facebook.

This followed a highly distinctive creative campaign designed to support the launch of KETTLE® Ridge Crisps and reach a younger audience for the brand. The 'Ridged for Extra Wallop' campaign had significant stand out and established the new range's position on-shelf. 'Ridged for Extra Wallop' was brought to life further through a creative PR and digital campaign that saw Ben Collins (previously Top Gear's The Stig) compete in the specially created Wallop to London Dodgem Derby – four purple dodgem cars racing in a contest of skill.

Brand Values

Kettle Foods insists on using the best potatoes it can find and hand cooking them with care in small batches. It blends real ingredients to create all of its seasonings for an authentic tasting crisp and remains true to its founding principle: no added MSG, artificial flavours or colours.

It's a simple formula but one that seems to work. Tasty chips, made with care, by people with a real passion and commitment to what they do.

RIDGED FOR EXTRA WALLOP

New KETTLE® Ridge Crisps are hand cooked with deep ridges that hold the flavour. No added MSG, artificial flavourings or colours. In great-for-sharing bags.

▶ **www.kettlechips.co.uk**

Brand History

▶ **1978:** Kettle Foods is founded by Cameron Healy in Salem, Oregon in the US. He starts with no working capital – but a lot of passion and an old camper van – selling cheese and roasted nuts to natural food stores along Interstate 5.

▶ **1982:** Inspired by tasting hand-fried potato chips on a beach in Hawaii, Cameron launches KETTLE® Chips in the US: a premium thickly sliced crisp, hand-cooked in sunflower oil, with seasonings made from authentic ingredients and absolutely no artificial ingredients or MSG.

▶ **1988:** KETTLE® arrives in the UK, setting up production in Norfolk. A pioneer of the new hand-cooked category, it soon expands its distribution network from delicatessens and fine food stores to include grocery retail.

▶ **1997:** KETTLE® Chips Sea Salt & Balsamic Vinegar launches.

▶ **1998:** KETTLE® introduces Butter & Mint seasoned chips, the first of many special editions.

▶ **2005:** The first KETTLE® Chips television commercial airs.

▶ **2007:** KETTLE® introduces its first multipacks.

▶ **2009:** KETTLE® Chips is voted a CoolBrand by a panel of experts and the UK public.

▶ **2010:** KETTLE® Ridge Crisps are introduced to the UK.

LLOYD'S

Lloyd's is unique. It's not an insurance company; it's a marketplace offering insurance products tailored to specific risks. Like any market, Lloyd's brings together those with something to sell (underwriters, who provide insurance coverage) with those who want to buy (brokers, working on behalf of their clients who are seeking insurance). Lloyd's operates in more than 200 countries and territories and its policyholders come from all over the world.

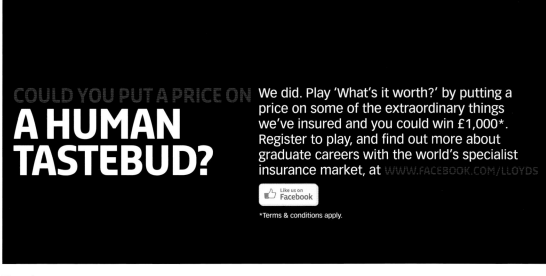

Market

Lloyd's can trace its beginnings back to the 17th century. Edward Lloyd's coffee house was first mentioned in the London Gazette in 1688. It swiftly became the place to go for ship captains, owners and merchants to get reliable shipping news and equally reliable insurance. This principle of a face-to-face way of doing business has remained throughout its history. Even today, business at Lloyd's is undertaken in person on its famous underwriting floor, known as 'the Room'.

In 2010 Lloyd's wrote more than £22.5 billion gross written premium globally. Eighty per cent of Lloyd's business comes from outside the UK and Lloyd's underwriters can delegate authority to intermediaries in other countries, allowing them to benefit from more than 75 global licences and a secure capital base.

Did You Know?

Lloyd's has insured some weird and wonderful things, such as: the first privately manned space trip, for US$100 million; Bruce Springsteen's voice, for £3.5 million; Ugly Betty star America Ferrera's smile, for US$10 million; and the tongue of Costa's Italian Master of Coffee, for £10 million.

Product

The attraction of Lloyd's lies in the way risks are expertly calculated by specialist underwriters, its consistently high ratings from financial institutions, and its capital strength – which Lloyd's describes as its 'chain of security'.

Lloyd's currently has around 85 syndicates offering policies that cover everything from property damage in the event of an earthquake to the construction of new windfarms. Lloyd's underwriters are renowned for devising tailored, innovative solutions to complex risks. From oil rigs to ocean-going liners, taste buds or tiaras – whatever the risk, it's likely Lloyd's has insured it.

Achievements

Lloyd's has been established for more than three centuries. During that time it has provided vital information about shipping to the British Admiralty during the Napoleonic Wars, provided a lifeline for policyholders facing the devastation of the 1906 San Francisco earthquake, insured the ill-fated Titanic in 1912, and paid out billions of dollars in the aftermath of the attack on the World Trade Center in 2001.

In between, it created the first insurance policies for jewellery, burglary and motor cars as well as the very first space risk. Alongside its global reputation for innovation, Lloyd's has an outstanding reputation for paying valid claims.

Recent Developments

The global balance between existing and emerging economic powers is changing. In 2008 Lloyd's became the first reinsurer to be granted 'admitted' status in Brazil. In 2007 it received its licence to write onshore reinsurance business in China, writing its first direct policy there in 2011.

A prudent investment strategy and strict market oversight ensured Lloyd's emerged relatively unscathed from the global financial crisis of 2008/09. Lloyd's was able to post record profits in 2009, with 2010 being another profitable year.

2011 proved an exceptional year for the frequency and severity of natural catastrophes, with floods in Australia, Brazil, Sri Lanka and Thailand; earthquakes in New Zealand, Japan and Turkey; and tornadoes and hurricanes in North America. Throughout, Lloyd's continued to pay valid claims to help businesses and communities rebuild.

Brand History

▶ **1688:** Lloyd's coffee house is recognised as the place for obtaining marine insurance.

▶ **1803:** Lloyd's responds to the growing number of wounded soldiers from the Napoleonic wars by setting up its first charity, the Lloyd's Patriotic Fund.

▶ **1904:** Lloyd's writes its first motor policy, cementing its reputation for innovation.

▶ **1906:** Faced with the devastation caused by the San Francisco earthquake, Lloyd's underwriter Cuthbert Heath issues the urgent instruction: "Pay all of our policyholders in full, irrespective of the terms of their policies." Lloyd's reputation for reliability is established in the US.

▶ **1911:** Lloyd's writes its first policy for aviation.

▶ **1965:** The space race is underway and Lloyd's underwrites the first ever space risk.

▶ **2005:** In the aftermath of Hurricane Katrina, Lloyd's emerges with only a small market loss and reinforces its commitment to help a devastated region rebuild.

▶ **2010:** Lloyd's is granted a licence to write direct business in China.

▶ **2011:** Lloyd's celebrates the 25th anniversary of its iconic building.

Promotion

Lloyd's is unlike any other business. A vital part of promoting Lloyd's, therefore, is helping the world understand what Lloyd's is, how it works, what it stands for and why it is so different from other insurance companies or markets.

Alongside this, Lloyd's is positioning itself as a global leader on risk. Its Risk Insight hub brings together the views of the world's leading business, academic and insurance experts in one place to analyse the latest material on emerging risk. In 2011 it published the second edition of the Lloyd's Risk Index, highlighting global business leaders' attitudes to risk and their ability to cope with it.

Also in 2011, Lloyd's celebrated the 25th anniversary of the iconic Lloyd's building; located in the financial heart of London, the building is a true monument to the brand. On its open day (as part of the Open House London architectural festival) more than 6,500 people visited the building, seeing the Underwriting Room, the Nelson Collection, the 18th century Adam Room and the view of London from the external glass lifts.

Brand Values

Lloyd's never underestimates the major asset its brand provides, not just for Lloyd's itself but for all the businesses that work in the market. It is recognised worldwide as a leading global market that is able and trusted to take on the

world's toughest risks. A highly distinctive brand, it is known for its history, unique way of doing business and ability to meet highly specialised requirements.

The Lloyd's brand values are summed up by the phrase: Constant Originality. That is, good faith and reliability coupled with creativity, authenticity and adaptability.

▶ **www.lloyds.com**

As 'the lighter way to enjoy…chocolate'™, MALTESERS® has become one of the UK's most popular confectionery brands and continues to grow its product portfolio through innovative developments. Having reached its milestone 75th year in 2011, MALTESERS® is continuing its anniversary celebrations in 2012. In what is set to be an unforgettable year for the brand, 2012 will also see the Fairtrade certification rolled out across its range for the first time.

Market

MALTESERS® is the third biggest confectionery brand in the UK (Source: Symphony IRI 52 w/e 3rd December 2011) and was supported by a £7 million media spend throughout 2011.

In the UK, the chocolate market is valued at £3.344 billion and is growing at 3.3 per cent year-on-year. MALTESERS® also plays a key role in the substantial bitesize category, which is valued at £515 million and is growing at 4.1 per cent (Source: Symphony IRI 2011). Seventy per cent of chocolate is consumed in the company of others, making it no surprise that sharing products continue to perform well.

Mars Chocolate UK, which owns MALTESERS®, has a 49 per cent share of the bitesize category and five of the top 10 selling bitesize products (Source: MAT 52 w/e 1st January 2011). MALTESERS® is the number one selling bitesize product in the UK (Source: Symphony IRI 2011).

Did You Know?

Each second, an average of two individual bags of MALTESERS® are sold in the UK.

Every hour, the Slough factory produces enough MALTESERS® to fill 10 Olympic sized swimming pools.

There are lots of theories as to how the perfect roundness of MALTESERS® is created, but to date it remains a closely guarded trade secret.

Product

MALTESERS® were first produced in the UK in 1936 at the Mars Chocolate UK factory in Slough. The brand's portfolio has since been bolstered by the introduction of numerous variants, but the original format – the MALTESERS® box – has the largest shopper base of all MALTESERS® brand extensions. It is the biggest selling boxed confectionery brand in the UK, worth £29 million (Source: Symphony IRI 2011).

MALTESERS® are available in single bag, box and pouch formats, as well as funsize and multipacks to cater for a variety of consumer needs – they also feature in the CELEBRATIONS® selection alongside other favourites from the Mars Chocolate UK portfolio.

When it comes to seasonal ranges, the MALTESERS® brand has a strong offering. Easter and spring now include the popular

Brand History

▶ **1936:** Forrest E Mars creates MALTESERS® and introduces the light and airy chocolate balls to the UK.

▶ **1943:** The product is temporarily discontinued due to World War II; production resumes in 1951.

▶ **1959:** The first TV advertisement for MALTESERS® hits the screen in black and white.

▶ **1985:** The MALTESERS® gift box is introduced for the first time.

▶ **1993:** The brand's ballerina advertisement is launched, with the tagline: 'Chocolate before the performance? No, MALTESERS®.'

▶ **2002:** MALTESERS® Ice Cream launches, followed by MALTESERS® White the following year.

▶ **2006:** The 'Naughty' 190 calories campaign is unveiled.

▶ **2007:** MALTESERS® engages in daytime television programme sponsorship for the first time.

▶ **2009:** The MALTEASTER® Bunny is introduced as part of the brand's seasonal offering.

▶ **2011:** MALTESERS® and Comic Relief partner for Red Nose Day, raising more than £1.2 million.

▶ **2011:** Mars Chocolate UK announces an agreement with the Fairtrade Foundation and the MALTESERS® brand reaches its 75th year.

▶ **2012:** MALTESERS® continues its anniversary celebrations and the Fairtrade certification appears on-pack.

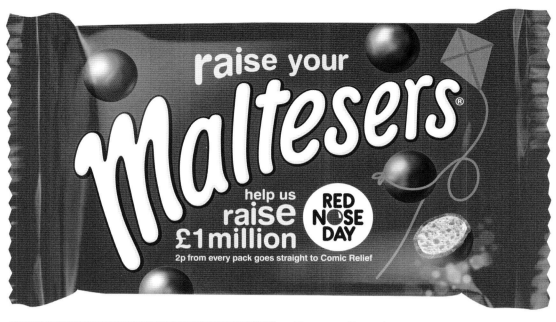

MALTEASTER® Bunny – a milk chocolate bunny with a crunchy and creamy MALTESERS® centre. The MALTEASTER® Bunny, now in its fourth year, offers consumers light-hearted fun in the run up to Easter and complements the brand's range of MALTESERS® Easter Eggs. At Christmas consumers can choose from a range of advent calendars, selection boxes, stocking fillers and boxed gifts with a seasonal design.

The portfolio also boasts MALTESERS® White, MALTESERS® Ice Cream, MALTESERS® Hot Chocolate and a MALTESERS® frothy cold milk drink.

Achievements

Spring 2011 saw MALTESERS® partner with Comic Relief for Red Nose Day in a bid to raise £1 million for charity, with at least 2p from every special pack purchased going straight to Comic Relief.

The playfulness of the MALTESERS® brand made it the perfect Red Nose Day partner, and to celebrate it set out a challenge for the public: Raise your MALTESERS®. Consumers were encouraged to suspend or raise their MALTESERS®

in funny and innovative ways, and invited to share videos and pictures of their efforts on the brand's website for the once in a lifetime chance to see their entry appear in TV adverts for the campaign.

MALTESERS® communicated its Red Nose Day initiative with a new on-pack design, while a TV advertising creative drove awareness and encouraged people to get involved. More than £1.2 million was raised through the partnership, beating the initial target.

Recent Developments

In September 2011, Mars Chocolate UK and the Fairtrade Foundation announced an agreement to introduce the first Fairtrade labelled Mars Chocolate UK product. As part of the initial roll-out, MALTESERS® will become the first product to carry the Fairtrade mark.

Fairtrade MALTESERS® will appear in stores during 2012 in the UK and Ireland. The move is expected to contribute in excess of US$1 million in annual Fairtrade premium funds for cocoa farmers to invest in their farms, business organisations and communities.

Mars Chocolate UK and the Fairtrade Foundation have a shared long-term ambition to make cocoa farming more sustainable, and the partnership is expected to increase total UK Fairtrade sales by approximately 10 per cent.

Promotion

MALTESERS® has always had a strong association with film, and in 2011 Mars Chocolate UK launched its 'Bag a Million Movies' on-pack promotion across its bitesize range, including packs of MALTESERS® singles, pouches and 'more to share' pouches.

The promotion offered consumers the chance to win one of a million DVDs, in association with Twentieth Century Fox. The promotion built on the existing heritage of Mars Chocolate UK's bitesize movie partnerships and was the chocolate manufacturer's biggest ever DVD giveaway.

Brand Values

MALTESERS® has always been associated with a light, playful treat and at its heart is about light-hearted fun and spontaneous, shared moments. To celebrate '75 years of Lightness' a commemorative limited edition box will be supported by an exciting media campaign as the brand's anniversary celebrations continue into 2012.

▶ **www.maltesers.com**

Marshalls
Creating Better Landscapes

Marshalls is the UK's leading hard landscaping manufacturer and has supplied some of the most prestigious landmarks in the UK with hard landscaping solutions since the 1890s. Marshalls strives to improve landscapes for everyone by using its expertise to create spaces that promote well-being, from using fairly traded stone and providing products that alleviate flood risks, to creating innovative anti-terrorist street furniture.

Market

Sustained growth has seen Marshalls expand to become the market leader in its sector. It supplies superior natural stone and innovative concrete hard landscaping products along with street furniture and water management solutions to the construction, home improvement and landscape markets. Its brand manifesto pledges a commitment to 'bring to life' the visions of architects, contractors, town planners, landscapers, civil engineers, builders' merchants, paving installers and homeowners.

Marshalls recently announced its expansion into Europe under the trading name Marshalls NV, which will supply products to a range of customers in Benelux, France and Germany, providing an ideal platform for launching its specialist landscaping products into the European market.

Product

Marshalls is committed to producing new products that better any existing market offering; to make them from the best materials it can source; and to care about the impact that the company and its products have on society and the environment. Investment in innovation continues to be a priority, both to develop new products and to reduce the environmental and social impact of its operations.

In the public sector and commercial end market, Marshalls satisfies the needs of a diverse customer base that spans local authorities, commercial architects, specifiers, contractors and house builders. Its integrated product range evolves to

> **Did You Know?**
>
> Marshalls supplied hard landscaping to the Northern Spectator Transport Mall at the site of the London 2012 Olympic Games; end-to-end the five million paving blocks would stretch 1,000 km, from London to Munich.

> **Did You Know?**
>
> Marshalls' quarry in Stainton, South Yorkshire, became the first operating site in the UK to be awarded the Biodiversity Benchmark from The Wildlife Trusts.

meet the exacting standards and sustainable requirements of developments in areas such as public realm, education, new house building and transport. Innovations such as its recently launched linear paving offering demonstrate the company's commitment to improving and extending the product range.

For the domestic market, Marshalls provides the inspiration and product ranges to create gardens and driveways that integrate seamlessly with people's lifestyles; the recent extension of its popular Fairstone product range underlines the brand's stance on ethical sourcing.

Achievements

Sustainability is at the heart of everything Marshalls does, whether it's becoming the first company to carbon label an entire product range or working with partners in India to ensure that there are safeguards against the

Brand History

▶ **1890:** Solomon Marshall starts to quarry in Southowram, Halifax and in 1904 establishes S. Marshall & Sons Ltd in West Yorkshire.

▶ **1947:** A second production site is opened to manufacture lintels, steps and fence posts. The following year an engineering division is established.

▶ **1964:** Marshalls becomes a plc with shares quoted on the London Stock Exchange.

▶ **1972:** New product development sees the introduction of block paving and the famous 'Beany Block', which combines drain and kerb.

▶ **1988:** Brick manufacturer George Armitage & Sons is acquired and goes on to become Marshalls Clay Products.

▶ **2004:** Marshalls acquires Woodhouse, expanding the Group's product offering to include design-led street furniture, lighting and signage.

▶ **2009:** More than 2,000 of Marshalls' commercial products now have a Carbon Trust Carbon Reduction Label.

▶ **2010:** Marshalls launches its first iPad app.

▶ **2011:** Marshalls announces a European venture, Marshalls NV.

use of child labour. In May 2011, Marshalls was awarded Best Collaboration at the Ethical Corporation Responsible Business Awards in recognition of the company's work with Indian non-governmental organisation Hadoti. Since 2007, Marshalls and Hadoti have established eight free schools and six free health centres in the heart of the quarrying area in Bundi.

Marshalls also became the first organisation in its industry to gain reaccreditation to the Carbon Trust Standard in 2011 after achieving a 15 per cent reduction in carbon emissions.

The company's longstanding history of strong CSR initiatives continued in 2011 with a varied programme of fundraising, product donation and staff volunteering activities. In June, Marshalls chief executive Graham Holden was named The Prince's Ambassador to Yorkshire and Humber by HRH The Prince of Wales in recognition of the organisation's commitment to responsible business.

Recent Developments
A key recent development for Marshalls is its work for the London 2012 Olympic and Paralympic Games. Promoted as 'the greenest games ever', sustainable venue construction is crucial and Marshalls has supplied hard landscaping products to the infrastructure, public realm, Olympic Village and satellite venues.

Recent developments also extend to the brand's CSR activities. In 2009 Marshalls joined the United Nations Global Compact (UNGC) – a framework for businesses committed to aligning operations and strategies with human rights, labour, the environment and anti-corruption – and in October 2011, hosted the UK's first UNGC supplier event.

Promotion
In 2011 Marshalls' commercial marketing team launched The Scapes: an integrated landscape offering that takes a holistic approach to the needs of clients and users of the landscape. The Scapes provide seamless product solutions

and present customers with simple, relevant information all in one place.

The commercial marketing team also ran a successful campaign in the early part of the year to highlight the benefits of its PAS68 anti-terrorist street furniture. The public safety campaign focused on the growing desire to create safe, beautiful public spaces, and featured a high profile interview on the BBC Culture Show with group marketing director, Chris Harrop on the aesthetics of the anti-terrorist landscape.

In recent years the brand's marketing strategy has become increasingly linked to social media. It has produced a set of popular 'How to' videos and directed promotional resources at Facebook, Twitter and YouTube, encouraging users to ask questions, share information and access Marshalls' expertise.

Did You Know?

In 2010, work was completed on the UK's largest concrete block paving installation at the port of Felixstowe. Marshalls supplied 13.3 million blocks to the site – that's the equivalent of 37 Wembley football pitches.

Brand Values
Marshalls believes that we all need places that make us feel safer, happier and more sociable; places to be ourselves, where we can live, play, create and grow. Its core brand values are based on trust, honesty and integrity.

Marshalls' vision is to be the supplier of choice to the landscape architect and contractor, and to the consumer for garden and driveway improvement projects. Marshalls is committed to conducting its business to achieve sustainable growth, while incorporating and demonstrating a high degree of social and environmental responsibility with an experienced, qualified and flexible workforce.

▶ **www.marshalls.co.uk**

As the world's largest chain of quick service restaurants, McDonald's serves more than 64 million people in 117 countries each day. In the UK, there are 1,200 restaurants serving around 2.5 million people daily and employing 88,000 staff, with £36 million invested in training and development each year. As a part franchised organisation, more than 60 per cent of McDonald's UK restaurants are owned and operated by independent businesspeople.

Market

McDonald's UK business falls into the informal eating out sector and sits alongside key players such as KFC, Burger King, Subway and Greggs.

In the third quarter of 2011 McDonald's UK moved into its 22nd consecutive quarter of growth, displaying consistency throughout a challenging global economy. Its resilience reflects the brand's ongoing strength and demonstrates that continued customer focus and investments aimed at modernising the restaurant experience are driving profitable market share growth. In the third quarter of 2011, global comparable sales increased by five per cent; US sales were up by 4.4 per cent, Europe by 4.9 per cent, and Asia Pacific, the Middle East and Africa by 3.4 per cent.

Product

As a restaurant McDonald's believes in the integrity of its end product – its food – the quality of which depends on the raw ingredients used at the first stage of the supply chain. The McDonald's Agricultural Assurance Programme ensures one consistent set of standards and requirements exists throughout its supply chain, which means that the same or comparable standards are applied to all of its menu items regardless of where they are sourced.

All raw ingredients are produced to exacting specifications and the highest possible standards. In its UK restaurants, for instance, all eggs are free-range and since May 2009, McDonald's has used only those that have been stamped on-farm to enhance traceability. McDonald's signature French Fries are made predominately from four key varieties of UK-grown potatoes (Pentland Dell, Russett Burbank, Shepody and Innovator), contain no animal extracts and are cooked in 100 per cent non-hydrogenated vegetable oil. The milk used by McDonald's UK mainland restaurants – in products ranging from sundaes to McFlurrys – is also sourced from British farms, and only 100 per cent British and Irish pork and beef burger patties are used in UK products.

All McDonald's fish menu items are certified by the Marine Stewardship Council (MSC) and the company works closely with the MSC on its sustainable seafood strategy to ensure that its offering does not feature endangered species. Hoki, fished in the southern hemisphere, is currently the only fish used in its Filet-O-Fish and Fish Finger menu items.

Achievements

McDonald's employs 88,000 people across the UK, having created 8,000 new jobs in the last two years alone. Its commitment to being a modern and progressive employer has garnered numerous accolades for the brand, including Investor in People Gold Status for the past three years and being named one of The Sunday Times 25 Best Big Companies to Work For in 2011.

In addition, McDonald's has topped the Best Business to Employee category at the 2011 European Sponsorship Association Awards, has featured in the Great Place to Work® Top 50 consistently since 2007, and has placed in The Times Top 50 Places Where Women Want to Work since 2006.

Recent Developments
People are fundamental to the success of McDonald's and over the past five years it has developed a 'learning ladder' that offers employees a clear progression plan through nationally recognised qualifications. In 2008 McDonald's obtained Awarding Body status, enabling it to offer an A Level-equivalent management diploma to more than 3,500 of its shift managers. Its latest addition is a foundation degree in managing business operations for restaurant managers, which was launched in 2011 in partnership with Manchester Metropolitan University.

In 1984, McDonald's became the first UK quick service restaurant company to publish detailed nutritional information about its food. Over the years it has added nutritional information to its tray-liners and packaging, and in September 2011 went further by ensuring that all McDonald's UK restaurants display the calorie content of all menu items on the menu boards – the point at which people choose their food.

Did You Know?

All 1,200 McDonald's restaurants in the UK recycle their used cooking oil for conversion to biodiesel to power the McDonald's delivery fleet.

Over the last 20 years, 14 Ronald McDonald Houses have been built which, along with 29 sets of Ronald McDonald Family Rooms, provide more than 400 bedrooms every single night of the year.

The restaurant experience was further enhanced in 2011 through the roll-out of a contactless payment system, which introduces added convenience for customers. Launched jointly with Visa Europe in all 1,200 UK restaurants, it is one of the UK's largest roll-outs of the technology.

Promotion
In line with its ethos of putting people at the heart of everything it does, McDonald's has been The FA's Community Partner since 2002. It has helped drive the training and recruitment of more than 20,000 community coaches, offering two million hours of free football training to young players across the UK.

As the Presenting Partner of the London 2012 Games Maker programme, McDonald's is supporting the selection and training of up to 70,000 volunteers who will lend their time, energy and expertise to help make London 2012 a success.

Brand Values
McDonald's is founded on its belief in a 'three legged stool' approach, with franchisees, company staff and suppliers all working together for mutual benefit.

McDonald's has always had a strong sense of social responsibility, with its founder Ray Kroc believing in the duty of businesses to put something back into the communities in which they operate. This principle is incorporated into McDonald's culture by placing the customer experience at the heart of the brand, through its ethical operations, and in its commitment to contributing to local communities.

▶ **www.mcdonalds.co.uk**

Brand History

▶ **1973:** McDonald's Golden Arches Restaurants Ltd is founded in the UK.

▶ **1974:** The first UK restaurant opens in Woolwich, London.

▶ **1984:** McDonald's becomes the first UK quick service restaurant group to introduce nutritional information countrywide for the benefit of customers.

▶ **1989:** The company's name changes to McDonald's Restaurants Ltd and the Ronald McDonald House Charity (RMHC) is created, providing parents with 'home away from home' accommodation at hospitals. The following year, the first Ronald McDonald House opens at Guy's Hospital, London.

▶ **1994:** McDonald's celebrates 20 years in the UK and raises £1.1 million for RMHC's Big Smile Appeal.

▶ **2000:** McDonald's UK launches its website.

▶ **2003:** A new global campaign is launched – 'I'm lovin' it'.

▶ **2004:** Salads are introduced – the biggest change to the UK menu for 30 years. WiFi is introduced in around 500 restaurants.

▶ **2007:** McDonald's becomes the UK's biggest retailer of coffee from Rainforest Alliance certified farms and commits to running its entire delivery fleet on 100 per cent biodiesel.

▶ **2010:** McDonald's UK becomes a Presenting Partner of the London 2012 Games Maker initiative; it is the first commercial partner to sponsor an Olympic volunteer programme.

On your side

Nationwide is more than 160 years old and is the world's largest building society. Unlike its bank competitors it has no shareholders so its only focus is its 15 million members. This 'On your side' approach has helped it to become a top three provider of mortgages and savings in the UK.

Market

The financial services market is served by a number of providers. Distinguished from its banking competitors, Nationwide is a building society or mutual, and so owned by and run for the benefit of its members (i.e. customers). With no external shareholders to pay dividends to, profits are reinvested in the business for the benefit of those members.

Nationwide has more than 10 million savings customers, five million current account customers and, as one of the UK's largest mortgage providers, issues a new mortgage every two minutes. In recent years it has grown substantially through its amalgamation with a number of other mutual societies across the UK.

Did You Know?

The Nationwide ATM in Coronation Street is the first product placement deal for a prime-time ITV soap.

The Society continues to demonstrate its support for first time home buyers, both with new products and through the free and impartial advice provided by its First Time Buyers' Guide. In the last year, one quarter of all Nationwide mortgages were for first time buyers.

Despite a climate of low interest rates, Nationwide savers continue to enjoy good rates; the Society's products consistently appeared in 'best buy' tables throughout 2011. As part of its Savings Promises (first announced in 2010), Nationwide took the unique step of writing to each of its savings customers to detail their current interest rates, therefore enabling them to make better informed decisions about their savings.

Product

Nationwide builds every product with mutuality in mind: understanding what members want and adapting its products accordingly. While its core market is traditionally mortgages and savings, Nationwide also offers a wide range of other products including current accounts, credit cards, investments, insurance – in the form of home, car, life and lifestyle – and personal loans.

Achievements

Nationwide receives numerous accolades for its consumer friendly products. In 2011 its current account received a five-star rating from Defaqto for the sixth consecutive year, recognising the excellence of the product's features and costs. Nationwide's main current account customers enjoy a variety of exclusive offers and benefits for no monthly fee, including free travel insurance. Thanks

to its current account, Nationwide has also garnered Recommended Provider status from Which? magazine.

Providing excellent products is only one part of the equation for Nationwide; the provision of top quality customer service is also critically important to the way it does business. Against its peer group of high street competitors,

Brand History

▶ **1846:** Provident Union Building Society is founded in Ramsbury, Wiltshire.

▶ **1848:** Northampton Town and County Freehold Land Society is founded.

▶ **1884:** The Southern Co-operative Permanent Building Society opens.

▶ **1967:** Northampton Town and County merges with Leicestershire Building Society to form Anglia Building Society.

▶ **1970:** The Co-operative Permanent Building Society changes its name to Nationwide Building Society.

▶ **1987:** FlexAccount is launched – the first full service current account to pay interest – and Nationwide merges with Anglia to become Nationwide Anglia.

▶ **1991:** The brand's name is shortened to Nationwide and a new logo launches.

▶ **2007:** Nationwide merges with the Portman Building Society.

▶ **2008:** Nationwide merges with Derbyshire and Cheshire Building Societies, and acquires the Dunfermline Building Society the following year.

▶ **2010:** Nationwide launches a new campaign starring David Walliams and Matt Lucas.

▶ **2011:** The brand launches its 'On your side' positioning and campaign.

Sleep well Britain.

Nationwide is a top performer for customer satisfaction in the combined areas of current accounts, savings and mortgages as measured by an independent industry benchmark (Source: GfK NOP Financial Research Survey (FRS), three months ending September 2011).

Nationwide has an 18-year relationship with Macmillan Cancer Support and has raised more than £6 million over the years. It is also supporting Disability Sport Events through a £1 million sponsorship deal over seven years. This is helping the charity increase opportunities for disabled people to realise their sporting potential on the road to the London 2012 Paralympic Games.

Recent Developments

Nationwide continues to expand its offering of banking products, with 2011 seeing the introduction of two new credit card products. It received the award for Most Responsible Credit Card Lending Practices for the fourth successive year at The Card & Payments Awards 2011.

The Society also remains focused on the customer experience, working to ensure flexible and convenient access to its products and services. Indeed, 2011 saw the launch of Nationwide's new internet banking solution, designed to give customers greater control of their finances.

Nationwide has also launched a new member engagement online portal: Your Nationwide.

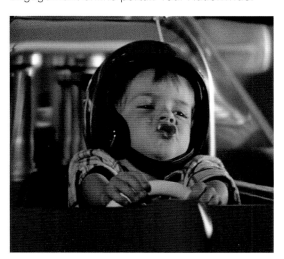

Did You Know?

Nationwide publishes the longest running series of house price data in the UK, going back as far as 1952, when the price of an average house was just £1,891.

The site provides an information resource for members, including how to submit feedback, how comments are being acted on, and the latest Society news and community initiatives. Nationwide also uses the site to openly publish its complaints-handling record and levels of customer service satisfaction. The move won support from The Mail on Sunday, which cited it as one from which Nationwide's competitors should learn.

Promotion

In 2011, Nationwide relaunched the brand with a new strapline – 'On your side' – highlighting the importance of putting customers first, rather than shareholders.

'On your side' is Nationwide's promise to help the hard-working people of Britain get on better with their money. The campaign features a magical 'carousel' that is made up of the moments of everyday life in which Nationwide helps people, whether it's better managing their day-to-day finances or saving for the big things in life.

The integrated launch began with a 60-second TV execution during the series premiere of ITV's Downton Abbey, followed by a London-focused digital out-of-home campaign and an online partnership with AOL. Further 30-second product-centric spots extended the campaign across TV. Nationwide will continue to communicate 'On your side' through a range of TV, press, digital, direct marketing, radio and outdoor media.

Brand Values

'On your side' is delivered and sustained internally and externally with PRIDE, Nationwide's set of shared values and behavioural principles that are embedded in its culture: Putting members first; Rewarding relationships; Inspiring trust; Delivering great service; Exceeding expectations. The brand promise ensures that members are put first in everything Nationwide does, underlining the company's fundamental difference from its key competitors.

▶ **www.nationwide.co.uk**

Every two minutes we help make someone happier with a new mortgage.

October 2011

A modern four-star hotel brand, Novotel has been responding to the needs of business and leisure travellers for more than 40 years with its own concept in contemporary hotel experiences. From the beginning, Novotel hotels were conceived as places of relaxation; today the network comprises almost 71,900 rooms and more than 400 hotels set in the heart of 60 countries across the globe.

Market

In 1967 Novotel launched the very first standardised hotel, revolutionising the hotel industry. As the mid-scale hotel brand within the Accor group, Novotel remains at the forefront of an intensely competitive marketplace with ever evolving brands.

Product

Consistency is the cornerstone of the Novotel brand, with guests having the assurance of high standards of service wherever they are in the world: attentive staff and a modern living space bedroom that is designed to be comfortable for both work and relaxation. A variety of restaurant solutions provide a choice of balanced cuisine 24/7, while additional innovative concepts include the Web Corner on a Mac, digital art and the Eureka meeting room.

As a specialist in business meetings, Novotel provides customised facilities for small and medium sized meetings through its Meeting@Novotel concept. All hotels have meeting facilities and there are more than 2,800 meeting rooms around the world.

Novotel gives special consideration to families through its Family&Novotel concept, which includes free accommodation and breakfast offers for children, welcome gifts, room reductions, baby equipment, play areas and healthy children's menus.

In addition, the hotels provide leisure areas designed to help guests relax and re-energise. The health and fitness concept, InBalance by Novotel, encompasses wellness and recreational leisure areas such as swimming pools, saunas, steam rooms and gym facilities.

Novotel rewards its guests via A|Club, the unique loyalty scheme from Accor. Members earn points at more than 2,300 hotels worldwide and can redeem them for reward vouchers or airline miles.

Achievements

Novotel is a pioneer in sustainable development and all hotels participate in the EarthCheck programme. A worldwide environmental and social certification programme, EarthCheck recognises the most responsible tourism products and services. These commitments to sustainable development are the result of listening to customers across a wide range of sectors and of holding internal employee think-tanks. Operationally this means that Novotel UK is committed to paperless communication and bookings, printing on recycled paper when printing is unavoidable, and providing water bottled on-site in reusable glass bottles in its meeting rooms.

Recent Developments

Novotel is continuing its expansion into the world's major destinations with openings in 2011 including a new flagship hotel in

Auckland, New Zealand and a new opening in London Blackfriars in 2012.

The online NovotelStore (novotelstore.com) enables guests to bring the Novotel experience into their own homes by purchasing furniture and accessories used within the hotels.

In line with Accor's strategic objective to become the global benchmark in hotels and to revolutionise the guest experience, Novotel has embarked on a partnership with Microsoft to define the hotel room of the future. The Room 3120 concept redefines the use of space and adds cutting-edge technologies such as an Xbox 360 console and the revolutionary Kinect sensor. The room was bookable online at novotel.com/room3120 for 90 days and was located in the centre of Paris in the four-star Novotel Vaugirard Montparnasse.

Did You Know?

Novotel employs 30,000 people worldwide.

In 2009 Novotel welcomed 1.9 million children as guests.

The hotel chain has the world's largest collection of private swimming pools, set across 75 per cent of its properties.

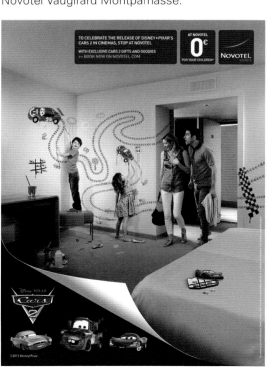

Brand History

▶ **1967:** The Novotel brand is born, with the opening of the first hotel in Lille Lesquin, France.

▶ **1972:** The first Novotel hotels outside France open – Neufchâtel in Switzerland and Brussels in Belgium.

▶ **1977:** Novotel expands to South America, with the opening of Novotel São Paulo Morumbi in Brazil.

▶ **1978:** The 100th Novotel opens, in Amsterdam. Novotel reaches 120 hotels by the end of the year. The following year Novotel opens in the Middle East.

▶ **1982–92:** Novotel opens hotels in Singapore, Toronto, Beijing, Sydney and Moscow.

▶ **1997:** Novotel now has 320 hotels in 53 countries.

▶ **2000:** The Meeting@Novotel concept is introduced and gradually implemented across the whole of the Novotel network.

▶ **2006:** Novotel expands to India, with the opening of Novotel Hyderabad.

▶ **2007:** The brand celebrates its 40th year across 60 countries around the world, and the first Novotel in Turkey opens in Istanbul.

▶ **2009:** Novotel continues to develop and opens its doors in Buenos Aires and Taipei.

▶ **2010:** Novotel opens hotels in Munich, Barcelona and Rio de Janeiro, and its Facebook page launches.

▶ **2011:** Novotel continues to expand its social media presence with the launch of its YouTube channel.

In 2011 Novotel unveiled a groundbreaking new room design. This innovative room is designed to create a sanctuary for guests. The new Novotel room uses technology to enable guests to tailor the space to their needs. The rooms focus on spaciousness and transparency; for example, a glass wall between the bedroom and bathroom can be frosted at the touch of a button.

Novotel invests not only in its product development, but also in its people. A global HR programme has therefore been developed to ensure staff are trained to deliver the best service, with a belief that happy staff mean happy customers.

More recently, the brand has launched Suite Novotel, composed exclusively of suites.

Did You Know?

The name 'Novotel' is a contraction of 'nouvel hôtel' (new hotel). At the chain's inception in 1967 the name was originally intended to be 'Ami', with the supporting slogan, 'Votre Ami sur la route' (Your friend on the road); but Citroën beat the brand to it by naming a new car model 'Ami 6'.

Designed as real living quarters, the spaces can be arranged to suit guests' needs. Suites are equipped with the Suite Box, giving guests high-speed internet access, unlimited phone calls, and free videos and music. The concept also offers a well-being space and a 24-hour fitness room, while guests staying for more than four days are offered free use of a Smart car.

Promotion

In 2011 Novotel celebrated the release of Disney Pixar's movie Cars 2 with a successful global partnership. The partnership highlighted the special focus Novotel gives to families with guests receiving Cars 2 memorabilia as welcome gifts. The Cars 2 Xbox game was available across the network, the hotel restaurants offered children Cars 2 games on their table mats,

and the movie trailer was shown on the screens in the reception area.

Novotel is committed to supporting various sports teams around the world. In France, Novotel is an Official Partner of the golf French Open, and also of the Danone Nations Cup, a children's football competition. To accompany its Buenos Aires opening, Novotel is the Official Hotel of The Dakar: the off-road car race taking place in 2012 in Argentina, Chile and Peru.

Novotel also engages with social media to strengthen its relationship with customers, launching its official Facebook page and YouTube channel in 2010/11.

Brand Values

The highest standards of service, a commitment to the environment, a dedication to creative contemporary design and intelligent use of technology are at the heart of the Novotel brand.

▶ **www.novotel.com**

The UK's leading nappy brand, Pampers® has been helping to care for the happy and healthy development of babies for 50 years (Source: IRI October 2011). The brand's range of products is specifically designed for each stage of a baby's development from newborn to toddler. Pampers is at the forefront of nappy technology, ensuring comfort and dryness for babies.

Market

Pampers is the leading brand within the UK nappy market (Source: Information Resources Incorporated (IRI) October 2011). The brand continues to fuel category growth with a steady pipeline of product innovation, designed to serve babies and their parents.

Product

Pampers products are designed for each stage of a baby's development and innovation is at the heart of parent group Procter & Gamble's philosophy for the brand. Its aim is to provide reliable products for all price brackets. In the past two years, Pampers has brought the new Simply Dry range to the value tier while the recent launch of Dry Max has bolstered the premium end.

The product line-up also features Pampers New Baby nappies with Total Care technology, which lock wetness and mess away from a baby's delicate skin, helping keep newborns snug and dry while they adjust to their new surroundings.

Pampers Baby Dry nappies have extra absorbent zones to lock wetness away and help provide up to 12 hours of 'golden sleep' for babies.

Pampers Active Fit with Dry Max are the driest nappies ever offered by the brand and with 20 per cent less bulk, the nappy helps enable a baby's active play.

Did You Know?

Pampers developed the first commercial disposable nappy in the 1960s.

In developing Dry Max, Pampers worked with more than 20,000 mothers and babies around the world, and studied more than 300,000 nappy changes.

Pampers Easy Ups, which can be pulled up like pants, can help toddlers make the transition away from nappies while still locking wetness away.

Achievements

In 2011 Pampers took double honours at the Prima Baby Reader Awards with both Pampers New Baby

and Pampers Active Fit with Dry Max receiving Platinum Awards. Pampers Active Fit was also named Nappy Product of the Year; 11,300 people from the UK and Ireland took part in the TNS survey.

Did You Know?

The latest Pampers nappies can absorb 300 ml of fluid and remain dry to the baby's touch.

The super-absorbent core used inside Pampers can hold 25 times its weight compared to paper pulp absorber, which holds only four times its weight.

Recent Developments

For the sixth consecutive year, Pampers partnered with UNICEF for the 'One Pack = One Vaccine' campaign in 2011. Together with UNICEF, Pampers is committed to eliminating maternal and neonatal tetanus by 2015. The long-term partnership is rooted in the heart of the Pampers brand and year-on-year, makes a huge

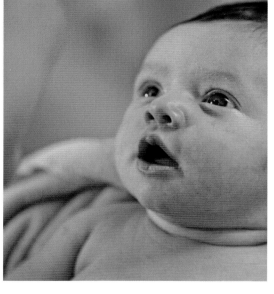

difference to the people most in need of vaccines. More than 100 million vaccines have been donated worldwide as a result of the campaign.

The Pampers brand is also committed to Procter & Gamble's long-term environmental sustainability vision, announced in 2010. This includes powering manufacturing facilities with 100 per cent renewable energy; using 100 per cent renewable materials in all products and packaging; sending zero consumer and manufacturing waste to landfill; and designing products that meet consumer demand but maximise the conservation of resources.

Promotion

Pampers brand campaigns centre around the mission to see the world through a baby's eyes. Recent campaigns have featured the company's core promise of 'peaceful nights, playful days', with Baby Dry and Active Fit products at the forefront.

The brand has also built its online presence; Pampers Village is an online community offering support to expectant and new mothers and fathers. Full of information, forums, expert advice, pregnancy calendars, potty training suggestions and links to online shopping, it extends the expertise around the Pampers brand to provide a one-stop-shop for parenting information.

Brand Values

Pampers is committed to the happy and healthy development of babies. It aims to deliver on this commitment through products that are designed specifically for each stage of a baby's development, as well as through the information it provides via the Pampers Village Parenting Panel. The Panel is formed of a group of professionals specially selected from various areas of expertise within pregnancy and baby development to help provide information to support parents and babies as they grow and develop together.

▶ **www.pampers.co.uk**

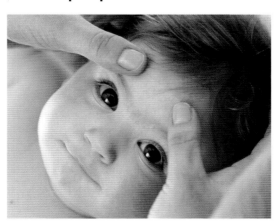

Brand History

▶ **1961:** Victor Mills, a Procter & Gamble engineer, develops the first disposable nappy after looking for better products to use for his grandson.

▶ **1975:** The shape of the nappy is updated for a better fit, changing from a rectangular shape to an hourglass shape.

▶ **1983:** Elastomerics improve the fit of the nappy by adding elastic to the waist as well as the legs. A frontal tape is also developed, which introduces the added convenience of being able to open and close the nappy a number of times. The concept of 'breathability' is also successfully introduced.

▶ **1984:** The super-absorbent core is first introduced, leading to a new generation of high performance, thinner nappies.

▶ **1990s:** Many new features are added, including a new material for the inner cuffs of the nappy for improved leakage prevention; a two-layer film for improved softness and comfort; and a Skin Care Top Sheet, which includes a protective layer of aloe vera for increased skin protection.

▶ **2010:** Pampers unveils Dry Max technology for the super-thin, next generation, Active Fit nappy.

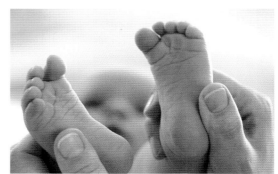

Since it opened in 1986 Pret A Manger has become the UK's leading independent retailer of premium sandwiches. Operating like a restaurant, all sandwiches, wraps, baguettes and salads are made from scratch on the day, avoiding the addition of chemicals, additives and preservatives. Pret is committed to sourcing natural ingredients and is unwilling to compromise on freshness or quality.

Market

It has been suggested that the UK sandwich market has reached maturity in recent years. The economic downturn saw a general sales dip in 2009, followed by a marginal recovery to an estimated value of £4.25 billion in 2010 (Source: 'Sandwiches and Lunchtime Foods' Mintel 2011). Pret A Manger performs well ahead of these market trends, however; the company adapts to cater for changes in consumer demand, yet keeps its trademark 'formula' consistent.

As a private company Pret A Manger is able to set its own agenda for development; unlike many of its public company competitors it is not under pressure to expand too quickly. Currently it has 290 shops, 240 of which are in the UK, turning over in excess of £350 million per year.

Product

Since its launch Pret A Manger has revolutionised the sandwich market through the company's founding principle: serving freshly prepared good, natural food.

Each shop (bar a few of the smaller ones) runs its own kitchen. 'Sell-by' dates are redundant as sandwiches and salads are prepared fresh, with any unsold at the end of the day going to homelessness charities and shelters rather than being kept over to the following day. Since its inception the brand ethos has been, and remains, to create simple, delicious, confident flavours from natural source ingredients.

Pret continues to innovate within its range and 2011 saw many new additions to its hot food category, from toasties to soups and porridge. Bold new flavours were also added to its popular sandwich range, a development that saw Pret awarded New Sandwich of the Year for its Sweet Chilli Crayfish & Mango Bloomer at The British Sandwich Awards 2011.

Achievements

Pret A Manger's longstanding association with homelessness charities is an integral part of the company ethos, and part of this has been its long-established tradition of donating money raised from sales of Christmas sandwiches. In 2011 the company went further, donating 25p from every Christmas sandwich and festive

Did You Know?

Pret A Manger was the first retailer to move from plastic sandwich boxes to cardboard back in the 1990s.

In 2011 The Pret Charity Run donated 2.4 million sandwiches to more than 100 homelessness charities and shelters.

Pret sells more than 50,000 bowls of its Proper Porridge every week; that's about 200,000 bags of oats per year.

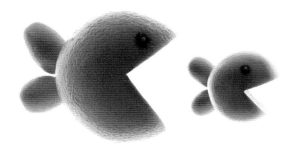

Brand History

▶ **1986:** Pret A Manger is founded by entrepreneurs Julian Metcalfe and Sinclair Beecham. The first shop serves more than 7,000 customers per week in its first year.

▶ **2001:** The McDonald's Corporation buys a minority stake in Pret A Manger, although it has no direct influence over what is sold, or how.

▶ **2003:** Soup, salad, sushi and hot drinks exceed 35 per cent of sales as Pret adjusts to changing eating habits.

▶ **2004:** The Pret DIY campaign is launched, in which Pret publishes its sandwich recipes for customers to try at home, and the brand introduces its quirky food images for the first time.

▶ **2008:** Bridgepoint, a European private equity firm, acquires a majority share in Pret, bringing an end to its relationship with McDonald's.

▶ **2011:** Pret celebrates its 25th year of making good, natural food in its shops in the UK, New York and Hong Kong, and looks to the future with its expansion into France.

gingerbread man sold from the beginning of November to the end of December. The money raised provides support for homelessness projects across the UK and also helps to fund Pret's own project: The Simon Hargraves Apprenticeship Scheme.

The scheme aims to break the cycle of homelessness by offering a three-month working placement to those often marginalised from conventional ways into employment – for instance, people with no fixed address or with prior criminal convictions. The scheme has taken more than 40 apprentices to date, 81 per cent of whom have graduated to become permanent Pret A Manger employees.

Recent Developments
Pret A Manger is the only UK high street cafe brand to use a 100 per cent Higher Welfare British chicken, a standard applauded by animal protection charities and key organisations. Indeed, Pret holds the Compassion in World

Farming Good Chicken Award. The Suffolk-reared chickens enjoy 20 per cent more space than the current industry standard and meet RSPCA recommendations for stocking density.

The company is also leading the way in its commitment to the Food Standards Agency's trial of placing calorie counts next to products on shelves, menus and tills. Pret A Manger displays calories and saturated fat content next to all its food products.

Pret holds a Green500 Platinum Award for carbon reduction, which was granted by the London Mayor in 2010. The award recognises the importance Pret A Manger places on sourcing good local food and reducing rather than offsetting carbon. Similarly, the company's ongoing commitment to avoiding landfill has seen it establish a back-of-house recycling scheme, a front-of-house separation scheme, and organic waste collections for composting from its kitchens. In 2011 all of Pret's London non-managed estate shops achieved a 100 per cent diversion from landfill target.

Promotion
Pret A Manger believes it has a lot to say, a lot to be proud of, and a lot to communicate.

Real stories about Pret's shop teams, ingredients, suppliers and attitude towards food cover the walls of its shops, packaging and website. Pret's philosophy is to communicate with its customers without the aid of traditional marketing platforms such

as television. Rather, its marketing spend is used to give customers free coffee and treats. The Pret A Manger shop experience is Pret's advertising: good, natural food and excellent service, time after time.

Brand Values
Pret A Manger's success relies on staff pride in their work, a culture fostered from within. The egalitarian hands-on approach filters down from the CEO to shop assistants and emphasises the importance Pret A Manger places on training and retaining good staff. The brand personality is underpinned by its core values: passion for food, enthusiasm, integrity, honesty and belief in its convictions, with an uncompromising stance on quality and commitment to innovation.

▶ **www.pret.com**

prontaprint
trusted to deliver, every time.

Prontaprint supplies design and print services to corporations, small and medium sized businesses, and public sector organisations. Adopting a 'partnership' approach, Prontaprint goes far beyond the typical print supplier relationship by investing time to understand each client's unique needs. It can cater to a wide range of design and print requirements, and is increasingly being relied on for e-communications design and implementation services.

Market

The UK 'on demand' print market currently generates total revenues of £1 billion per annum and Prontaprint is a major force within the sector.

Prontaprint was originally established to help business customers overcome the high prices, large minimum orders and long lead times associated with traditional commercial printers – without customers having to suffer any loss of print quality or service levels. From the outset, the brand took on the role of improving standards within the on demand market, identifying opportunities to offer a wider range of professional quality products and services than were typically provided by smaller print suppliers.

Product

Prontaprint is capable of delivering all of the materials necessary for a seamlessly integrated, multi-element communications

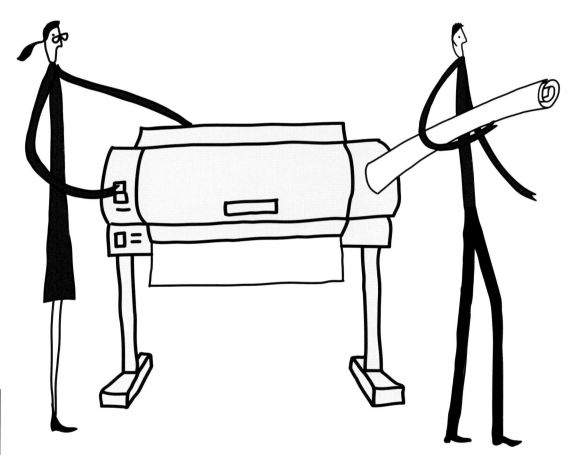

Brand History

▶ **1971:** The first Prontaprint Centre opens in Newcastle upon Tyne.

▶ **1973:** The first Prontaprint Franchise Agreement is signed.

▶ **1980s:** The Prontaprint network expands across the UK and into international markets.

▶ **2009:** Prontaprint completes the roll out of a new brand positioning.

▶ **2010:** Prontaprint Gateway is introduced, offering customers the convenience of web-to-print services.

▶ **2011:** Prontaprint celebrates its 40th anniversary, and announces its Entrepreneur of the Year competition for 2012.

campaign or promotion. If it can be designed and printed, the chances are Prontaprint can produce it.

The company's focus on offering a wide range of products and services can generate significant efficiency benefits for its customers; liaising with just one team for the production of a range of items leaves customers free to focus on other activities.

Prontaprint's wide-reaching product range encompasses four areas. Business identity – Prontaprint's design teams help businesses to create a strong identity and then apply it consistently across all printed materials and e-communications. Business operations – Prontaprint can design and print the myriads of business forms, invoices, statements, training manuals and price lists that help make a

business tick. Business promotion – Prontaprint designs eye-catching flyers, banners, advertising, tenders and annual reports to help businesses convey vital messages to their chosen audiences. Conferences and events – Prontaprint can supply everything from exhibition kits to personalised invitations, name badges and large format displays.

Achievements

As a founder member of the British Franchise Association (BFA), Prontaprint has played a crucial role in establishing a regulatory body for the franchise industry. The company is a former winner of the BFA Franchisor of the Year award and was appointed to the Association's board in 2005.

A cornerstone of Prontaprint's success is a genuine understanding that its business model

includes two equally important tiers of customers – and that each must be served well. Prontaprint recognises that the key is to work closely with its Franchisees, supporting them at every stage of their business development. In turn, the training will help empower Franchisees to deliver higher quality services to their end customers.

Prontaprint is all about building long-term, mutually beneficial relationships. Established Franchisees continue to receive business and marketing support, which helps each Prontaprint Centre to keep innovating and exceeding customer expectations.

Recent Developments

As a design and print 'trusted adviser' to many start-up companies and rapidly growing enterprises, Prontaprint is well-versed in the techniques that can help organisations spread the word about their capabilities and communicate more productively with their marketplace. In late 2011, the company launched its Entrepreneur of the Year competition to recognise business success. The judging panel for the 2012 award includes representatives from the Financial Times and PrintWeek magazine, as well as Levi Roots, the entrepreneur who achieved success with his Reggae Reggae Sauce brand in BBC Two's Dragons' Den.

In 2010, Prontaprint launched its bespoke web-to-print service, Prontaprint Gateway, across the UK and Ireland. The system provides clients with 24-hour access to an online gateway, where they can personalise pre-approved artwork templates, view proofs and place print orders. The service is especially suited to large organisations and multi-site operators that want individual outlets to be able to order customised printed materials at a local level, but also need the guarantee that their brand integrity is maintained.

Promotion

As the range of design and print services provided by Prontaprint Centres has continued to grow, there has been an increasing need to ensure that existing customers and new prospects are kept informed of the latest

Did You Know?

Prontaprint was the first print brand to be selected as a Business Superbrand.

Prontaprint is a former winner of the British Franchise Association's Franchisor of the Year award.

Prontaprint's central brand management team won a prestigious Franchise Marketing Award in 2008.

offerings that could bring value to their business. In 2011 this led Prontaprint to devote additional funding and resources to its marketing campaigns. These are now helping Prontaprint Centres to communicate the efficiency benefits for customers of using one supplier for a wider range of services.

With an ever-growing list of products and services, it's essential that potential customers are able to engage with the company efficiently. Work is underway on a new website that will make it easy for customers to assess different product options and make informed decisions. In addition to the new central website, each local Prontaprint Centre will have its own microsite.

Brand Values

Prontaprint's 'four Cs' describe the core values that underpin the Prontaprint brand. 'Close' illustrates the brand's focus on building long-term relationships with clients, on a peer-to-peer business level. 'Connected' refers to

the way in which the collective talent across the Prontaprint network can work together to cover complex requirements. 'Can do' reflects Prontaprint's flexible approach and its spirit of judging its own performance in terms of how much Prontaprint achieves for its business customers. 'Collaborative' serves as a reminder of Prontaprint's commitment to working with customers as a virtual partner, not just as a supplier.

Prontaprint's marketing strapline – 'trusted to deliver, every time' – sums up the company's belief that business integrity is vital in winning each client's trust and that customers' expectations have to be met on each and every project.

▶ **www.prontaprint.com**

RIBA

The RIBA is known to millions through the televised RIBA Stirling Prize, and from the work of more than 27,000 RIBA Chartered Architects and 3,300 RIBA Chartered Practices who bear its gold standard. A trailblazer for design quality and driven by a passion to promote architecture through its exhibitions, talks, world-class collections and online, the RIBA champions better buildings, communities and the environment through architecture and its members.

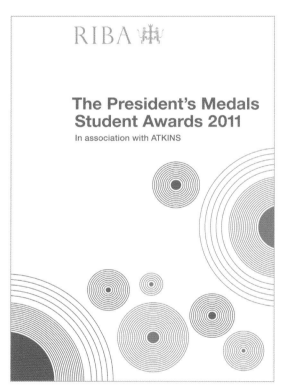

NewcastleGateshead
Shaping the City

Market

The Royal Institute of British Architects (RIBA) provides support for its members through advice, training, and technical and business services. Its knowledge and information resources are backed by one of the greatest architectural libraries and collections in the world, and the RIBA's commercial activities make it the leading provider of information to the construction industry.

The RIBA has a regional network of 11 offices in England, plus the Royal Society of Architects in Wales (RSAW), and works with fellow Institutes in Scotland and Northern Ireland. The Institute also has a growing number of members and activities in the US and the Gulf.

Did You Know?

Each year around 1,000 RIBA Chartered Architects give their time to support Architect in the House, a collaboration between the RIBA and the housing and homelessness charity Shelter. The scheme has raised more than £1 million to date. Donations help Shelter provide essential advice and support to those in need across the UK.

Product

Through its commercial ventures, the RIBA is the leading source of technical expertise for those working in the built environment sector. Under the NBS brand, it delivers the de facto national building specification system for buildings in the UK.

As RIBA Publishing and RIBA Bookshops, it is the industry's leading publisher and re-seller of books, contracts and forms, while RIBA Insight is in demand for its unique marketing opportunities that enable product manufacturers and service providers to promote their products to architects and other construction professionals.

Every year, RIBA Client Services helps around 4,000 clients who are looking to find an architect, matching their needs with local RIBA Chartered Practices. The RIBA also validates architecture courses across the globe, with one-third of the world's architects qualifying through a RIBA validation system.

The RIBA helps the public, decision-makers and clients learn more about the built environment, and encourages engagement with key issues of the day. It does this through exhibitions, talks, televised awards and in 2012, the teaching initiative Inspired by Design. Aimed at

Brand History

▶ **1834:** The Institute of British Architects is founded.

▶ **1934:** King George V and Queen Mary open the RIBA's new Art Deco-style headquarters.

▶ **1996:** The inaugural RIBA Stirling Prize Award takes place.

▶ **1997:** The RIBA and Shelter collaboration, Architect in the House, is launched.

▶ **2004:** The V&A+RIBA Architecture Partnership is established at the Victoria and Albert Museum, London.

▶ **2006:** RIBA Library is designated an Outstanding Collection by the government.

▶ **2007:** The RIBA Lubetkin Prize is established.

▶ **2008:** Ruth Reed is elected as the RIBA's first female president.

▶ **2009:** RIBA celebrates its landmark 175th birthday.

▶ **2011:** The RIBA and Bradford University establish the RIBA MBA, a groundbreaking new course.

11–19 year-old students, the venture focuses on the architecture of the London 2012 Games.

A major digitisation project is also underway at ribapix.com, making the RIBA's world-leading collection of architectural drawings and photographs increasingly accessible online.

Achievements

The launch of the 'Good design – it all adds up' report in July 2011 was a landmark for the profession. At a time when the value of architecture and design has been increasingly questioned, the RIBA demonstrated through illustrated case studies that good design is not a luxury; it makes economic sense and brings tangible benefits to society. Indeed, with the UK coalition government committed to localism, which will see much more decision-making at a local level, the RIBA has worked with central government to influence the national framework so that the need for design quality is integral to planning. Many RIBA Chartered Architects will be at the forefront of this change and the RIBA has published a number of guides to show how their expertise can be used to best effect.

Recent Developments

The introduction of Building Information Modeling (BIM) will transform the way that architects and construction teams collaborate. Virtual buildings can be created from a single set of product data and everyone involved in the project is able to examine and learn from the model before construction commences. The use of BIM also provides a valuable data set for the ongoing management of the asset throughout its life. RIBA Enterprises is at the forefront of BIM with its new software, NBS Create, and its new free BIM object service, the National BIM Library. These services will help architects to work more efficiently and enhance collaboration across the whole project team.

The RIBA is also bringing construction professionals together every day of the year through the RIBA Knowledge Communities: the ever-growing online platform that sees specialists from more than 80 countries debate and collaborate with each other on built environment issues. These range from highly focused technical issues to topics that affect the whole industry, such as sustainability and government construction strategy.

'Better homes for Britain' is the rallying call behind the RIBA's HomeWise campaign, supported by extensive research into how homes are used in the 21st century. Promoted online and in print, through an extensive media campaign, to government

and at party conferences, RIBA HomeWise is aimed at improving the quality of the nation's new-build housing.

Promotion

The RIBA brand is driven through its press and marketing activity, the high profile taken by its president, its lobbying of government and by RIBA Enterprises' marketing of its products to the whole construction industry. RIBA members play a central role in developing the brand as they too practice using the RIBA letters and crest – while industry partnerships also help to maintain the RIBA profile. On the consumer-facing side, Architect in the House sees the RIBA working with the housing and homelessness charity Shelter.

RIBA Building Futures is the Institute's thinktank and addresses 'big picture' issues. 'The Future for Architects?' examined how the global economy is transforming business practice, and projected the evolution of these trends into 2025. Such innovation builds the brand through media coverage.

RIBA 卅

The RIBA **champions** *better* **buildings, communities** *and* *the* **environment** *through* **architecture** *and* **our members**

Brand Values

The brand is crystallised in the letters 'RIBA', which represent architecture's gold standard and are valued by RIBA members and the public alike. The RIBA aims to be responsive to its stakeholders and audiences; to be influential through its advocacy and campaigning; to be bold as it addresses 21st century challenges of design and construction; and to be authoritative at all times. In all that it does, it aims to inspire trust, demonstrate competence and show leadership.

▶ **www.architecture.com**

RICOH

Ricoh is a leading global provider of technology and services that help businesses be more productive and profitable. A service-oriented company, it transforms high transaction business processes for its clients, from small domestic businesses to multinationals. No matter where in the world, or what industry, Ricoh has the global network to support organisations in achieving their business goals.

Market

Ricoh works in partnership with organisations to make business processes more efficient and secure, and flexible enough to meet the needs of the future. Engagement with customers is a critical part of its approach and once a solution is up and running, emphasis is placed on educating users to ensure maximum productivity alongside minimal environmental impact. Ricoh believes that all product parts should be designed and manufactured so they can be recycled or reused.

A Fortune Global 500 company, Ricoh's EMEA operations achieved revenues in the region of 3.5 billion euros in March 2011, with worldwide sales totalling 16.4 billion euros. The company has a workforce of more than 109,000 people across Europe, America, Asia Pacific, China and Japan.

Product

Ricoh built its reputation by producing hardware that brought documents to life such as printers, copiers and fax machines. In fact, one in four multifunction products in the UK is a Ricoh device (Source: InfoTrends 2011).

Today, Ricoh specialises in streamlining and managing high transaction information flow; a term that encompasses all regular, repetitive and document-heavy business processes. Examples include consolidating a company's entire invoicing function, helping a hospital administration make the most effective use of its patient records, and helping CSR managers to monitor and manage the environmental impact of their business.

Ricoh's UK call centre is based in Northampton, but all service engineers work on a local basis to ensure swift response times and minimum downtime for clients.

Achievements

Historically, Ricoh has claimed many 'firsts' in its business sector. It created the first digital copier using pioneering technology that remains widely used today; it developed the first dot matrix printer for use with calculators, which was then incorporated in mainstream printers and is still used today; and it introduced the world's first 'write once, read many' (WORM) optical disc media in 1986, using organic dyes.

Being at the forefront of its business is a quality that continues to the present day. In October 2011, Ricoh was identified as a Leader in Gartner's Magic Quadrant guide for multifunction products and printers worldwide. The Magic Quadrant serves as a guide for mid to large organisations, enabling them to identify and evaluate technology providers that can help reduce their costs, control printer fleets and reduce their environmental impact.

The year also saw Ricoh's ethical and environmental policies recognised. It was named one of the World's Most Ethical

Did You Know?

Ricoh consumable items can be granulated and reprocessed into high quality polymers for use in the manufacture of washing machines, electrical casings and many other items. Used toner powder is removed and used in the production of asphalt concrete, tile resin, anti vandal paint and construction boards.

Companies by the Ethisphere Institute for a third consecutive year, for going beyond legal minimums, and featured in the Corporate Knights Global 100 Most Sustainable Corporations list for a seventh consecutive year. Ricoh's commitment to minimising its environmental impact is further illustrated by all of its major UK production sites having achieved a zero waste to landfill target.

Recent Developments

In 2011 Ricoh launched Europe's first eco-board: a billboard powered entirely by wind and solar power that lights up only when sufficient power has been collected. The board is located on the M4 motorway between London and Heathrow Airport, and is powered by 96 solar panels and five wind turbines.

Ricoh's Global Eco Action Month, which took place in June, saw UK employees take part in

numerous activities to support the company's commitment to sustainability and biodiversity, and its endorsement of the UN's World Environment Day.

Also in 2011, Ricoh launched three light production, colour digital printing presses that allow companies to print in colour for a similar cost to printing in black and white. The presses, which enable companies to offer more competitive rates or to increase their margins, come in two scanner models and one printer-only model.

Did You Know?

Ricoh's eco-board on the M4 in West London is the first billboard in Europe to be powered by wind and solar energy.

Promotion

Ricoh's promotional mix blends online and social media work with more traditional corporate sponsorships and partnerships. Ricoh is an Official Partner of the tennis ATP World Tour and the sponsor of the Ricoh Women's British Open Golf tournament.

In January 2012 it launched a blog spot, ricohcommunity.com, which features views and discussions from Ricoh and other experts on issues affecting all aspects of document management across industry. Ricoh's Twitter feed incorporates abridged versions of the blog's content, while also keeping followers up to date with daily company news and thinking on key business issues.

Brand Values

Ricoh cares about its people, profession, society and the planet, and it combines a winning spirit, innovation and teamwork to sharpen its customer-centric focus. As a global brand, Ricoh is committed to the highest standards of ethics and integrity.

▶ **www.ricoh.co.uk**

Brand History

▶ **1936:** Riken Kankoshi Co. Ltd is formed to make and market sensitised paper.

▶ **1938:** Riken Kankoshi Co. Ltd becomes Riken Optical Co. Ltd; production of optical devices and equipment begins.

▶ **1963:** The company changes its name to Ricoh Company Ltd.

▶ **1971:** Ricoh introduces its first office computer, the RICOM 8.

▶ **1973:** The first high-speed facsimile machine for offices – the RIFAX 600S – succeeds in transmission between Tokyo and New York via satellite communications.

▶ **1975:** Ricoh launches the RICOPY DT1200, a wet-type plain-paper machine that becomes the world's best-selling copier.

▶ **1983:** Ricoh UK Products Ltd is formed.

▶ **1993:** Ricoh UK Products Ltd becomes the first recipient of the Queen's Award for Environmental Achievement.

▶ **2002:** Ricoh is ranked first in the world for corporate responsibility by Oekom Research.

▶ **2009:** Ricoh produces the world's first biomass toner, to be used in the imagio MP 6001GP in Japan.

▶ **2011:** Ricoh features in the Corporate Knights Global 100 Most Sustainable Corporations in the World list for the seventh year in a row.

RICS | the mark of
property
professionalism
worldwide

RICS provides the world's leading professional qualification in land, property and construction, with more than 100,000 qualified members and around 75,000 students and trainees in over 140 countries. An independent organisation, RICS acts in the public interest: setting the highest standards of competence and integrity among its members; and providing impartial, authoritative advice on key issues for business, society and governments worldwide.

Market

In a world where the public, governments, banks and commercial organisations demand greater certainty of professional standards and ethics, attaining RICS status is the recognised mark of property professionalism. RICS brings quality assurance to the marketplace through the qualifications and standards it sets, underpinned by regulation, and its requirements for lifelong learning for all members.

Product

RICS members are trained to understand the whole lifecycle of property – from land management and measurement, through planning, environmental impact assessment and investment appraisal, to managing the construction process and advising on the most efficient use and disposal of buildings.

RICS ensures its members are at the cutting edge of practice by producing relevant professional standards, guidance and information. RICS offers a comprehensive portfolio of specialist products and services, as well as professional tools for the industry such as BCIS (RICS' Building Cost Information Service), which is the leading provider of cost information for construction.

In a record output for RICS, 2011 saw the completion of 60 new official publications across the many specialisms of land, property and construction. The ambitious production programme – managed by expert members and staff from the organisation's 17 professional groups – has created a wealth of knowledge that is available to RICS members and the public alike.

Did You Know?

RICS operates the world's largest online library for land, property and surveying texts.

The government's response to the Low Carbon Construction Innovation and Growth Team report (in June 2011) named RICS as the lead body for developing standards on more issues than any other organisation.

Brand History

▶ **1792:** The Surveyors Club is formed, comprising city-based surveyors to represent the rapidly growing property profession.

▶ **1868:** Offices are leased at 12 Great George Street, Parliament Square, London. They remain the organisation's headquarters to the present day.

▶ **1881:** Queen Victoria grants a Royal Charter to the Institution of Surveyors, requiring it to 'maintain and promote the usefulness of the profession for the public advantage'.

▶ **1905:** The organisation establishes scholarships for pre-graduate and postgraduate study at British universities, and gives substantial grants to agricultural, forestry and economics schools.

▶ **1946:** The 'Royal' prefix is granted; the organisation becomes known as the Royal Institution of Chartered Surveyors (RICS).

▶ **1951:** James Nisbet publishes a controversial new method of cost planning building work. The method goes on to become an industry standard.

▶ **1999:** LionHeart, the RICS benevolent fund for surveyors, celebrates its 100-year anniversary.

▶ **2005:** RICS launches the Sustainability Commission to produce guidance for the profession.

▶ **2011:** RICS Futures is launched to gather and demonstrate opinion on the future of the property sector and the profession over the next 20 years.

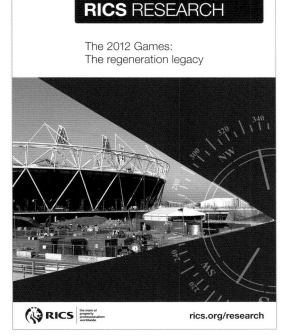

RICS RESEARCH

Report **September 2011**

The 2012 Games:
The regeneration legacy

RICS | the mark of property professionalism worldwide

rics.org/research

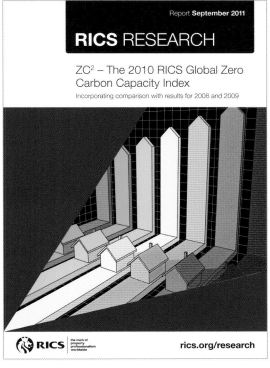

RICS RESEARCH

Report **September 2011**

ZC² – The 2010 RICS Global Zero
Carbon Capacity Index
Incorporating comparison with results for 2008 and 2009

RICS | the mark of property professionalism worldwide

rics.org/research

RICS also produces seminars, conferences and events to enable practitioners to maintain their professional competence, keep up-to-date in best practice and access networking opportunities. RICS' recent programme included more than 1,000 separate functions, which attracted nearly 45,000 delegates. Additionally, RICS' local groups organise regional events that help members in the most remote areas to find cost-effective ways to share views, maintain their knowledge and develop contacts.

Achievements

In response to the changing landscape of academic learning, the organisation recently launched RICS Online Academy. The e-learning platform teaches through 'webinars' and podcasts, which are hosted by experts from each specialism, and provides easy access to guides and templates for RICS candidates undergoing their Assessment of Professional Competence. The Online Academy also enables RICS to provide professionals with leading edge training and information tailored to many world markets.

RICS continues to influence policy for the public good, from hosting high profile government minister debates and policy launches to providing up-to-date and independently funded research into a range of issues – such as sustainability in the built environment, construction procurement and housing needs for an ageing society. As a result, RICS is regularly called upon to provide commentary and thought leadership articles.

In addition to RICS' high profile work, its members and staff work closely with politicians and officials outside of the media glare to ensure that legislation is balanced and practical.

Did You Know?

In 1922 Irene Barclay became the first woman to qualify as a Chartered Surveyor in the UK.

Famous surveyors include Captain James Cook, Thomas Jefferson, Lawrence of Arabia, Walt Disney, Abraham Lincoln, Leonid Brezhnev and Sir George Everest.

Recent Developments

As part of its commitment to protect the public interest and continually raise the standards to which its members work, RICS launched its Valuer Registration Scheme in 2010. Valuations underpin nearly all financial decisions, from home mortgages to major investment and corporate finance transactions or stock exchange listings. Through the new designation, 'Registered Valuer', the scheme provides assurance in the quality of valuations and raises the credibility of valuers, enabling clients to identify the best regulated and qualified professionals in the field.

In its partnership with the Chartered Surveyors Training Trust, RICS has been working to deliver an apprenticeship scheme aimed at 16–24 year-olds, which will count towards RICS associate membership. RICS is also looking

at new routes to membership and recently launched Professional Experience, which enables experienced professionals in land, property and construction to become chartered RICS members. The new route benefits the public interest as it ensures more property professionals will work to high standards and be bound by RICS' ethics and rules of conduct.

Promotion

The RICS brand is promoted widely through the work of RICS itself, with its strong focus on recognition of professional standards, and through its 100,000 members delivering standards in more than 140 markets.

A recent survey cited that 87 per cent of the UK's key employers, business leaders, decision-makers and opinion formers recognised RICS as 'the mark of property professionalism worldwide' (Source: UK RICS Survey 2011).

The reputation of the brand is supported by a comprehensive communications and engagement plan aimed at RICS members and their clients, opinion formers, politicians, business leaders, and consumers of RICS' products and services.

Brand Values

Integrity, passion, innovation and drive are the guiding forces of the RICS brand, upholding its motto: Est modus in rebus (There is measure in all things).

▶ **www.rics.org**

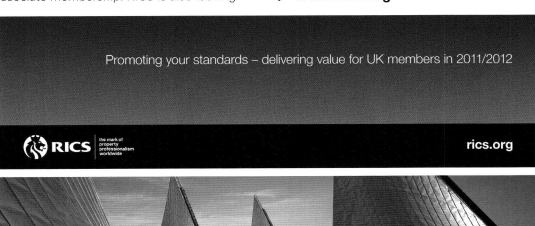

Promoting your standards – delivering value for UK members in 2011/2012

RICS | the mark of property professionalism worldwide

rics.org

Rolls-Royce

Rolls-Royce is a global business providing and supporting integrated power systems for use on land, at sea and in the air. The group has a broad customer base including more than 500 airlines, 160 armed forces, 4,000 marine customers and energy customers in 120 countries. Rolls-Royce has facilities in over 50 countries and employs nearly 40,000 people, of whom 11,000 are engineers.

Market

Rolls-Royce annual revenues are £11 billion, half of which comes from services. The group's announced order book by the end of 2011 was £61 billion.

The group operates in four long-term global markets – civil and defence aerospace, marine and energy. These markets create a total opportunity worth some US$2 trillion over the next 20 years. The markets have a number of similar characteristics: they have very high barriers to entry; they offer the opportunity for organic growth; and they feature extraordinarily long programme lives, usually measured in decades.

The size of these markets is generally related to world gross domestic product growth or, in the case of the defence markets, global security and the scale of defence budgets.

Did You Know?

Rolls-Royce invests nearly £1 billion annually in research and development.

The company has announced a new business to address the expanding market for civil nuclear power.

Product

Rolls-Royce is one of the world's biggest aero engine manufacturers and its Trent family of engines is a leader in modern widebody aircraft. Rolls-Royce is also a market leader for business jet engines.

In civil aerospace, Rolls-Royce powers more than 30 types of commercial aircraft, from business jets to the largest widebody airliners. A fleet of 13,000 engines is in service.

The group is also the leading military aero engine manufacturer in Europe and the number two military aero engine manufacturer in the world, powering approximately 25 per cent of the world's military fleet.

In the marine market, its products include established names such as Kamewa, Ulstein, Aquamaster and Brown Brothers which, together with a strong focus on research

Brand History

▶ **1904:** Henry Royce meets Charles Rolls, whose company sells high quality cars in London.

▶ **1914:** At the start of World War I, Royce designs his first aero engine, the Eagle, which goes on to provide half of the total horsepower used in the air by the allies.

▶ **1940:** Royce's Merlin powers the Hawker Hurricane and Supermarine Spitfire in the Battle of Britain. Four years later development begins on the aero gas turbine.

▶ **1953:** Rolls-Royce enters the civil aviation market with the Dart in the Vickers Viscount. It becomes the cornerstone of universal acceptance of the gas turbine by the airline industry.

▶ **1966:** Bristol Siddeley merges with Rolls-Royce.

▶ **1976:** Concorde, powered by the Rolls-Royce Snecma Olympus 593, becomes the first and only supersonic airliner to enter service.

▶ **1987:** Rolls-Royce is privatised.

▶ **1999:** Rolls-Royce acquires Vickers for £576 million, transforming Rolls-Royce into the global leader in marine power systems.

▶ **2004:** A milestone year, Rolls-Royce celebrates its centenary.

▶ **2010:** The new Trent XWB engine for the Airbus A350 XWB runs for the first time.

▶ **2011:** Rolls-Royce Trent 1000 engines power the new Boeing 787 Dreamliner into service.

and development, have made Rolls-Royce a pioneer of many important technologies, including aero-derivative marine gas turbines, controllable pitch propellers and water jets. The company is a world leader in the design of offshore support vessels.

The Rolls-Royce energy business is a world-leading supplier of power systems for onshore and offshore oil and gas applications, with a growing presence in the electrical power generation sector. It supplies products to customers in more than 120 countries and its main products include the industrial Trent and industrial RB211 gas turbines.

Achievements

Rolls-Royce is highly ranked in several external indices that benchmark corporate responsibility performance, including the Dow Jones

Did You Know?

Rolls-Royce reactor plants power all of the nuclear submarines for the Royal Navy.

Rolls-Royce's UT offshore vessel design is the most successful in the world, with sales in excess of 500 units.

Sustainability World and European Indexes; it has retained its position in both for nine consecutive years. The group scored 100 per cent for environmental reporting.

In 2010 it achieved Gold status for the third year running in the Business in the Community Corporate Responsibility Index; the group's dedication to reducing its environmental and social impact translated into an overall score of 93 per cent.

For the third consecutive year, Rolls-Royce has been included in the FTSE 350 Carbon Disclosure Leadership Index, run by the Carbon Disclosure Project (CDP), in which the quality and depth of a company's response to the annual CDP questionnaire is scored.

Recent Developments

Among its ongoing corporate social responsibility activities is the Rolls-Royce Science Prize: an annual awards programme that helps teachers implement science teaching ideas in their schools and colleges. There is a total of £120,000 worth of prizes to be won each year. The competition builds on the group's commitment to Project ENTHUSE: a £30 million partnership between industry, the government and the Wellcome Trust that provides teachers with funding to cover the cost of attending courses at the National Science Learning Centre.

At major Rolls-Royce sites, the group also sponsors a range of education projects. Employees get involved with local schools to support young people and promote STEM subjects – Science, Technology, Engineering and Maths.

Promotion

The strategy for Rolls-Royce centres on five key elements: addressing the four global markets; investing in technology, infrastructure and capability; developing a competitive portfolio of

products and services; growing market share and installed product base; and adding value to customers through product-related services.

Rolls-Royce invests close to £1 billion annually in research and development and it invests more than £30 million annually in training.

The group is determined to give an effective response to the problem of climate change and other environmental concerns and is committed to a programme of continuous improvement for its production and service activities around the world.

Similarly, it is committed to significant annual investment in research and development in order to provide leading-edge technologies that reduce fuel burn, emissions and noise across all its products. It is also at the forefront of research into advanced technologies that could provide entirely new approaches to low carbon energy solutions.

Brand Values

Rolls-Royce is one of the most famous brands in the world. The Rolls-Royce brand means more than engineering excellence – it is a standard of quality across all the company's activities. The brand is at the heart of everything Rolls-Royce does. Its brand values are reliability, integrity and innovation and its brand positioning statement is: 'Trusted to deliver excellence'.

▶ **www.rolls-royce.com**

ROYAL ALBERT HALL

Opened in 1871, the Royal Albert Hall is one of the world's most famous stages. Each year its breathtaking auditorium hosts more than 360 shows, and the magical atmosphere combined with some of the world's greatest artists creates legendary events. A registered charity that operates without public funding, the Hall also programmes more than 120 events a year outside the main auditorium, which broaden its appeal to younger artists and audiences.

Market

The Royal Albert Hall operates in the highly competitive entertainment, leisure and tourism sectors. It is a registered charity and receives no public revenue funding. Its competitors are the other leading UK performing arts and entertainment venues and organisations, many of which receive central or local government funding. It also faces more general competition for a customer's leisure time and pound, especially in the age of digital media, home entertainment and the current economic situation.

Product

Built as part of Prince Albert's vision for a centre for the arts and sciences, the Royal Albert Hall hosts performances by artists from around the world and promotes productions in collaboration with partners. Events in the Hall's auditorium encompass classical music, jazz, world music, circus, rock and pop, ballet, opera, comedy, tennis, film premieres, corporate dinners, science talks, children's performances, charity concerts, award ceremonies and occasions of national importance, such as the Royal British Legion's Festival of Remembrance.

The Hall also promotes performances in its state-of-the-art Elgar Room and offers daytime tours of the building, free music in the Café Consort and a free exhibition series. These events, combined with extensive education work, enable the Hall to be true to Prince Albert's founding ambitions within a modern context.

Achievements

The Hall celebrated its 140th birthday in March 2011, an achievement that was complemented by several industry awards. The Hall was named International Theatre of the Year at the prestigious Pollstar Concert Industry Awards for a record 13th time and also picked up Best Venue Teamwork at the Live UK Music Business Awards for the second year running. In addition to achieving Superbrand status, the Hall was also voted a CoolBrand for the third successive year.

The Hall's founding Charter requires it to maintain its iconic Grade I listed building and through it, to promote the understanding and appreciation of the arts and sciences. The Hall's education programme, launched in 2004, has now provided opportunities for around 200,000 young people from many different backgrounds to engage in the arts and sciences, the cultural industries and live performance. The Hall has also extended its partnership with the charity Music for Youth.

The Hall supports other registered charities with their fundraising activities and offers itself free of charge to a charity each year, awarding the 2011 opportunity to the Spirit of London Awards. Other highlights have included concerts in support of the Teenage

Brand History

▶ **1871:** The Royal Albert Hall is opened by Queen Victoria in March.

▶ **1912:** The Titanic Band Memorial Concert takes place at the Hall, featuring 500 performers and the conductors Sir Edward Elgar, Henry Wood, Landon Ronald and Thomas Beecham.

▶ **1941:** The first BBC Proms season at the Hall takes place.

▶ **1963:** The Beatles and The Rolling Stones appear on the same bill on 15th September.

▶ **1970:** Tennis is first played at the Hall.

▶ **1996:** Work begins on the Royal Albert Hall's eight-year major building development programme.

▶ **2004:** The official 're-opening' of the Hall by Her Majesty The Queen takes place.

▶ **2006:** Bill Clinton speaks at the Hall about his vision for leadership in the 21st century.

▶ **2007:** Swarovski Fashion Rocks is broadcast to more than 40 countries around the world.

▶ **2010:** The UK premiere of Cirque du Soleil's Totem takes place at the Hall.

▶ **2011:** The Phantom of the Opera stages a special performance at the Hall to celebrate its 25th anniversary.

Registered charity number: 254543

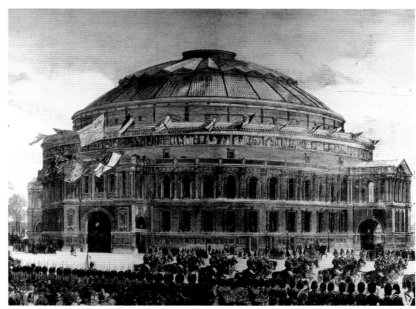

Cancer Trust, the Prince's Trust Rock Gala and events in support of Leukaemia & Lymphoma Research and Comic Relief.

Recent Developments

2010 was a record-breaking year for the Hall: 381 events in the main auditorium played to audiences of more than 1.3 million, with an attendance of over 81 per cent across the year. It was also a year that saw further rapid expansion of the Hall's own artistic programming, maximising its public benefit and encouraging both new and younger audiences and artists into the building.

Did You Know?

In 1909 a full indoor marathon was run at the Hall – a total of 524 circuits of the auditorium's arena.

It took six million bricks and 80,000 terracotta blocks to build the Hall.

For 2012, the Hall is co-promoting a brand new production of Verdi's Aida, the return of the Imperial Ice Stars with Swan Lake on Ice, the first ever Beethoven Piano Concerto Cycle by Lang Lang in the UK, a piano recital by YouTube star Valentina Lisitsa, and the European premiere of the re-mastered film of West Side Story with the score performed live.

A new partnership with 'rhubarb' has ensured a comprehensive catering operation within the Hall, and the strengthened in-house hospitality team is now able to offer bespoke public-facing and corporate packages for most

Brand Values

The Hall's brand values are encompassed in the positioning statement, 'Entertaining the World'. It is the Hall's ambition that everyone, young and old, from every nation and culture, should feel welcome at the Hall and able to enjoy the shared experience of live performance on one of the world's most famous stages.

The Royal Albert Hall is proud of the building, its heritage and its unrivalled history of performance. It is passionate about offering all its customers the best possible experiences, creating memories and ensuring that it continues to develop and protect this magical building for future generations.

▶ **www.royalalberthall.com**

The Hall's success continued in 2011 with an extremely busy and diverse programme in the auditorium as well as additional series and events in the Elgar Room, which has now established itself as an integral part of the Hall's programming and a small-scale entertainment venue for London. Highlights of the Hall's own programming in the auditorium included Puccini's Madam Butterfly, Strictly Gershwin with English National Ballet, Nitin Sawhney's unique commission for the Hall's great organ, a high definition screening of The Matrix accompanied by the live score, and The Wonderful World of Captain Beaky in support of UNICEF.

events in the Hall's calendar. Branded bars provided by partners include Moët & Chandon, Asahi, Cloudy Bay, Spitfire Ale and Aspall Cyder.

Promotion

The Royal Albert Hall markets its own initiatives and works with its event promoters, assisting them with their ticket sales through the Hall's marketing channels. Over the last year, the Hall has seen a great increase in its online marketing initiatives, especially the use of its social media channels. The Hall also works in partnership with other brands to reach new audiences and is interested in exploring new corporate collaborations.

the Luxury Included® holiday

Since opening its first resort in 1981, Sandals Resorts has been at the forefront of the Caribbean all-inclusive travel sector by offering luxury, innovation and choice. In an industry brimming with new contenders, the combined knowledge and experience of Sandals' management team and resort staff has kept the company at the head of the expanding all-inclusive market. After all, it was Sandals that introduced the Luxury Included® concept.

Market

In recent years the concept of luxury travel has steered away from conservative, off-the-shelf five-star packages towards tailor-made individualism. Right from the outset, Sandals Resorts set itself apart from its competitors by placing an emphasis on personal choice, always aiming to offer more. Where others had inclusive buffet-style meals and rooms at a set rate, Sandals' prices covered gourmet speciality restaurants and white-glove service, premium drinks, tips and taxes, in addition to all recreational and water sports activities, including scuba diving.

Currently there are 13 Sandals resorts aimed at 'two people in love' located in Jamaica, Saint Lucia, Antigua and the Bahamas. Its sister brand, Beaches, comprises four resorts in Jamaica and Turks & Caicos, and caters for couples, families and singles.

Product

Sandals prides itself on its top-of-the-range products, from à la carte restaurants and Beringer® wines, to an extensive range of

Did You Know?

All Sandals resorts in Jamaica, Saint Lucia, Antigua and the Bahamas, and Beaches resorts in Jamaica, are proud holders of Gold Travelife status, which recognises their efforts for environmental sustainability in the region.

water sports, including the most comprehensive scuba diving programme in the Caribbean. Its butler service, available to top suite guests since 2004, is offered in partnership with the Guild of Professional English Butlers and represents the ultimate in luxury pampering.

Sandals was one of the first operators in the Caribbean to offer full-service spas. The exclusive Red Lane® Spas now feature in all of its establishments and are an enduring signature of the brand, offering exotic indigenous therapies alongside Dermalogica treatments.

The brand's unique Luxury Included® holiday concept encompasses a collection of luxurious suites in Jamaica, Saint Lucia, Antigua and the Bahamas. The experience features an extended range of premium services, as well as partnerships with the likes of fine-living expert Martha Stewart and golfer Greg Norman.

The family oriented Beaches Resorts provide an exclusive Sesame Street® activities programme with daily games and weekly shows for children, while Xbox 360 Game

Garage Centres and the Scratch DJ Academy® cater for their tween and teen guests.

Achievements

Both Sandals Resorts and Beaches Resorts continue to accrue industry awards that reaffirm the brand's leading position across the luxury travel market.

A consistent winner at the World Travel Awards, Sandals Resorts has claimed the coveted title of World's Leading All Inclusive Company no less than 14 times, and has been named the Caribbean's Leading Hotel Brand/ Group for 18 consecutive years. Beaches Resorts has been voted World's Leading Family All Inclusive for 13 successive years. Recognition for individual resorts includes Sandals Grande Antigua Resort & Spa being voted World's Most Romantic Resort

Brand History

▶ **1981:** Gordon 'Butch' Stewart buys a dilapidated hotel in Jamaica. Despite having no prior hotel experience, he opens Sandals Montego Bay several months later.

▶ **1985:** Sandals unveils its signature swim-up pool bar.

▶ **1988:** Sandals Negril opens its doors. Three years later Sandals becomes the largest operator of all-inclusive resorts in the Caribbean and opens its first resort in Antigua.

▶ **1993:** Sandals Regency Saint Lucia is launched in April, offering guests the opportunity to split their stay between two islands, Antigua and Saint Lucia.

▶ **1994:** WeddingMoons® is launched – a concept combining a holiday wedding with an inclusive honeymoon.

▶ **1996:** Sandals Royal Bahamian Resort & Spa opens. The following year the first Beaches Resort opens, Beaches Negril in Jamaica.

▶ **2008:** Sandals Negril is the first hotel in the world to be awarded Platinum Certification by EarthCheck in recognition of its sustainable practices.

▶ **2009:** Beaches Turks & Caicos Resort Villages & Spa opens its Italian Village. The Sandals Foundation is also established, continuing the company's on-going philanthropic activities within Caribbean communities.

▶ **2010:** Sandals Weddings by Martha Stewart™ launches, Sandals Emerald Bay opens in February, and Royal Plantation Ocho Rios is rebranded as a Sandals Resort.

▶ **2011:** Sandals celebrates its 30th birthday, while its two-year-old sister company, Island Routes Caribbean Adventure Tours, continues to grow by adding Barbados and the Cayman Islands to its programme.

(previously World's Leading Honeymoon Resort) for the 14th consecutive year in 2010, and Beaches Turks & Caicos Resort Villages & Spa claiming World's Leading Family Resort.

Some of the brand's many other accolades include Sandals Resorts being voted Best All Inclusive Resort at the Travel Weekly Globe Awards for six consecutive years and in 2010, claiming Best All Inclusive Hotel/Resort Company at the British Travel Awards. In 2011 Sandals Emerald Bay, Great Exuma, Bahamas was voted Best Golf & Spa Resort of the Year by Caribbean World Magazine.

Recent Developments

In 2011 Sandals unveiled a US$500 million investment programme, with enhancements to seven of its 13 Luxury Included® resorts. Sandals Grande Riviera Beach & Villa Golf Resort in Jamaica received a US$60 million upgrade and now comprises the Riviera Villas & Great House and the Riviera Seaside & Beach Club, offering two holidays in one. Additional renovations include new and redesigned restaurants, high-tech in-room upgrades, and a facelift for the resort's Red Lane® Spa.

As well as enhancing its resorts, Sandals continues to invest in the communities in which it operates, through the Sandals Foundation, its philanthropic arm. 2011 saw the introduction of the company's first volunteering programme for guests, the Reading Road Trip, which aims to improve the listening, reading and comprehension skills of local children.

Promotion

Brand promotion comes in the form of a multimillion-pound advertising campaign that supports the efforts of travel agents and tour operators to market both the Sandals Resorts and Beaches Resorts brands. The campaign encompasses a broad range

of media: flyers, brochures, posters, signage and window displays for travel agents, in addition to the more high profile television and ecommerce activities, consumer and trade advertisements, and national billboards.

Did You Know?

Sandals was the first Caribbean brand to offer Jacuzzi® baths, satellite television, swim-up pool bars and to equip every room with a king-size bed.

Sandals' visual brand identity is evolving to suit global markets in the ever-changing face of luxury world travel. The new brand image is more sophisticated and lifestyle focused, hence able to deliver the Luxury Included® ethos with more success. Sandals Resorts and Beaches Resorts operate a sophisticated CRM programme, which includes a highly attractive loyalty scheme: Sandals Select.

Brand Values

Sandals is one of the best-known luxury resort brands in the world. It continues to build on its leading position in the Caribbean hotel industry with innovations such as the Luxury Included® concept, making it well positioned to address consumers' growing demands for luxury choices to be included in their package holiday. Sandals offers more included luxuries than any other resort brand worldwide, and throughout its history has striven to create the ultimate Sandals experience: luxury, service and uncompromising quality delivered in picturesque beachside locations.

▶ **www.sandals.co.uk**

savills

Savills is a global real estate services provider listed on the London Stock Exchange. With more than 200 offices and associates throughout the Americas, Europe, Asia Pacific, Africa and the Middle East, Savills offers a range of specialist advisory, management and transactional services to clients worldwide. Its 26,000-strong workforce combines entrepreneurial spirit and a deep understanding of specialist property sectors with the highest standards of client care.

Market

Within the global Savills framework, the UK-wide operation encompasses 200 service lines, 99 offices and more than 3,200 staff, with its reach extending nationwide. Indeed, the firm was voted best in class across four regional categories at the Estates Gazette Awards 2011. In central London, Savills is at the leading edge of residential sales over £5 million. While competitors have been seen to consolidate or merge, Savills has continued its organic growth by securing key talent across the UK; it's a strategy that has enabled the company to retain zero debt.

Outside the UK, Savills not only works closely with domestic investors across the world but also alongside many international investors to introduce foreign capital from the US, Australia and Hong Kong into London's property arena.

> **Did You Know?**
>
> **Savills Asia Pacific accounts for 41 per cent of group revenue.**
>
> **Savills has 12 offices in China and the largest property management business in Hong Kong and China.**
>
> **The Savills investment management business, Cordea Savills, attracted equity inflows and client commitments of more than US$1 billion in Europe during 2011.**

Product

During its 157-year history, Savills has grown from a family firm of chartered surveyors into an international property services group. Savills is at the forefront of the global markets and in 1997, became the first among its peers to enter the Asia market; its Asian business is now a significant force in the firm's global growth. Such expansion enables Savills to maximise the benefits of cross-border business, providing investment, leasing and consultancy services to overseas clients in the UK.

Savills will continue to strengthen its presence in the Far East and Europe through organic expansion and acquisition, extending its property expertise across a wide spectrum of markets and disciplines.

Achievements

Savills is the only UK real estate adviser to feature in the top 10 of the FTSE 350 Carbon Disclosure Leadership Index 2011, and stands alongside major property companies such as British Land and Great Portland Estates. The firm was commended by the government-supported Carbon Disclosure Project for its approach to the disclosure of climate change information.

Savills consistently achieves number one positions for its financial, brand and recruitment performance. Recent accolades include National Property Adviser of the Year at

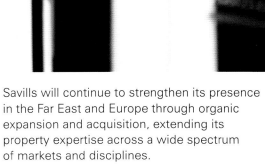

Brand History

▶ **1855:** Savill & Son is founded by Alfred Savill.

▶ **1972:** The firm is rebranded as Savills and moves to premises on Grosvenor Hill in Mayfair, London – which remains its head office to the present day.

▶ **1988:** Savills is listed on the London Stock Exchange and begins trading as a plc, which enables the company to raise equity capital for expansion and acquisition.

▶ **1997:** A 20 per cent share of Savills is sold to First Pacific Davies – one of Asia's foremost property companies – and the subsidiary is rebranded FPDSavills. Savills acquires a majority shareholding in the Spanish, German and French companies trading as Weatherall Green & Smith.

▶ **2000:** Savills plc is listed in the FTSE 250 and acquires First Pacific Davies in April.

▶ **2004:** To coincide with the company's 150th anniversary in 2005, the decision is made to drop 'FPD' from FPDSavills. The rebrand will bring all the subsidiaries back under the Savills umbrella.

▶ **2013:** Savills will relocate its two London West End offices to new headquarters just north of Oxford Street – 33 Margaret Street, W1.

the Estates Gazette Awards; Best International Property Consultancy Marketing at the Bloomberg International Property Awards, for a campaign by Savills Vietnam; Hong Kong's Best Property Agency in GoHome's luxury property service category; and Shanghai Post's Best Agency. It has also repeatedly retained number one graduate employer titles from both TARGETjobs and The Times, and is the first real estate company to feature in The Times Top 100 Graduate Employers league table.

Recent Developments

The 21st century Savills is a leading international property services brand with around half its revenues and profits now earned from outside the UK.

Having established a market leading position with its prime residential brand in the UK and Hong Kong, Savills launched a residential service through its Singapore business in 2011, establishing a dedicated workforce of more than 550 brokers. The firm is earmarking key global cities for further expansion.

The Savills investment management business, Cordea Savills, provides international fund specialised expertise, and its European business has attracted equity inflows and client commitments of more than US$1 billion during 2011. It has recently reopened its

Nordic fund and launched a prime London residential development fund.

In a further commitment to boost its leasing platform, 2011 saw Savills form a strategic alliance with the largest tenant representation firm in North America, Cresa Partners.

Promotion

Brand recognition and visibility are key to the success of Savills and it invests heavily in promotion. The strategy includes traditional offline advertising in trade magazines and broadsheets, as well as a focus on maintaining the brand's online presence.

In order to enhance its clients' online experience, Savills relaunched its website in 2010. The first six months saw traffic to the site increase by 40 per cent, propelling it into the market leading position of the most visited national estate agency website (Source: Hitwise March 2011). Its success is ongoing, picking up Best Corporate Website at the Property Marketing Awards 2011. A new

iPhone app bolstered the online experience and was awarded a five-star rating in The Times.

Trade fairs are also key in helping Savills engage with its client base, enabling it to highlight the many property sectors in which it operates.

Brand Values

Savills attracts the best individuals within its market, and through its careful selection and preservation of a unique culture, provides a global platform from which their talents and expertise can not only benefit clients but also the wider community.

The firm's vision is to be the real estate adviser of choice in the markets it serves. Savills does not wish to be the biggest, just the best (as judged by its clients). Its values capture commitment not only to ethical, professional and responsible conduct but also to the essence of real estate success; an entrepreneurial value-embracing approach.

▶ **www.savills.co.uk**

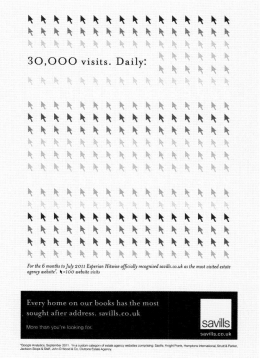

SIEMENS

As a leading global engineering and technology services company, Siemens provides innovative solutions to help tackle the world's major challenges, across the key sectors of energy, healthcare, industry, and infrastructure and cities. In the UK, Siemens has been operating for 169 years and today employs around 13,000 people. UK revenues for 2011 were £4.4 billion, which includes inter-company revenue.

Brand History

▶ **1843:** The 19-year-old William Siemens arrives in England to sell the rights to his brother Werner's electroplating technique.

▶ **1853:** William Siemens takes over the running of the UK business, which primarily involves the selling of water meters.

▶ **1858:** The independent company known as Siemens, Halske & Co. is set up with its own workshops. It is renamed Siemens Brothers in 1865.

▶ **1873:** The first Atlantic cable is laid by Siemens Brothers, with the Faraday cable steamer built specially for this purpose.

▶ **1984:** A Siemens sales company is founded under the name Siemens Ltd.

▶ **1989:** The Plessey Company is taken over jointly by Siemens and General Electric Company.

▶ **2008:** In London, Siemens and McKinsey publish a study on sustainable infrastructure.

▶ **2009:** Siemens helps develop the world's first floating wind turbine, Hywind, enabling turbines to be installed in deeper waters offshore.

▶ **2010:** Siemens invests in the UK's first tidal turbine to extract energy from tides around the UK; it is located in Strangford Lough, Northern Ireland.

▶ **2011:** Siemens signs an order with Eurostar for 10 Velaro high-speed trains, depot modifications and 10 years of service. The Department for Transport awards Siemens preferred bidder status for 1,200 Desiro City rail vehicles and two new depots for the Thameslink route.

Market

In the UK, around 5,000 Siemens employees work in manufacturing, with products including superconducting magnets for MRI scanners, industrial gas turbines and variable speed drives – all of which are exported worldwide.

In other sectors the company's performance is also strong. Siemens is the leading supplier of offshore wind turbines in the UK. More than 40 per cent of the electricity from wind power in the UK is generated using its technology. In fiscal year 2011 global revenue generated by the Siemens environmental portfolio contributed around 30 billion euros to the company total. Siemens aims to exceed the 40 billion euros revenue mark with green technologies by the end of fiscal year 2014.

In the healthcare sector, Siemens is an integrated healthcare business with innovative solutions in imaging, workflow and diagnostics. Siemens is also the most experienced managed equipment services (MES) provider in the UK healthcare market. Every working day, 15,000 women in the UK are screened for breast cancer; in excess of 6,000 are screened on Siemens medical equipment.

As part of its newest sector, infrastructure and cities, Siemens manufactures and maintains more of the UK's road traffic infrastructure than any other company, and maintains over 350 electric and diesel trains.

Product

The Siemens product portfolio – including its environmental portfolio – is divided into four sectors: industry, energy, healthcare, and infrastructure and cities.

Siemens Industry is a leading supplier of innovative, environmentally friendly products for industrial customers. Its solutions include automation technology, industrial controls, drive technology and industrial software.

In energy, Siemens is the only company worldwide with the know-how and technologies along the entire energy conversion chain, from the production of oil and gas, to power generation, the transmission and distribution of electrical energy, and renewable energy technologies.

Siemens Healthcare provides solutions to increase efficiency and improve patient care along the patient pathway. The company is pioneering new innovations

Did You Know?

Red Bull Racing uses Siemens PLM software to design its F1 car.

More than one million people cross the road safely every day thanks to Siemens Traffic Solutions technology.

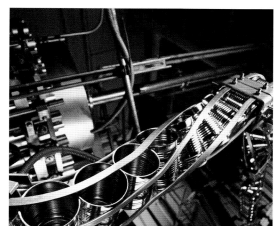

such as the world's first fully integrated PET MR system, the Biograph mMR, and low-dose computed tomography (CT) imaging.

A new era began for Siemens on 1st October 2011, with the launch of its newest sector: infrastructure and cities. Combining the expertise of existing businesses in the industry and energy sectors, it provides cities with joined-up technical solutions for sustainable mobility, environmental protection and energy savings. Infrastructure and cities comprises five divisions – Rail Systems, Mobility and Logistics, Low and Medium Voltage, Smart Grid and Building Technologies – and has a clear market focus on local authorities, airports, harbours, rail operators and utilities. The sector joins up Siemens' capabilities to make buildings and energy distribution grids 'smart'; to enable fast and energy-efficient transport for people and goods; and to make cities sustainable. Siemens' global Centre of Competence for Cities will be based at its sustainable cities initiative – the Crystal (pictured below) – in East London.

Achievements
Siemens realises that young people are the drivers of economic development and actively demonstrates its commitment to enthuse young people in science and technology subjects. Siemens plans to recruit 140 apprentices and at least another 140 graduates in 2012.

Recent Developments
On 1st January 2012 Roland Aurich (pictured above) became the new chief executive of Siemens plc and Cluster North West Europe. Mr Aurich is the former president and CEO of Siemens in Canada, prior to which he served as CEO of Siemens in Sweden.

In the past three years, Siemens has invested £8 million in an Energy Services Centre in Newcastle, which includes £3 million for a Wind Power Training Centre at the same location.

Continuing the company's focus on sustainability, building work is well under way on the Crystal in East London. As part of the Green Enterprise District, the £30 million centre will enable Siemens to explore how to

Did You Know?

Siemens makes and maintains Heathrow Express trains, which carry 16,000 passengers each day between Paddington railway station and Heathrow Airport.

More than one-third of the UK's mainland electricity supply is generated using Siemens equipment.

create a better future for our cities. Opening in summer 2012, it will be home to the world's largest exhibition focused on urban sustainability, bringing together city decision-makers and the public.

Promotion
Siemens is High Performance Partner to the GB Rowing Team. It also sponsors the team's Start programme, a talent identification and development initiative looking for the elite athletes of the future.

Siemens is also a principal sponsor of the Science Museum's climate science gallery, 'atmosphere...exploring climate science' and sponsors the Royal Academy of St Martin in the Fields.

Brand Values
The Siemens brand values are: responsible, excellence, innovative and zero harm.

▶ **www.siemens.co.uk**

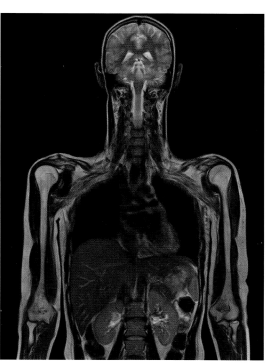

Every body deserves one

Silentnight Beds is the leading mass-market bed brand with a wide consumer profile and is continually updating its product range to give its customers a comfortable night's sleep. Silentnight is famous for its Hippo and Duck characters, first created to demonstrate the unique 'no roll together' property of its beds and a now familiar feature of its advertising.

Brand History

▶ **1946:** Tom and Joan Clarke form Clarke's Mattresses Ltd in Skipton, North Yorkshire.

▶ **1949:** As demand grows, the company relocates to a larger manufacturing site in Barnoldswick.

▶ **1951:** The company changes its name to Silentnight Ltd and is soon producing more than 4,000 divan beds a month.

▶ **1986:** The Ultimate Spring System launches – the first new spring system in the UK for more than three decades – and the brand icons, Hippo and Duck, are introduced.

▶ **1990s:** The spring system is improved and renamed Miracoil® Spring System.

▶ **2008:** mattress-now® launches – the first Silentnight 'convenience' mattress.

▶ **2009:** Silentnight launches Miracoil®7 and PocketZing®, and the new CGI Hippo and Duck are introduced.

▶ **2010:** Silentnight returns to television screens with sponsorship of American Idol, and the Best for Bedsteads range is launched.

▶ **2011:** The brand's parent company, Silentnight Group, is acquired by HIG Europe. PocketZing®3 and SleepHealthy® launch, and the brand's Facebook and Twitter communities are developed.

Market

The branded bed market is a large, stable market mostly driven by replacement purchases. In 2010 it was worth £1.1 billion in the UK with 4.2 million purchases (Source: GfK December 2010). As the number one in the market, Silentnight Beds has significant brand awareness: spontaneous awareness is 37 per cent, rising to 83 per cent when prompted by the Hippo and Duck images.

In 2011 Silentnight Group was bought by HIG Europe, the European arm of global private equity firm HIG Capital. The deal secures the future of the Silentnight Beds brand alongside its sister brands Sealy (UK), Rest Assured, Pocket Spring Bed Company and Layezee Beds.

Product

In the 1980s Silentnight Beds launched an innovative new spring system into the UK market; more than 20 years later, it remains the bedrock of the brand's product offering. Formed from a continuous coil of springs, the system offers three key benefits: no roll together, no roll off and extra back support in the centre of the mattress.

In 2009 it was relaunched as Miracoil®3, with its three-zone spring system providing increased support for the lower back and greater pressure relief. In the same year Miracoil®7 was added to the range, providing seven support zones for 'total body relaxation' and more advanced materials such as Cirrus Airflow fabrics to maintain comfortable sleeping temperatures.

Silentnight's products also cater to the established pocket spring sector. The PocketZing® range features improved technology to provide zoned support for different parts of the body. A natural pro-biotic treatment called Purotex® has also been added to the mattresses, keeping them hygienic and free from dust mites. Silentnight has received the Allergy UK Seal of Approval for all mattresses containing Purotex®.

Prompted by consumer desire for immediately available products, and the entry of supermarkets and general retailers into the bed market, Silentnight launched mattress-now® in 2008. The full size memory foam mattress

> **Did You Know?**
>
> **Silentnight Beds was originally called Clarke's Mattresses Ltd. In 1951 the company ran a competition among employees to come up with a new name, offering a £5 prize for the best suggestion. Joan Clarke, wife of company founder Tom, won with her suggestion 'Silentnight' – she never claimed her prize.**

is tightly rolled, shrink-wrapped and boxed, ready for immediate sale.

A licence agreement with Comfy Quilts has enabled Silentnight to extend its brand into pillows, duvets, mattress protectors and toppers, while further areas of product development for Silentnight include its SleepHealthy cot mattresses. Introduced in 2011 and available exclusively in Mamas & Papas, they make use of the Purotex® treatment and provide a cool and comfy sleeping environment for babies. Silentnight also licenses its My First Little Bed cot mattresses to Rochingham.

Achievements
Silentnight Beds is a full member of the Furniture Industry Sustainability Programme, having shown commitment to social, economic and environmental sustainability across its business. Indeed, Silentnight has implemented a programme of changes to make its bed manufacturing process more sustainable and in 2011, achieved FSC certification for all the timber used in the production of its divans and headboards.

Each month more than 2,100 old mattress are sent to landfill in the UK; in 2011 Silentnight launched its Collect & Recycle service to

provide an alternative disposal solution for its customers. When Silentnight delivers a new bed, it removes and recycles the old one – no matter what its condition or age.

Recent Developments
In line with its reputation for innovation and increased sustainability in the sector, Silentnight Beds has launched two new materials for use in its products: EcoComfort Fibre® and EcoMemory Fibre®.

EcoComfort Fibre® is a polyester pad made from 50 per cent recycled material. A special vertical structure provides the same support and comfort as an equivalent foam pad, but retains less heat thanks to the breathable polyester, therefore keeping the user cool and helping to prevent disturbed sleep. EcoMemory Fibre® is an alternative to visco-elastic memory foam – which is popular for its body-moulding and pressure-relieving properties – and also makes use of polyester's heat-regulating properties.

Promotion
While Silentnight Beds has had an online presence for some time, in 2011 it turned its focus to increasing consumer engagement via social media. The brand's Twitter and Facebook presences were further developed, with regular

competitions, jokes from Hippo and Duck, and dedicated content all leading to a community of more than 2,000 followers.

In 2010 Silentnight became the sponsor of ITV2's American Idol. The two-year sponsorship included 15 idents featuring the brand's Hippo and Duck characters. Each 19-week campaign delivered more than 22 'opportunities to see' among Silentnight's target audience of 25–45 year-old C1 and C2 women.

Additional advertising activity in 2011 included a three-month press ad campaign in which the brand utilised mobile technology for the first time by including a QR code. An online collaboration with Tesco Direct, meanwhile, helped consumers find their ideal bed via the Perfect Match Finder tool.

Brand Values
The Silentnight Beds brand promises comfort, support and pressure relief for all shapes and sizes – as demonstrated by Hippo and Duck. The business has consistently invested in its products, plant and marketing to ensure that it is at the forefront of bed manufacturing in the UK, offering the very best in products, service and delivery.

▶ **www.silentnight.co.uk**

Stretch out, without splashing out. Buy a king-size for the price of a double.

Silver Cross®

Silver Cross is passionate about offering parents the highest levels of quality, baby comfort and safety, coupled with chic, contemporary design. A British brand with more than 130 years of heritage, Silver Cross now operates not only in the UK, but also sells products throughout the world, offering fashionably designed prams and pushchairs, furniture, bedding, car seats, nursery toys and gifts.

Market

The UK baby market, which is defined as households with babies and children under the age of four years old, is currently worth an estimated £1 billion. Already a world leader in the design, development and production of high quality nursery products, Silver Cross is continuing to gain an increased share of the nursery goods market. The focus for the brand in recent years has been to offer new parents across the globe a truly international selection of quality nursery products.

Product

All Silver Cross products are created by in-house designers and product development specialists based in the brand's UK head office, with the aim of supporting parents and their children on the journey from delivery room to school gates.

The highly acclaimed travel collection comprises a contemporary range of prams and pushchairs including the recently launched Surf: an all-terrain from-birth pram system with state-of-the-art air sprung suspension and ultra compact fold. In addition, the collection

includes three of the UK's best-selling pram and pushchair combinations: Sleepover, Freeway and 3D. The pram systems are joined by lightweight strollers: Dazzle, Fizz, Zest and the best-selling Pop, which provides unsurpassed build quality and style at an affordable price.

Silver Cross offers a collection of five car seats including the multi-award-winning Ventura Plus group 0+, which combines with all Silver Cross prams to make travel systems and is now available with an ISOFIX base. The range also contains the Explorer Sport, which is a two-stage car seat that grows with the child; the Explorerfix, which uses a push–click ISOFIX installation; the Navigator, a fully adjustable group 2–3 car seat; and the Navigator Fix, Silver Cross' latest ISOFIX group 2–3 seat for older children.

The world-famous Heritage collection is handmade in England to the same high standards employed in the 19th century. Each pram comes with an individually numbered plaque and certificate of authenticity, including

the craftsman's signature. The Balmoral pram has become a global style icon, favoured by the Royal Family and A-list celebrities, while the Kensington is defined by a sweeping, curved, hand-painted steel body and highly polished chrome chassis.

Silver Cross' toy collections include doll's carriages (miniature replicas of the Balmoral), classic teddy bears and rag dolls, a range of owl and pussycat themed nursery gifts, and a soft activity collection that develops young children's key skills.

Achievements

Silver Cross' leading British design and high manufacturing quality continues to be put through its paces by parents across the country, with the brand's full collection continuing to win numerous high profile parenting magazine awards. In particular, the Surf won a host of awards in 2011, including the illustrious Junior Design Award and Prima Gold Award.

The brand's popularity and heritage in the UK has aided growing recognition of its products internationally. With distributors operating across the world, Silver Cross now sells prams

Brand History

▶ **1877:** Silver Cross is founded by William Wilson, a prolific inventor of baby carriages who gains a reputation for producing the world's finest carriages.

▶ **1920s–30s:** Silver Cross becomes incorporated and is crowned the number one baby carriage for royals, supplying its first baby carriage to George VI for Princess Elizabeth.

▶ **1951:** Silver Cross launches a new shape; the forefather of the Balmoral, it becomes synonymous with the name 'pram'.

▶ **1977:** Silver Cross celebrates its centenary by flying customers and buyers around the world in its new centenary aircraft, and by presenting a baby carriage to Princess Anne.

▶ **1988:** The Wayfarer is launched. It becomes Britain's best-selling pushchair for a decade, selling more than 3,000 per week.

▶ **2002:** Entrepreneur and businessman Alan Halsall purchases Silver Cross and relaunches the famous Balmoral.

▶ **2006:** Silver Cross goes global, forging partnerships with distributors in Europe, America, Canada and Japan.

▶ **2009:** Silver Cross launches its Home Collection and a range of soft activity and gift toys.

▶ **2010:** The Surf pram and pushchair are launched, and Silver Cross enters the nursery furniture and bedding market.

▶ **2011:** The Silver Cross brand continues to expand online, with a blog and presences on Facebook and Twitter. The international operation also develops further.

in more than 30 countries. Products can be seen in cities as diverse as Tokyo, where the lightweight strollers are particularly popular; Moscow, where the Sleepover has been a notable success; and Melbourne, where the new Surf has been a hit.

Recent Developments
During 2011 Silver Cross continued to drive forward with modern designs. The Surf range has been extended to include blue and pink options as well as the Special Edition Petals, which features intricate design details and co-ordinating accessories. Fizz is the latest addition to the lightweight travel collection.

2011 also saw further expansion of Silver Cross' classic toys and gifts. The new Cherished doll's carriage features a personalised plaque, and the owl and pussycat toy range now includes a selection of baby gifts.

In 2010 Silver Cross launched a furniture, bedding and décor collection. The furniture features three wooden styles – Devonshire, Nostalgia and Porterhouse – and is designed to grow alongside a child. The white glove delivery service adds a further dimension of customer care. The complementary styles of bedding and décor – Classic, Cherished and So Pretty – combine high quality fabrics, trims and embroideries to make the ranges both practical and beautiful.

Silver Cross has a long history of charity work and continues to fund two bursaries at the Genesis Research Trust. Under the leadership of Lord Robert Winston, the Genesis Research Trust is involved in cutting-edge medical research into the prevention of premature birth.

Promotion
Silver Cross invests heavily in marketing. Communications activities include: extensive consumer advertising; a presence at major nursery trade and consumer events; in-store

displays; plus wide ranging online activity. Recently, Silver Cross has built an online community through Facebook, Twitter and blogger outreach, creating a new channel through which consumers can communicate with the brand on a daily basis.

Silver Cross communications are straightforward, open and honest. Its strongest marketing tool has always been word-of-mouth. From royalty and trendsetters in the film and music world to mums around the globe, the brand is endorsed by those who have first-hand experience of Silver Cross products.

Did You Know?

Silver Cross is the oldest nursery brand in the world.

More than 1,000 individual hand operations are required to manufacture each Balmoral pram.

Brand Values
Silver Cross is one of the UK's most loved and trusted brands. In 2012, more than 130 years after its launch, Silver Cross still stands for elegant and desirable British design. It is passionate about providing the best start in life and strives to be known worldwide for its experience and knowledge in producing original and imaginative products.

▶ **www.silvercross.co.uk**

SKANSKA

Skanska is involved in some of the UK's most prestigious projects in both the private and public sectors, from large high-profile schemes to smaller projects including public realm improvements, hard and soft landscaping as well as hundreds of utilities projects each year. It is a UK leader in private finance initiative and public–private partnership schemes, and has recently established a residential development business in the UK: Homes by Skanska.

Market

Skanska is one of the world's leading project development and construction groups with expertise in construction, development of commercial and residential projects, and public–private partnerships. Based on its global experience in green construction, Skanska aims to be the client's first choice for environmentally friendly solutions.

Headquartered in Stockholm, Sweden and listed on the Stockholm Stock Exchange, the Group currently has 52,000 employees globally.

The Group's operations are based on local business units, which have good knowledge of their respective markets, customers and suppliers. These local units are backed by Skanska's common values, procedures, financial strength and Group-wide experience. Skanska is thereby both a local construction company with global strength and an international constructor and developer with strong local roots.

The company undertakes approximately £1.5 billion worth of work in the UK each year and prides itself on being able to combine the best in British engineering with the best in Swedish innovation and design. It works throughout the UK, integrating the skills of its operating units in a collaborative style in order to deliver real benefits to its clients.

Did You Know?

Globally, Skanska undertakes about £11 billion of work a year.

Skanska is the only Swedish contractor in the UK.

In 2011, Skanska was named the UK's Best Green Company across all sectors by The Sunday Times.

Product

In the UK, Skanska carries out all aspects of the construction, development and infrastructure process – from financing, design and construction right through to facilities management, operation and maintenance. UK construction operations include building, civil engineering, utilities and infrastructure services, piling and ground engineering, mechanical and electrical, ceilings and decorative plasterwork, and steel decking. By combining the skills and experience of its construction operations and those of its Infrastructure Development Business Unit, Skanska has become a UK leader in private finance initiative and public–private partnership schemes covering healthcare, education, defence, transportation and street lighting.

During 2011, the company officially launched its residential business in the UK – Homes by Skanska – and purchased two development sites in Great Kneighton, Cambridge. Skanska's first homes will be available for sale during early summer 2012.

The company works on a number of major projects each year in both the private and public sectors, and has undertaken some of the most technically challenging schemes across the UK. These have included the London landmarks 30 St Mary Axe (the Gherkin) and

Heron Tower, which is the tallest new building in the City. Skanska is also responsible for the redevelopment of Barts and The London hospitals, and is currently working on the M25 Design Build Finance and Operate contract in a joint venture.

Skanska's focus is on creating sustainable solutions and it aims to be a leader in green construction, health and safety, and business ethics. Skanska acknowledges that almost everything it does affects both the environment and the lives of people in the communities in which it operates, both now and in the future. It employs community liaison managers to work closely with those communities, keeping them fully informed of the activities on Skanska sites. The company also employs local labour and trade contractors wherever possible.

Skanska works strictly in accordance with the Skanska Code of Conduct and to its Five Zeros, which reflect its core values: zero loss-making projects, zero accidents, zero environmental incidents, zero ethical breaches and zero defects.

Achievements

The company's commitment to contribute to a more sustainable world is resolute. In June 2011 it was named the Best Green Company

in the UK across all industries by The Sunday Times. It seeks to use its position to influence clients and its supply chain to make more sustainable decisions, taking a longer-term view over the infrastructure it develops.

Skanska is proud of its third-party recognition, which it considers a true measure of the value and performance of the company and the brand. In the last few years, Skanska has received more than 100 external awards not only for the projects it has constructed, but also for key areas of its performance including health and safety, the environment and sustainability. 2011 saw Skanska receive a string of awards from the Considerate Contractors Scheme.

Promotion

While the company does occasionally promote its services and skills in the traditional way with advertising and exhibitions, this is secondary to the way in which the company prefers to be seen and recognised. Rather, Skanska is focused on being truly recognised for the way it lives up to its brand values.

It achieves this through the performance and behaviour of its people – Skanska people are 'team players who care and want to make a difference to the way their projects are delivered' – and the creation of facilities that its staff, clients, partners and the communities in which it works, are proud of. Every office and major Skanska construction site in the UK is planned using a bespoke approach according to its specific needs, creating a 'shop window' for the company's visual brand identity.

Brand Values

Skanska's key responsibility is to develop and maintain an economically sound and prosperous business. It is committed to the countries, communities and environments in which it operates, and at the same time, its employees and business partners.

Skanska stands for technical know-how and competence combined with an understanding of its customers' needs. The ability to apply these skills to new areas enables it to produce the innovation that its clients demand. Skanska aims not only to develop, build and maintain the physical environment for living, working and travelling, but also to be the leading green developer and constructor. By achieving this, Skanska believes it will be the client's first choice in construction-related services and project development.

▶ **www.skanska.co.uk**

Brand History

▶ **1887:** Aktiebolaget Skånska Cementgjuteriet, later renamed Skanska, is founded by Rudolf Fredrik Berg. Its first international order is received from Great Britain's National Telephone Company.

▶ **1927:** Sweden's first asphalt-paved road is constructed in Borlänge in central Sweden – a milestone in Skanska's role in building Sweden's infrastructure.

▶ **1965:** Skanska is listed on the Stockholm Stock Exchange.

▶ **2000:** Skanska enters the UK construction market by acquiring Kvaerner's construction business, which had previously been part of the Trafalgar House Group.

▶ **2010:** Skanska celebrates a decade of operation in the UK.

▶ **2011:** Skanska officially launches its residential development business in the UK – Homes by Skanska.

▶ **2012:** Skanska celebrates 125 years of operation.

Starbucks Coffee Company is one of the leading retailers, roasters and brands of speciality coffee in the world. It is committed to offering customers the highest quality coffee and the finest coffee experience, while operating in ways that produce social, environmental and economic benefits for the communities in which it does business. Starbucks entered the UK market in 1998 and now employs more than 11,000 partners in more than 700 coffeehouses.

Market

The branded coffee chain market has demonstrated remarkable buoyancy during the recent economic downturn, comfortably out-performing the wider retail sector. It is estimated that there are more than 4,600 outlets in the UK with an estimated £1.9 billion turnover. Starbucks remains the most recognised coffee brand and has reported sales growth throughout 2011 (Source: Allegra Strategies).

Product

Starbucks coffeehouses offer high quality whole bean coffees; fresh, rich-brewed, Italian-style espresso drinks; a variety of pastries and confections; and coffee-related accessories. In addition, Starbucks retails whole bean and ground coffees, chilled coffees and bottled Frappuccino through selected UK supermarkets, and has an established business in the UK foodservice sector. Starbucks also sells its instant coffee, Starbucks VIA™ Ready Brew, across the UK in supermarkets, on trains and through a number of airlines.

Achievements

Since the company opened its first store, Starbucks has been committed to doing business responsibly. In the UK and Europe, all Starbucks espresso – which is used in every latte, cappuccino, and so on – is 100 per cent Fairtrade certified. In addition to its Fairtrade commitment, Starbucks provides agronomy experts, based in Rwanda and Costa Rica, to share technical and environmental expertise with farmers. This investment enables farmers to increase their yields and income, building sustainability into production. Starbucks also provides funding to organisations that make loans to coffee growers, which help them to sell their crops at the best time to get the right price and to make capital improvements. Over the years, Starbucks has committed more than US$15 million to a variety of farmer loan funds.

Starbucks also continues its longstanding relationships with humanitarian and development organisations including Conservation International (CI). In a five-year partnership, Starbucks is working with CI to

Did You Know?

The name 'Starbucks' comes from the first mate's name in the classic novel, **Moby Dick**.

The Starbucks logo, with its twin-tailed mermaid, is based on a 16th century Norse woodcut.

Starbucks offers more than 87,000 possible drink combinations.

address climate change, contributing to the search for global climate solutions.

Additionally, Starbucks invests in young people; nationally through partnerships with The Prince's Trust and the National Literacy Trust, and locally through the work its partners (employees) do from stores around the country. The company is also backing young people through Starbucks Youth Action; the partnership with a leading youth charity, UK Youth, aims to empower young people to bring community projects to life in their local areas. The programme includes skills training, seed funding and service hours from Starbucks partners. In 2011 Starbucks Youth Action supported more than 50 local community projects across the UK and Ireland.

The 2011 launch of Starbucks University, meanwhile, now gives partners the chance to gain externally recognised qualifications to help them to progress in their career.

Recent Developments

Starbucks continually strives to innovate and offer customers an even better experience. In March 2011, Starbucks marked its 40th anniversary by unveiling a new look and logo at its refurbished flagship store on Knightsbridge's Brompton Road, London. Additional customer perks are available across

its stores, such as free easy-access WiFi and free iTunes downloads, while the introduction of mobile payment technology – introduced in January 2012 – brings added convenience for customers.

March also saw the launch of a collection of premium coffees called Starbucks Reserve™. Baristas have been specially trained to prepare the coffee by hand using the 'pour over' method.

In May, the company launched its Starbucks Frappuccino However-You-Want-It range. With more than 35,000 combinations now available, customers are able to tailor their Frappuccino by choosing between different types of milk, adding extra coffee shots, opting for decaf coffee, and selecting from an array of syrups and flavours.

Additional product development in 2011 included the launch of new breakfast and lunch options including Bistro Boxes. Developed with popular eating trends in mind, each serving contains fewer than 500 calories.

Promotion

Storytelling is key to the Starbucks culture. The success of the company's communication strategy is rooted in its partners' passion for and involvement in its innovative product and experience.

The Starbucks UK Facebook site is well established with a fan base of more than 450,000. Globally, Starbucks has over 30 million Facebook fans, making it one of the most successful brands in social media.

The company has established the popularity of seasonal favourite drinks in the UK and Ireland, offers beverage customisation and has been at the forefront of innovating the coffeehouse experience in the UK for more than 10 years. Starbucks coined the phrase,

the 'third place' – a restful environment between home and work in which to relax, take time for yourself and enjoy a freshly made cup of high quality coffee. Partnerships with BT OpenZone and The Guardian newspaper further enhance the Starbucks experience.

Brand Values

The Starbucks mission is to 'inspire and nurture the human spirit – one person, one cup, and one neighbourhood at a time', which is supported by a passionately held set of principles that guide how partners in the company live every day.

▶ **www.starbucks.co.uk**

Brand History

▶ **1971:** Starbucks is founded in Seattle by three friends who met at the University of San Francisco in the 1960s.

▶ **1982:** The first store is a success and catches the attention of Howard Schultz, who joins the company. With the backing of local investors he purchases Starbucks in 1987.

▶ **1991:** Bean Stock is introduced – a stock option scheme for all employees to make them 'partners'.

▶ **1998:** Starbucks enters the UK market through the acquisition of 60 stores from Seattle Coffee Company.

▶ **2000:** The Starbucks Christmas Bookdrive is first launched with the National Literacy Trust. In the same year, Starbucks begins to sell Fairtrade certified coffees in-store.

▶ **2003:** The Starbucks Coffee Master Programme is launched.

▶ **2007:** Starbucks is named one of the Great Place to Work® Institute's top 10 Best Workplaces in the UK.

▶ **2008:** Starbucks Shared Planet™ launches, detailing the company's global goals in the areas of ethical sourcing, environmental stewardship and community involvement.

▶ **2009:** Starbucks Card Rewards and Starbucks VIA™ Ready Brew are introduced. Starbucks is ranked as one of the 100 Best Companies to Work For by Fortune.

▶ **2010:** Starbucks celebrates a year of offering 100 per cent Fairtrade espresso by taking baristas to Tanzania to meet farmers and learn more about coffee.

▶ **2011:** Starbucks celebrates its 40th anniversary with a redesign of its famous logo, and is named Most Ethical Company in the coffee industry in Europe for a third year.

Sudocrem®

The Sudocrem brand encompasses skin care products. Having celebrated its 80th birthday in 2011, Sudocrem Antiseptic Healing Cream has an illustrious heritage and has proved itself as a product that can be trusted to soothe, heal and protect babies' skin from nappy rash. Instantly identifiable, thanks to its familiar grey tub, this multiple award-winner is recognised as the nation's favourite nappy rash cream and has been market leader in its sector for decades.

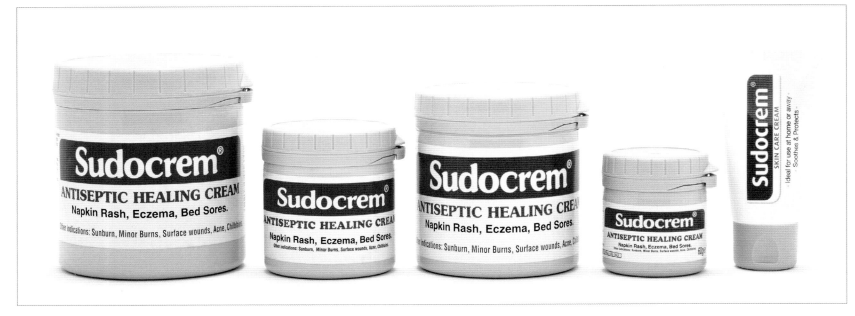

Market

The UK baby nappy rash market is worth £24 million (Source: Information Resources Incorporated (IRI) October 2011) and is on the increase; between 2010 and 2011 market growth was seven per cent (Source: IRI 2011). Sudocrem Antiseptic Healing Cream has dominated this category for the past 30 years and holds 62 per cent of total category volume sales (Source: IRI 2011). Even with the increasing popularity of disposable nappies, Sudocrem Antiseptic Healing Cream remains as popular today as ever.

Product

Sudocrem Antiseptic Healing Cream is for the treatment of nappy rash; however, the cream's combination of ingredients makes it a versatile product for use by the whole family. As well as treating a baby's nappy rash, it can help teenagers treat their acne, and older people treat skin problems such as incontinence dermatitis. It is also recommended as a first aid box treatment for minor burns, sunburn, cuts and grazes thanks to its antiseptic and mild anaesthetic properties.

Sudocrem Antiseptic Healing Cream is available over the counter in a range of classic tub sizes to suit every need, and is also available via prescription. Generations of healthcare professionals have put their trust in Sudocrem Antiseptic Healing Cream and more than 700,000 prescriptions were written in the UK in 2010 (Source: IMS Health November 2011).

Sudocrem Skin Care Cream – which uses similar ingredients to the classic Sudocrem Antiseptic Healing Cream, but in slightly different proportions – is aimed at helping to maintain healthy skin as part

Did You Know?

Although it's best known for helping to ease babies' nappy rash, Sudocrem Antiseptic Healing Cream can also be used for treating sunburn, minor burns, cuts, grazes, eczema, chilblains and acne.

More than eight million tubs of Sudocrem Antiseptic Healing Cream were sold in the UK between September 2010 and September 2011 (Source: Company Data).

of a daily skin care routine. The tube size is designed for people 'on the go', and is particularly useful when travelling as it is compliant with aeroplane hand-luggage restrictions. The cream is versatile and thanks to its gentle and soothing properties, can be applied as often as is needed. It can be used on problem skin, such as spot or blemish-prone areas, or dry patches common on elbows and knees, and is also suitable for use on skin that has been exposed to the sun.

Achievements

Sudocrem Antiseptic Healing Cream has been the market-leading nappy rash cream in the UK for more than 30 years and has achieved total penetration across the UK's pharmacies.

It has carved out a niche as a first aid cream that can be used at all life stages, from birth into old age. As well as being a mother's staple, it has earned recognition and a following among healthcare professionals.

Thanks to its consistent, reliable positioning and proven product performance, the Sudocrem brand has earned a plethora of top-class awards over the years – and continues to do so, year in year out.

Recent Developments

In 2012 Forest Laboratories launched two new additions to the brand portfolio: Sudocrem Kids & Babies mousses. Sudocrem Moisturising Mousse is a gentle, hypoallergenic mousse for young children and babies that helps prevent their skin from becoming dry. It uses Proderm Technology®, which is proven to gently soothe and care for delicate skin.

Sudocrem Sunscreen Mousse is a hypoallergenic high protection SPF 50 sunscreen. Using Proderm Technology®, it provides long-lasting protection and forms

a moisturising barrier that also allows skin to breathe. It has a superior four-star UVA rating and is water resistant.

Both mousses are specially formulated to protect a baby's delicate skin. Gentle enough to use every day, they are free from colours, fragrances, parabens and other preservatives.

Promotion

The brand makes use of a diversified range of promotional activities in order to communicate its unique selling points and illustrious brand heritage.

Consumer-facing promotion takes the form of traditional, above-the-line media such as television and parenting press. Sudocrem will continue to invest in television advertising aimed at mothers with young children (from birth up to five years of age) to communicate its growing range of products. In addition, new press executions will feature in the leading parenting magazines. Multi-platform, fully integrated social media campaigns – as well as the current online campaigns on leading parenting websites – will complement the classic promotional channels.

Alongside the consumer strategy, Sudocrem actively engages with primary healthcare professionals and pharmacists. Annually, Forest Laboratories attends more than 50 nursing and specialist exhibitions, reaching thousands of health visitors, midwives and district nurses. In addition, a dedicated sales team visits nursing homes nationwide to promote the benefits of Sudocrem Antiseptic Healing Cream in caring for elderly skin.

Brand Values

Through its consistent and robust formula, Sudocrem Antiseptic Healing Cream, in the classic grey tub, has become a consumer stalwart with a strong brand heritage. A clinically proven cream that can soothe, heal and protect, its key brand values are: gentle,

effective and trusted. Meanwhile, Sudocrem Skin Care Cream, in the white tube, is fast establishing itself as a 'use anytime, use anywhere', credit-crunch skin care cream.

Always read the label.

▶ **www.sudocrem.co.uk**

Brand History

▶ **1931:** Thomas Smith develops Smith's Cream in his Dublin pharmacy. The cream is distributed across Ireland.

▶ **1950s:** Smith's cream is renamed Sudocrem Antiseptic Healing Cream.

▶ **1960s:** Sampling to parents and healthcare professionals, to broaden the cream's appeal, begins.

▶ **1977:** Sudocrem Antiseptic Healing Cream is launched across the UK.

▶ **1985:** A new manufacturing facility opens in Dublin.

▶ **2007:** Sudocrem Antiseptic Healing Cream celebrates its 30th UK birthday and continues its reign as the number one selling nappy rash cream.

▶ **2009:** Sudocrem Skin Care Cream, for adults, launches in a distinctive white tube.

▶ **2011:** A milestone year for Sudocrem as the brand celebrates its 80th birthday.

▶ **2012:** The brand expands its product portfolio by launching two Sudocrem Kids & Babies mousses – Sudocrem Moisturising Mousse and Sudocrem Sunscreen Mousse – both of which use unique Proderm Technology®. Sudocrem products are now available in more than 41 countries worldwide, and counting.

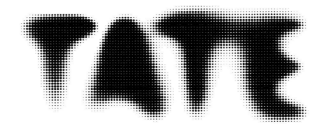

Tate's impressive pedigree dates back to the 19th century, but in recent years it has built an unparalleled reputation for increasing public access to national collections of both home-grown and international modern, contemporary art. This ambitious and trailblazing agenda has been achieved through challenging traditional ideas of gallery-goers and embracing innovation across its four sites: Tate Britain, Tate Modern, Tate Liverpool and Tate St Ives.

Market

Tate defines itself through a commitment to making art more accessible, moving away from the view of galleries as 'elitist' – a legacy from the past. Opening up the market in this way is key to the brand's ethos of making visiting galleries and exhibitions a more social, people-focused experience.

Tate works hard to ensure it appeals to and attracts new audiences. It has been particularly successful at making gallery attendance attractive to young audiences and family visitors, with London's Tate Modern boasting one of the youngest visitor profiles worldwide.

In an average year, around half of Tate Modern's visitors are from overseas, while at Tate Britain this figure is around one-third. All four galleries remain popular with indigenous audiences.

Did You Know?

Tate Britain was built in the 1890s on part of the site of the old Millbank Penitentiary, a vast 19th century prison.

The oldest work in Tate's collection is John Bette's A Man in a Black Cap, which was painted in 1545 and is on display at Tate Britain.

Product

At one time simply known as the Tate Gallery, expansion has seen the brand evolve into a family of four galleries, all united under the Tate umbrella: Tate Britain, Tate Modern, Tate Liverpool and Tate St Ives.

The current Tate brand was developed in partnership with Wolff Olins for the launch of Tate Modern and Tate Britain in 2000. The brief was to create a distinctive, worldwide brand that broadened the appeal of Tate's four gallery sites and conveyed its forward-thinking approach to experiencing art. It needed to unify the collection through the notion of 'one Tate but many Tates'.

The galleries were joined together under the single powerful idea of 'look again, think again', offering both an invitation and a challenge. This is epitomised by an ever-changing, four-faceted

Brand History

▶ **1897:** The National Gallery of British Art opens at Millbank, London – commonly referred to as the Tate Gallery in honour of its founder, Sir Henry Tate.

▶ **1917:** The Gallery is given responsibility for the national collection of international modern art and for British art dating back to about 1500.

▶ **1932:** The Gallery is officially renamed Tate Gallery.

▶ **1988:** On 24th May, Tate Liverpool is opened by HRH The Prince of Wales.

▶ **1993:** Tate St Ives opens. Within its first six months the 'Tate of the West', as it is dubbed by the press, receives 120,000 visitors, almost twice the expected number.

▶ **2000:** Tate Modern is created in a former London power station and the gallery at Millbank relaunches as Tate Britain.

▶ **2010:** Tate Modern celebrates its 10-year anniversary with a three-day arts festival, including a birthday procession.

logotype that reflects the fluidity and dynamic nature of the brand. In 2010 Tate refreshed its core values to focus on being open, diverse, international, entrepreneurial and sustainable. The invitation to 'look again, think again' remains relevant, reflecting the new trends in audience behaviour and the galleries' intention to provoke dialogue.

Tate's product offering is not limited to its four galleries, however, with Tate Entertaining, Publishing and Online Shop among its brand extensions.

Achievements

Since opening Tate Modern in 2000, visitor figures to the four Tate galleries have risen from four million to more than seven million per year. A key factor in achieving this significant increase has been the brand's emphasis on differentiation. Tate was the first major gallery in the UK to establish a distinct brand appeal through a pioneering approach to art that focuses on increased accessibility. It continues to lead the field internationally in regard to arts communication, through the democratisation of gallery-going (without dumbing down) and a shift of focus from 'the collection' to 'the experience', putting people before art.

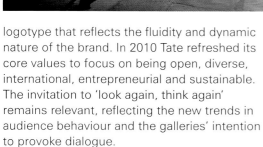

Did You Know?

The Turner Bequest includes more than 300 oil paintings and 30,000 sketches and watercolours painted by the artist, and represents the largest body of his work in the world.

Recent Developments

Tate's digital marketing, social media and interactive activities have increased significantly over the past year and Tate prides itself on its interaction with the public via its Twitter and Facebook channels. Since January 2010, Tate's Twitter following has risen from 14,000 to more than 505,000 followers, making it the leader in its sector, while Facebook fans now number around 320,000. Digital engagement with the public is prompted by posts such as the Tate 'weather forecast', in which a painting from the Tate collection reflects the forthcoming weekend's weather.

The public are encouraged to review exhibitions through all digital channels and Tate's blog is attracting an increasing number of visitor comments. The Tate Debate, hosted on the blog, regularly sparks further discussion. Tate Online is now the UK's most visited arts website, with more than 20 million unique visitors in 2010.

Promotion

Tate runs a number of campaigns throughout the year, some linked to its programme of events and exhibitions and some to the permanent collection. Core promotional activity centres on high profile press campaigns, Underground advertising and innovative strategies.

In September 2011, for example, Tate Britain embarked on an innovative marketing campaign to promote the John Martin: Apocalypse exhibition. The digital phase centred on a three-minute trailer, produced by Habana Creative, in which a young woman finds herself drawn inside one of Martin's apocalyptic works. It received more than 50,000 views, while SF Signal branded it "the best trailer [they'd] ever seen for an art exhibit".

Elsewhere online, a Spotify Facebook app – Apocalyptic Tracks – presented viewers with one of a number of John Martin's paintings, and invited them to choose a music track to complement the artwork. On Twitter, an interactive initiative encouraged people to follow the story of Elena Batham, a typical 19-year-old who became lost in the paintings. Followers were encouraged to help Elena solve puzzles to find her way home.

The campaign also saw Tate team up with Pandemonium Fiction to produce an anthology of short stories inspired by the John Martin: Apocalypse exhibition, with submissions from authors including renowned science fiction and fantasy writer Jon Courtenay Grimwood.

Brand Values

Tate's brand values are imbued throughout the organisation and include elements outside the presentation of art. The way Tate speaks in any form of communication reflects the spirit of the brand: inviting – it makes you curious and interested; intelligent but not academic – it doesn't underestimate your intelligence, but it's never obscure; challenging but not intimidating – it makes you think; and fresh – it has a contemporary point of view.

▶ **www.tate.org.uk**

At the start of the 20th century in Beaumont, Texas, two men were nurturing a small, fledgling enterprise that was to survive and grow, eventually expanding into one of the world's major petroleum companies, Texaco Inc. Today, the Texaco brand is an active force in UK society, fuelling industry and the economy, keeping people on the move, and participating in a range of community and environmental projects.

Market

The market is in a mature state and presents a challenging environment to major oil companies and independent operators alike. Change has been driven by a combination of high fuel taxes, low margins, aggressive hypermarket expansion and a subsequent fall in the total number of service stations in the UK. This contraction has focused primarily on company owned and operated service

stations, with the remaining dealer network being noticeably improved through the addition of non-fuel concepts. The market is now characterised by sophisticated shop formats, as well as alliances between traditional oil companies and convenience store operators.

In the UK, fuels are marketed under the Texaco brand by Valero Energy Ltd, which owns the oil refinery in Pembroke, Wales. Valero markets its fuel through around 900 Texaco-branded service stations – and it is testament to the strength of the Texaco brand that this represents the largest branded network of independently owned service stations in the UK.

Product

Texaco is best known for high quality fuels, providing standard grades and a Supreme product in both its petrol and diesel offering in the UK. Texaco Supreme petrol and diesel contain a chemical additive that helps to keep a car's engine clean and performing better. Industry standard engine tests have proved that in the UK, no other petrol or diesel keeps an engine cleaner (Source: Company Data).

Brand History

▶ **1901:** The forerunner of Texaco, the Texas Fuel Company is established in the US. Its first international shipment of one million barrels of crude oil is made to the UK the following year.

▶ **1903:** The first Texaco Company refinery begins operations in Port Arthur Works, Texas, and processes 318,364 barrels of oil in its first year.

▶ **1911:** Texaco opens its first service station on a street corner in Brooklyn, New York – the beginnings of a rapidly growing retail network.

▶ **1916:** Texaco Petroleum Products Company arrives in the UK.

▶ **1964:** Her Majesty Queen Elizabeth The Queen Mother opens the company's Pembroke refinery.

▶ **1970s:** Texaco-sponsored Formula One drivers Emerson Fittipaldi and James Hunt claim three World Champion titles between them: Emerson in 1972 and 1974, and Hunt in 1977.

▶ **1981:** Texaco introduces its star logo, which is used to the present day.

▶ **2001:** Chevron Corporation and Texaco Inc. merge to create ChevronTexaco Corporation, which becomes Chevron Corporation in 2007 – one of the largest corporations in the world based on market capitalisation.

▶ **2011:** Valero Energy Corporation acquires Chevron Corporation's UK and Ireland refining and marketing business; the Texaco brand is licensed to Valero Energy Ltd in the UK. Valero and the Texaco brand claim Best Oil Company Initiative at the Forecourt Trader Awards.

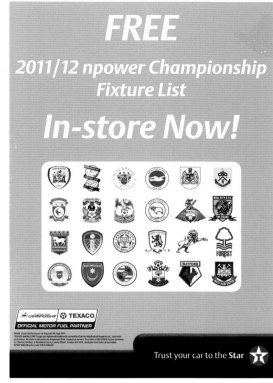

The Texaco brand also supplies fuels to major airlines and shipping customers as well as products and services for industrial, commercial and domestic use in the UK.

Achievements

As one of the largest employers in the Pembrokeshire region, Valero makes a significant contribution to the area's economy. The company actively supports the community in additional ways, however, making it a priority to work with a number of charities – both local and national – and business initiatives such as the prestigious Arts and Business Cymru Awards.

Valero has also supported the children's charity Action for Children (formerly known as NCH) for close to 20 years, and the amount raised by staff and customers to help vulnerable young people has reached more than £1 million.

Recent industry accolades for the Texaco brand include Best Branded Supplier in the Non-foods, Fuel and Drinks category at The Co-operative Retail Trading Group Supplier Awards 2011. Texaco beat competition from the likes of Diageo, Imperial Tobacco, Hallmark and Coca-Cola.

Did You Know?

The Texaco logo has its origins in 1903, when 19-year-old refinery employee JR Miglietta suggested that the five-pointed star on the Texas state flag be used as the Texas Company's symbol. He later recommended placing a green 'T' inside the red star. Company folklore suggests that Miglietta, an Italian immigrant, chose the colours of his native country's flag.

Recent Developments

The last few years have seen a significant increase in emphasis on both energy security and climate change awareness. Valero believes that biofuels will play an increasingly important role in transportation fuels. The company now has 10 state-of-the-art ethanol plants in the US, making it the first traditional refiner to enter ethanol production. Valero also has investments in several companies working to commercialise emerging alternative biofuels.

In 2011, Valero and the Texaco brand beat other major oil brands to claim the award for Best Oil Company Initiative at the Forecourt Trader Awards. The accolade recognises the success of Valero's service station rebranding programme in the UK, which includes the roll-out of a comprehensive and modern service station image, the introduction of Supreme fuels, and the implementation of retail programmes and marketing initiatives aimed at further developing Texaco's brand position.

The new service station image has been launched across the UK and the programme roll-out continues.

Promotion

The Texaco brand has been rewarding loyal customers for more than 30 years through a range of innovative loyalty schemes. In 2008, its loyalty programme relaunched as Star Rewards, a scheme that rewards customers with fuel and shopping vouchers when they purchase fuel at Texaco service stations.

The brand has been the official Motor Fuel and Motor Oil Partner of the Football League Championship since 2007, and over the years has been official fuel partner to 20 clubs within the Championship. Texaco-branded fuel and ticket competitions feature throughout the football season, as do local community

programmes that are run in partnership with a number of Championship clubs.

In addition, Texaco offers a range of competitive fuel cards that include The Business Card (for small to medium sized fleets), the Fastfuel Card (for larger fleets), and an authorised third-party fuel card via an alliance with BP.

Local site marketing support is provided in the form of Texaco-branded materials, aimed at helping retailers increase customer traffic to their sites and develop links with the local trading area.

Brand Values

The Texaco Star was designed to be a beacon on the road for motorists – an enduring symbol portraying a sense of performance, quality and trust for the Texaco brand.

Texaco aims to be a strong, reliable, trustworthy, iconic, knowledgeable, experienced, Americana brand known for enduring performance and established trust amongst customers who know and love their cars.

▶ **www.texaco.co.uk**

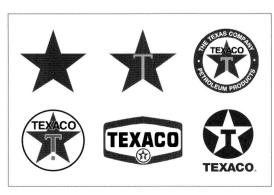

The **co-operative**
good for everyone

As the UK's largest co-operative, owned by its members, The Co-operative is built on trust and sound ethics. Under The Co-operative brand, its family of businesses is experiencing a renaissance as consumers increasingly see the value in its integrity. The rebrand of the Somerfield estate and the merger of the Britannia Building Society with The Co-operative Banking Group have cemented The Co-operative as one of Britain's strongest brands.

1844 — **First** shop opened by the Rochdale Pioneers.

1948 — **First** self-service supermarket in the UK.

1986 — Fat 2.0g | Sat 12. approx. pe — **First** to introduce customer friendly labelling.

1999 — .co.uk smile the internet bank — **First** internet bank launched in the UK.

2000 — FAIRTRADE — **First** Fairtrade bananas in the UK.

2001 — **First** UK pharmacy to use Braille on our own-brand medicines.

2005 — **Successful** brand pilot in Northampton and Hull.

2007 — We sell food **grown by us.**

2007 — **All** fresh beef, pork & poultry is 100% British.

2008 — RSPCA GOOD BUSINESS AWARDS 2008 LIFETIME ACHIEVEMENT — **First** ever RSPCA lifetime achievement award for animal welfare.

2008 — **First** to change all our own-brand hot drinks to Fairtrade.

2008 — **All** our own-brand fish is responsibly sourced.

2009 — Launch of our **biggest ever** brand campaign.

2009 — **First** UK travel agent to launch an ethical strategy.

2010 — **Over** 1 million members trading with more than 1 Co-operative business.

2011 — WE'RE TAKING ETHICS TO THE NEXT LEVEL. We unveiled our landmark **Ethical Operating Plan**

The **co-operative** good for everyone

Proud to serve **Britain** for over 165 years

Market

The Co-operative is now the clear leader in the community food sector – the fastest growing area of the grocery market. Since 2009, The Co-operative has become the fifth largest food retailer in the country. In its food business alone, more than 2,900 stores generate annual sales of more than £8 billion, with approximately 20 million customers per week.

With footholds in food, funerals, travel, pharmacy, electrical, motors, farms, financial services and legal services, The Co-operative's broad portfolio has helped it to increase both turnover and profits in a difficult climate. Its operating model, which means it does not answer to stock markets and speculators, has appealed to those concerned by the way in which big businesses operate, especially in light of the recent economic crisis.

More than four million new members have joined The Co-operative since it relaunched its membership scheme in 2006. There are now more than six million members, all of whom are entitled to a say in how the business operates and are rewarded by sharing in the organisation's profits. In 2010, the Group members earned £70.5 million as a share of profits.

> **Did You Know?**
>
> The Co-operative operates in every postal area in the UK.
>
> The Co-operative has turned away more than £1 billion of loans to businesses that contravened its Ethical Policy.

> **Did You Know?**
>
> The Co-operative was the first major retailer to adopt the RSPCA Freedom Food scheme, and today sells 73 accredited products.
>
> More than 5,000 branches of The Co-operative are powered by renewable energy.

Product

Now united under the umbrella brand, The Co-operative's businesses embrace multiple sectors and offer unparalleled reach across all areas of the country. Best known for its food stores, The Co-operative is also one of the most diversified financial businesses in the UK; is the third largest retail pharmacy chain; and has become Europe's leading funeral business.

Perhaps less well known amongst its activities is the fact that The Co-operative is the UK's largest farmer, with more than 50,000 acres in England and Scotland. It is also diversifying into wind farms and aims to generate 15 per cent of its own energy by 2012 through these and other renewable energy sources such as hydropower, biomass and ground-source heat.

In 2006, The Co-operative set out on the largest rebranding exercise in UK corporate history

JOIN THE GREEN SCHOOLS REVOLUTION

The bright young minds in our schools can lead the way to a greener future for all of us. Find out more and get involved at
www.greenschools.coop

The **co-operative**
good for everyone

GREEN SCHOOLS **REVOLUTION**

when it began the task of converting its entire estate to 'The Co-operative'. The £1.5 billion upgrading exercise involves refitting and rebranding its stores; to date, 4,400 of its outlets have undergone this transformation.

Achievements

The Co-operative has won an array of awards across its family of businesses. Some of its most notable in 2011 include being named Green Retailer of the Year at the Grocer Gold Awards for the second year running, and Responsible Retailer of the Year at the Oracle Retail Week Awards for the fourth consecutive year.

In 2010, The Co-operative Financial Services claimed the prestigious title of Financial Times Sustainable Bank of the Year, beating 110 financial institutions from 44 countries in the process.

Recent Developments

By the end of October 2011, The Co-operative had rebranded more than 600 Somerfield stores to its award-winning Co-operative brand. In another acquisition, The Co-operative Bank merger with the Britannia Building Society has created a business of real scale with £70 billion of assets, 7.8 million Banking Group customers, 10,000 employees, more than 300 branches and 20 corporate banking centres. The Britannia branch fascias have been updated to overtly link The Co-operative and Britannia on the high street.

Promotion

In 2011, The Co-operative took a great leap forward with the launch of a new Ethical Operating Plan, and the aim to be clearly recognised as the UK's most socially responsible business.

Every year it supports thousands of initiatives, both local and global, helping people to change the world around them. The Co-operative aims to inspire even more people to get involved and has set goals in eight key areas: democratic control and reward, supporting co-operatives, keeping communities thriving, inspiring young people, tackling global poverty, protecting the environment, responsible retailing, and ethical finance.

It's a challenging time to be a young person in Britain, so The Co-operative has established a community programme that will directly benefit 250,000 young people across the UK, and help them to change their world through active citizenship. In particular, The Co-operative's Green Schools Revolution raises young

people's awareness of how to create a clean, green, sustainable future.

Brand History

▶ **1844:** The Rochdale Pioneers create a local co-operative and open their first store to avoid exploitation by unscrupulous shopkeepers.

▶ **1872:** The Co-operative Bank is set up, initially as the CWS Loan and Deposit Department.

▶ **1942:** The London Co-operative Society opens the UK's first self-service shop. By 1950, 90 per cent of self-service stores are operated by co-operatives.

▶ **1965:** Dividend Stamps are introduced as an alternative to the traditional methods of paying the 'divi'. The CWS launches the national Dividend Stamp Scheme in 1969.

▶ **1985:** The CWS stops all animal testing on its own-brand toiletries and household products. It co-sponsors a Private Member's Bill to improve labelling for products tested on animals.

▶ **1992:** The Co-operative Bank becomes the world's first bank to introduce a customer-led Ethical Policy.

▶ **2003:** The Co-operative switches all own-brand coffee to Fairtrade, generating an extra £1 million each year for coffee farmers in the developing world.

▶ **2007:** The Co-operative Group and United Co-operatives merge, successfully becoming one business within one year.

▶ **2009:** The Co-operative acquires Somerfield, merges with Britannia Building Society, and launches its biggest ever brand campaign.

▶ **2010:** The rebrand of the 500th Somerfield store to The Co-operative takes place.

▶ **2011:** The Co-operative's landmark Ethical Operating Plan is unveiled.

Brand Values

The Co-operative's vision is to be 'Good for Everyone' with five key components forming the DNA of its brand: consistent quality, trustworthy, rewarding, championing and community.

The Co-operative is a consumer-owned business in which its members have a democratic say in the way the business is run, how its profits are distributed, and how it achieves its goals. Just £1 allows anyone to join The Co-operative and each member has an equal say: collective action lies at the heart of the business.

▶ **www.co-operative.co.uk**

Now a £6 billion brand, The UK National Lottery is the most cost-efficient lottery in Europe and delivers a higher percentage of revenue back to society, through returns to the Good Causes and duty to the government, than any other major lottery operator in the world. Innovation, integrity and transparency spearhead its success both in enabling thousands of people each year to win life-changing amounts of money and in helping to fund the Good Causes across the nation.

Market

The National Lottery has successfully operated in a highly competitive gambling market for more than 17 years in the UK and during that time has established itself as a national institution. Since a second operating licence started in 2002, total National Lottery sales have increased by more than 20 per cent. Now currently in its third licence period, after Camelot again won the right to operate The National Lottery, record half-year returns to both prize payouts and the Good Causes were announced in November 2011.

Product

The National Lottery features a portfolio of games that offer opportunities to win life-changing amounts of money every day of the week. Each game is designed to deliver a particular prize value, while positioning the games at relatively low price points helps ensure that players participate in The National Lottery responsibly.

The National Lottery offering ranges from Lotto (the original National Lottery game) to Thunderball, which offers the best chance of winning £500,000 on a £1 National Lottery game. EuroMillions, which is run in partnership with nine European lotteries, delivers the most sizable jackpots. Additionally, The National Lottery runs a broad range of Scratchcards and interactive instant play games that deliver instant win experiences to players through a variety of prize levels and game styles, both at retail and online. The National Lottery portfolio results in an average of four million winners each week.

In the period up to March 2012, The National Lottery will contribute around 28 per cent of every £1 spent to the Good Causes, enabling it to support communities across the UK in the charitable, heritage, arts and sport sectors.

Achievements

The National Lottery has created more than 2,800 millionaires since its creation in 1994; the biggest jackpot win to date took place in July 2011 when a couple from Largs in Ayrshire scooped £161 million on EuroMillions.

Brand History

▶ **1993:** The government sets up a licence for the UK's state-franchised lottery.

▶ **1994:** The National Lottery's licence to operate is awarded to the Camelot Group. The first National Lottery draw takes place on 19th November.

▶ **1995:** Scratchcards are launched to complement The National Lottery draw.

▶ **1999:** Thunderball launches to give players more chances of winning a smaller jackpot of £250,000.

▶ **2002:** Camelot begins its second seven-year licence to operate The National Lottery. The National Lottery game is renamed Lotto and Lotto HotPicks also launches, offering a chance to win bigger prizes for matching fewer Lotto numbers.

▶ **2004:** EuroMillions is launched in partnership with lotteries in France and Spain. The first draw is held on 13th February, with Austria, Belgium, Ireland, Luxembourg, Portugal and Switzerland subsequently joining.

▶ **2009:** Camelot begins its third operating licence – this time for 10 years – as it celebrates its 15th anniversary. A UK-only Millionaire Raffle is introduced to EuroMillions, guaranteeing the creation of a UK millionaire every week.

▶ **2010:** Camelot launches a new-look Thunderball game, with changes including an increased top prize of £500,000. The introduction of UK-only Super Raffles to EuroMillions help to make it a £1 billion brand.

▶ **2011:** A new Tuesday EuroMillions draw is launched.

Over the years, The National Lottery has paid out more than £40 billion in prizes, reinforcing its position as one of the most successful lotteries in the world.

To date, The National Lottery has raised over £27 billion for the Good Causes, with more than 370,000 individual grants being made across the UK. This amounts to an average of 120 per postcode district. The National Lottery has also funded British Olympic and Paralympic athletes since 1997 and by the summer of 2012, will have contributed £2.2 billion to the London 2012 Olympic and Paralympic Games. This money has gone towards the regeneration and development of venues and infrastructure within the Olympic Park in East London, and supports more than 1,200 UK athletes with training and living costs.

Recent Developments

In May 2011, The National Lottery launched a new Tuesday draw day for EuroMillions, alongside a new advertising campaign to introduce Hector Riva: the ultra-rich, suave millionaire and his world of parties, yachts and private jets. The draw provides players with a further opportunity to win a life-changing jackpot, while highlighting the glitz and glamour that a EuroMillions win might deliver.

Promotion

The National Lottery's promotional strategy is a combination of emotional imagery around winning and tactical messaging to highlight large jackpots and rollovers. Each game has a separate campaign strategy to underline its unique brand essence.

'Not What You'd Do? What Would You Do?' is one of the latest in a series of campaigns that invites players to dream about the possibilities of a Lotto win. As Lotto jackpots are often smaller than EuroMillions, the element of choice becomes more important to a Lotto winner.

Did You Know?

Around 70 per cent of adults play The National Lottery – giving it greater reach than any other FMCG brand in the UK (Source: Conquest Research 2011).

The National Lottery creates an average of 20 millionaires every month, and more than 12,000 people have enjoyed a share of the Lotto jackpot prize.

EuroMillions uses the phrase, 'Welcome to My World' to demonstrate what could be possible if you were to become a 'EuroMillionaire'. Previous strategies involved more tactical messaging around large jackpot sums; however, the new campaign helps bring EuroMillions to life by visually representing key elements of a millionaire's lifestyle.

Traditionally, each Scratchcard has had its own promotional strategy and campaign, highlighting the differentiating factors of the cards to help players choose which cards to buy. From 2012, Scratchcards will be consolidated under one brand proposition that delivers the benefit of an instant win.

In 2012, The National Lottery is launching a new brand promise under the 'Life Changing' strapline. This reinforces the brand's dual aims of creating exciting jackpots for a large volume of winners, alongside fulfilling its responsibility to the Good Causes that contribute to enhancing the lives of those in the UK. The promise will sit alongside the branding for each game, helping to combine the various tenets of The National Lottery family. It will run with TV, press, online and retail support.

Brand Values

The National Lottery is committed to providing life-changing opportunities for everyone, through both large prize payouts and its contribution to the Good Causes.

The National Lottery is also committed to responsible play and through its brand strategy, supports long-term and sustainable growth that encourages people to join in and play, while spending relatively small amounts.

▶ **www.national-lottery.co.uk**

Since Thomas Cook's inaugural trip in 1841, his name has come to represent a pioneering approach to tourism. Introducing the first overseas package tour in 1855, today Thomas Cook takes six million British holidaymakers abroad each year. Thomas Cook Group plc has a network of more than 3,400 stores across 21 countries and over 22.5 million customers, making it one of the world's leading leisure groups.

Market

In an increasingly competitive industry, Thomas Cook has ensured it is well placed to retain its position as one of the world's leading leisure travel groups.

Product

In addition to its leading mainstream brands such as Thomas Cook, Airtours, Cruise Thomas Cook and Direct Holidays, the company's diverse portfolio continues to evolve in response to market trends and changing consumer buying habits.

The Thomas Cook Style Collection comprises five unique and stylish holiday selections, each of which includes a range of value-added benefits within its price. The Collection includes Ultimate Style, a bespoke selection of luxury five-star hotels; Villas with Style, a range of high quality villas across the globe; and MyStyle, which comprises a selection of world-class hotels and resorts

Did You Know?

Thomas Cook personally conducted the first round-the-world tour in 1872/73. The tour took 222 days and cost around £300.

Thomas Cook's monthly European Rail Timetable, still published today, was first sold in 1873.

that offer a unique and affordable five-star experience in beautiful beachfront locations.

Thomas Cook caters for the family market with its hugely successful Aquamania water park and FamilyWORLD resorts. Exclusive to Thomas Cook customers in the UK, FamilyWORLD is a selection of family-friendly four-star resorts that offer a unique programme of activities for the whole family, hosted by a dedicated Thomas Cook team. Many hotels also offer KidsWORLD and KidsWORLD EXTRA; dedicated drop-in kids' clubs that provide non-stop activities under the supervision of fully qualified UK childcare staff.

Thomas Cook Sport, Europe's leading sports travel operator, is the Official Travel Partner for several top football teams, and Thomas Cook is also the official provider of short breaks to the London 2012 Olympic and Paralympic Games.

Achievements

Thomas Cook's values have stood the test of time since its founder described himself as "the willing and devoted servant of the travelling public". In 2011, its commitment to the industry was recognised through a host of awards including Short Haul Tour Operator of the Year for Thomas Cook, Best Consolidator for Gold Medal, and Best Ski/Activity Operator for Neilson at the Globe Travel Awards, as well as a host of accolades at The British Travel Awards.

The company remains committed to being a responsible business: working with the Travel

Brand History

▶ **1841:** Thomas Cook's first excursion, a rail journey from Leicester to a temperance meeting in Loughborough, takes place.

▶ **1855:** In his first continental tour, Cook leads two parties from Harwich to Antwerp, then on to Brussels, Cologne, Frankfurt, Heidelberg, Strasbourg and Paris.

▶ **1865:** Thomas Cook opens an office on Fleet Street, London, which is widely regarded as the UK's first high street travel agency.

▶ **1874:** Cook's Circular Note, the first travellers' cheque, is launched in New York.

▶ **1939:** Holidays by air on chartered aircraft are included in the summer brochure for the first time.

▶ **2003:** Thomas Cook rebrands its airline to Thomas Cook and launches a tour-operating brand under the same name.

▶ **2007:** Thomas Cook UK & Ireland becomes a FTSE 100 company on the London Stock Exchange, and Thomas Cook Group plc forms after a merger with MyTravel Group.

▶ **2009:** Thomas Cook becomes official provider of short breaks to the London 2012 Olympic and Paralympic Games.

▶ **2011:** Thomas Cook, The Co-operative Travel and Midlands Co-operative complete their retail joint venture, and in doing so become the UK's largest retail travel chain.

Foundation, contributing towards worldwide sustainable tourism projects, and through The Thomas Cook Children's Charity. The charity raised £1 million in 2011 through employee fundraising and customer donations, and aims to make dreams come true for sick and disadvantaged children worldwide.

Recent projects in the UK include involvement in Sport England's 'Inspired' initiative. Thomas Cook has committed £500,000 to help support children's sports initiatives around the country, with the aim of helping to deliver a legacy for the London 2012 Games.

Recent Developments
In 2011, Thomas Cook UK and The Co-operative Travel completed a merger of their retail and high street foreign exchange businesses. With around 1,400 stores, the joint venture is now the UK's largest high street travel chain.

Thomas Cook's new online travel agency celebrated its first year with a gross booking value of around £1 billion, as it strives to become one of the top three European online travel agencies. With online a key part of Thomas Cook's multichannel strategy, significant improvements have been made to its customers' online experience, with new layouts, clearer price presentation and new merchandising functionality, as well as regularly updated inventory content.

Did You Know?

Thomas Cook owned and operated a funicular railway at the top of Mount Vesuvius for more than 50 years.

In 1919 Thomas Cook became the first travel agent to offer pleasure trips by air.

Thomas Cook first advertised trips to the moon in 1950.

Promotion
Created in 1984 by advertising agency Wells Rich Greene, 'Don't just book it. Thomas Cook it.' quickly became one of Britain's better-known advertising slogans. The strapline, reintroduced in 2008, was extended in 2011's campaigns that explored what 'it' in the slogan is. The approach provided the springboard for one of the company's most successful advertising campaigns, featuring husband and wife celebrity couple Jamie and Louise Redknapp. What began as a dreamy, inspirational and accessible TV-led advertising campaign was extended in 2011 through further executions. The campaign was supported with press and cinema slots, and included the first London 2012 TV advert promoting Thomas Cook's role as official provider of short breaks to the Games.

The campaign improved overall brand awareness, reaching record levels of nearly 68 per cent – a significant increase on the previous year. Of customers who saw the TV advertising, first choice consideration to book with Thomas Cook increased by more than 50 per cent (Source: Conquest Research).

Brand Values
Committed to keeping the customer at the heart of everything it does, Thomas Cook believes that people are its greatest asset and key differentiator in a highly competitive marketplace.

A modern, forward-thinking business dedicated to finding new ways in which to pioneer, Thomas Cook takes pride in its heritage and trusted brand to drive results and add value.

▶ **www.thomascook.com**

tommee tippee®

simply intuitive™

Millions of families have grown up with Tommee Tippee®, the UK's best-known baby brand for nearly 50 years. Traditionally known for cups and tableware, in 2006 the brand's leading position was reinforced with the launch of Closer to Nature®, a newborn feeding range now credited with revolutionising the way mothers feed their babies. Closer to Nature is now the UK's number one selling newborn baby essentials brand (Source: IRI w/e 24th September 2011).

Brand History

▶ **1965:** Manufacturing rights are acquired for Tommee Tippee baby products in the UK and Europe.

▶ **1986:** Tommee Tippee introduces Pur, the first silicone teat, to the market.

▶ **1988:** Sip 'n' Seal, the first non-spill baby cup, is launched.

▶ **1997:** Tommee Tippee buys Sangenic – a patented nappy disposal system.

▶ **2001:** Easiflow becomes the first baby cup to be accredited by the British Dental Health Foundation.

▶ **2006:** The launch of Closer to Nature changes the face of newborn feeding through radical innovation.

▶ **2009:** Tommee Tippee's new 'star' brand identity is introduced.

▶ **2010:** The brand launches in the US and Canada.

▶ **2011:** The Explora toddler range is relaunched.

Market

The baby accessories market is estimated to be worth almost £200 million in the UK (Source: Information Resources Incorporated (IRI) 2011 and Company Data) and encompasses everything from bibs and bottles to monitors and harnesses. It does not include nappies, wipes, toiletries, formula milk or baby food.

Tommee Tippee is the leading brand in a fiercely competitive market. Three-quarters of consumers that buy products from the top three brands will only buy Tommee Tippee (Source: Kantar Worldpanel 2011). Tommee Tippee has more than one-third of the total market share by value.

The brand has more than 96 per cent distribution through all channels including specialist baby stores, nursery shops, supermarkets, independent chemists and department stores. Internationally, it is sold in more than 70 countries.

Product

Tommee Tippee has more than 700 products in its range and is the only baby accessory brand to cater for parents' and children's needs from pregnancy through to the reception class gates. The brand prides itself on its commitment to innovation and has patents in place for most products. Its offering is enhanced by a promise of quality, safety, simplicity, convenience and value.

The brand was the first to design a non-spill cup in the 1980s (Sip 'n' Seal), a groundbreaking bottle babies could hold themselves (the Nipper Gripper), and a teether filled with purified water that could be cooled for effective relief from the pain of teething.

In recent years significant additions to the product portfolio have included the Closer to Nature, Explora® and Sangenic® ranges. Closer to Nature feeding products have been designed to mimic the natural flex, feel and movement of a mum's breast, making it easier

to combine breast and bottle feeding. Explora products help the weaning transition from bottle/breast to cup and spoon, encouraging children to feed independently. The Sangenic range helps to ensure hygienic nappy disposal both in and out of the home, by wrapping dirty nappies in antibacterial film.

Achievements

Tommee Tippee is the fifth biggest baby accessories supplier globally. Out of the top 10 categories in the baby accessories market in which the brand operates, Tommee Tippee is number one in eight of them (Source: IRI 2011).

The Closer to Nature bottle and teat won a Gold Award from Practical Parenting &

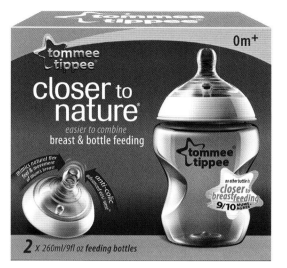

Pregnancy magazine for 2010/11 and claimed Platinum in the Prima Baby & Pregnancy Readers Awards 2011. Furthermore, in an independent online survey of 1,085 UK mums, respondents voted the Closer to Nature bottle as the best choice for their baby; 237 respondents were Closer to Nature users, with nine out of 10 agreeing that it made the transition from breast to bottle easy (Source: Mum's Views July 2011).

In 2006, the Sangenic Nappy Disposal system won The Queen's Award for International Trade in recognition of the outstanding growth achieved internationally. In an independent survey of 110 users of the Sangenic Nappy Disposal System, 99 per cent said they would recommend the product (Source: Swift Research September 2011).

Recent Developments
In January 2011 Closer to Nature digital baby monitors, including one with a sensor pad to relay a baby's every sound and movement, were introduced. This was followed in February

Did You Know?

Tommee Tippee's first product was a weighted base cup and was so named because it didn't tip over.

Sangenic products wrapped up more than 350 million nappies in over 50 countries in 2010.

by the addition of a new hygiene range to the Closer to Nature portfolio, including long-lasting germ-busting surface sprays, hand gels and sterilants – all featuring a groundbreaking antibacterial agent that is being used for the first time in specialist baby products. November saw the introduction of a Closer to Nature digital ear thermometer, for an accurate, one-second read of baby's temperature.

Innovations unveiled in 2012 will include the Closer to Nature Video Monitor with Movement Sensor Pad and a new development within the breastfeeding range.

The Explora range was relaunched in November 2011 to include new products that make feeding easier for mums and babies, such as a baby food blender, pop-up food freezer pots, soft-tipped weaning spoons, and bowls that are designed to help a baby scoop out food.

The Sangenic range saw the introduction of a new out-of-home solution to hygienically wrapping nappies: the Wrap & Go Dispenser with antibacterial film.

In January 2012, Tommee Tippee extended its distribution in the North American market by partnering with a new retailer (in addition to its existing relationship with Toys R Us® USA).

Promotion
Tommee Tippee is one of the key sponsors of the UK Baby Shows, a series of consumer exhibitions attracting more than 75,000 parents and pregnant women every year. The brand also works closely with the top parenting titles

and has invested in a dynamic social media programme. In addition, its online presence – tommeetippee.com – currently operates in 21 countries.

A trained midwife works as the brand's health liaison manager, enabling a strong relationship with health professionals directly involved in the care and welfare of new babies.

Brand Values
Tommee Tippee products are designed to be Simply Intuitive™, making life easier for parents at every stage of a child's development. The brand's established reputation and continuing commitment to quality and innovation ensures that brand loyalty is passed not only from generation to generation but also from parent to parent.

Did You Know?

If you took all the Tommee Tippee cups sold in the UK in 2010 and laid them end-to-end, the line would stretch from London to Manchester (209 miles).

▶ **www.tommeetippee.com**

TONI&GUY™

TONI&GUY has long been renowned as an innovator within the hair industry, bridging the gap between high fashion and hairdressing. Widely regarded as the number one global hairdressing brand, Toni Mascolo's franchise model has maintained the company's high education and creative standards, protected the brand and made thousands of TONI&GUY hairdressing entrepreneurs a success worldwide.

Market

In the years since the birth of TONI&GUY, hairdressing has become a sophisticated industry worth billions, spawning some of the most influential and creative artists in the beauty and fashion sector. From individual salons to global chains, competition is fierce with both men and women now seeking quality and service.

TONI&GUY has helped to change the face of the hairdressing industry on an international scale and today has an annual turnover in excess of £185 million, with 226 salons and 42 essensuals salons in the UK, and 207 salons in 42 countries worldwide.

Product

TONI&GUY salons aim to offer a consistent level of service, guaranteed quality, exceptional cutting and innovative colour – in simple but well-designed salons and at an affordable price. All techniques practised by the stylists are taught by highly trained and experienced educators in 24 academies around the world.

A client's in-salon experience is enhanced by extras such as TONI&GUY.TV, TONI&GUY Magazine, and samples of luxury brands to take away. In addition, products from the professional label.m range – created and endorsed by Sacha Mascolo-Tarbuck and her International Artistic Team – can

be purchased in salons, enabling clients to replicate fashion-inspired styling at home.

Achievements

TONI&GUY has a worldwide brand presence and is recognised for its strong education network, currently operating 24 teaching academies globally – two in the UK and 22 internationally.

An average of 100,000 hairdressers are trained each year, with more than 5,500 employees in the UK and a further 3,500 worldwide. This philosophy of motivation, inspiration and education is seen as fundamental to the brand's success.

TONI&GUY has won in excess of 50 British Hairdressing regional and UK awards including Best Artistic Team a record 11 times and

Did You Know?

TONI&GUY has published 30 video/DVD educational collections and 34 collection books.

TONI&GUY educates more hairdressers than any other company in the world.

British Hairdresser of the Year three times. Co-founder and chief executive Toni Mascolo is a former winner of London Entrepreneur of the Year and in 2008 received an OBE in recognition of his services to the British hairdressing industry.

Toni's daughter, global creative director Sacha Mascolo-Tarbuck, was the youngest ever winner of Newcomer of the Year at just 19 years old. Other awards since include London Hairdresser of the Year 1999; Hair Magazine's Hairdresser of the Year 2007; Creative Head's Most Wanted Look of the Year in 2006 and its Most Wanted Hair Icon in 2009; and Fashion Focused Image of the Year from the Fellowship for British Hairdressing in 2008 as well as its 2010 Hairdresser of the Year.

TONI&GUY branded haircare products have received recognition through numerous trade and magazine awards over the years including accolades from Hair Magazine, Pure Beauty, Grazia, FHM, Beauty Magazine and Cosmopolitan to name a few.

In addition, the company was the first ever winner of Hair Magazine's Readers' Choice Award for Best UK Salon Group in 2006, a title it has since also been awarded by both Reveal and Your Hair Magazine.

Recent Developments

Social networking has become an important part of TONI&GUY's communications in recent years, with a presence on both Facebook and Twitter enabling the brand to engage more fully with its customers.

Did You Know?

TONI&GUY co-founder and chief executive Toni Mascolo still cuts hair once a week, alternating between London's Sloane Square and Mayfair salons.

Promotion

As a brand, TONI&GUY juggles the need for consistency, the desire to be fashionable and the reassurance of solid service values, with the excitement of the avant-garde, supported by its philosophy of continual education.

TONI&GUY Magazine was launched in 2003 to echo and communicate the brand's heritage and philosophy, focusing on key trends in fashion, the arts, beauty, grooming and travel. Distributed in salons across Europe and globally as far afield as Australasia, the magazine promotes an inspirational yet accessible face of the company to customers, employees and franchisees alike. In November 2004 it was named Launch of the Year at the APA Awards, while more recent wins include Best Consumer Publication in 2010 and 2011.

TONI&GUY.TV also launched in 2003, enhancing clients' in-salon experience. Containing up-to-the-minute content, from music to fashion and travel, it receives more than 90,000 views per week in the UK. It has also become an outlet for associated, appropriate brands to communicate to this sought-after audience and in 2010, won Best Use of Video at the APA Awards.

TONI&GUY remains committed to its vision to link the fashion industry with hairdressing through its sponsorship of London Fashion Week and London Fashion Weekend, a partnership that began in September 2004. The TONI&GUY session team works on more than 70 shows per year in London, New York,

Paris, Milan, Tokyo and Shanghai and offers support to key British design talent including Giles Deacon and Todd Lynn.

Brand Values

TONI&GUY's reputation has been built on an impeccable pedigree and foundation of education, fashion focus and friendly, professional service. TONI&GUY aims to encompass the importance of local and individually tailored, customer-led service, promoting an authoritative, cohesive and – most importantly – inspiring voice.

TONI&GUY is one of the most powerful hairdressing brands in the world, offering some of the best education and guaranteeing innovative cutting and colour. It aims to be fashionable but friendly to provide the ultimate link between fashion and hair – pioneering, passionate and inspirational.

▶ **www.toniandguy.co.uk**

Brand History

▶ **1963:** TONI&GUY is launched from a single unit in Clapham, South London by Toni Mascolo and his brother Guy.

▶ **1982:** The launch of the TONI&GUY Academy takes place.

▶ **1985:** TONI&GUY's first international salon opens in Tokyo, Japan.

▶ **2001:** The TONI&GUY signature haircare range is launched. The following year Toni and Pauline Mascolo launch the TONI&GUY Charitable Foundation.

▶ **2003:** TONI&GUY Magazine and TONI&GUY.TV are launched in the UK. The brand also expands into different markets, opening an optician and a deli-café.

▶ **2004:** TONI&GUY becomes Official Sponsor of London Fashion Week.

▶ **2005:** The professional haircare range, label.m, launches. It grows to include more than 45 products that are distributed in over 47 countries.

▶ **2007:** The Model.Me haircare range is launched, as is the TONI&GUY electrical line.

▶ **2008:** Toni Mascolo is awarded an OBE for his services to the British hairdressing industry.

▶ **2010:** Sacha Mascolo-Tarbuck and James Tarbuck join the British Fashion Council/Vogue Designer Fashion Fund, which supports new design talent. The company comprises 267 salons in the UK and 229 internationally.

▶ **2011:** TONI&GUY becomes Official Sponsor of the British Fashion Awards.

WARWICK BUSINESS SCHOOL

Warwick Business School (WBS) is the UK's top provider of finance and business research and education, and has the ambition and the capability to become Europe's leading university-based business school. Its mission is to publish leading-edge research that has real impact; to produce world-class business leaders; and to provide a lifelong return on investment for students, alumni and partners.

Market

WBS is one of the largest business schools in Europe, and offers the UK's top pure finance course (as ranked by the Financial Times in 2011). As the largest department of the University of Warwick, WBS offers both excellent facilities and a prestigious reputation to students and delegates who come from around 120 countries to learn at undergraduate, masters, MBA and PhD levels.

WBS academics produce world-leading research in all fields of management, which is why it attracts the very best PhD candidates. Ninety-seven per cent of full-time faculty who teach and research at WBS have PhDs and their doctoral community is thriving.

With recognised leaders in disciplines as diverse as behavioural science, innovation strategy, public sector governance, entrepreneurship, knowledge management, business strategy and finance,

Did You Know?

Professor Mark Taylor, Dean of WBS, was previously a managing director at BlackRock and is one of the most cited researchers in the world for finance and economics.

people go to WBS to explore grounded, well researched ideas that work in the real world. WBS research and expert opinion is valuable, sometimes crucial, to the success of corporations, not-for-profit organisations, the government and society.

Product

WBS has something to offer individuals at every stage of their career and currently offers 26 courses to more than 6,500 students, 65 per cent of whom are from outside the UK. It provides a range of business and management undergraduate degrees; a growing portfolio of specialist masters courses; a full-time MSc

in Management; the unique Warwick Global Energy MBA as well as the popular and flexible Warwick MBA; and one of the world's most respected PhD programmes.

For corporate clients and individuals, it also offers a range of diplomas, short courses and customised programmes. WBS consults with industry to keep its programmes fresh, relevant and accessible. The fact that many graduates return for further study at WBS later in their careers demonstrates its effective blend of academic research with the practicalities of the workplace. Alumni members, who number over 30,000, have cited the combination of a highly intelligent and internationally diverse cohort as being a major benefit of their learning experience.

Reduce your education miles: buy local, go global

Warwick Business School, based at the University of Warwick in Coventry, is in the top 1% of business schools worldwide.

Development & training – retain your staff
Recruitment opportunities – fresh talent hot off the press
Consultancy – sometimes free, always enlightening
Network – join our international business community

Call Kathryn Chedgzoy today
024 7615 0515
wbs.ac.uk/go/doorstep

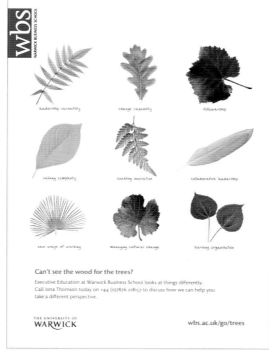

Can't see the wood for the trees?

Executive Education at Warwick Business School looks at things differently.
Call Iona Thomson today on +44 (0)7876 218157 to discuss how we can help you take a different perspective.

THE UNIVERSITY OF
WARWICK

wbs.ac.uk/go/trees

Achievements

WBS has achieved a global reputation for excellence in just 45 years. It has one of the broadest subject bases and most highly regarded faculty of any business school in the world. Its commitment to research is fundamental to its culture and differentiates it from teaching colleges and commercial training companies.

Its portfolio of 14 masters courses provides highly specialised learning in areas of business and management that are increasingly important in the search for sustainable competitive advantage.

More than 30 years of combined learning experience enables WBS to deliver the Warwick MBA to nearly 2,500 experienced managers each year, wherever they are in the world. The Warwick Global Energy MBA,

Did You Know?

WBS academics have written more than 120 books in the last five years and 3,857 papers in the last 12 months.

WBS is culturally diverse; more than a third of faculty have qualifications from international institutions, have worked abroad, or hold non-UK or joint nationality.

which is a groundbreaking programme that develops strategic leadership for the future energy industry, continues to expand and grow.

The reputation of WBS means its graduates are highly sought after by business leaders and can be found in senior positions around the world. Its expertise is clear from its diverse list of clients, partners and sponsors, including The Bank of England, Deloitte, E.ON, IBM, Islamic Bank of Britain, Johnson & Johnson, Nestlé, PepsiCo, Procter & Gamble, Rolls-Royce, the Royal Shakespeare Company, Santander and Vodafone.

Recent Developments

WBS celebrates its 45th anniversary in 2012 and its course portfolio continues to refresh, expand and diversify every year.

In 2011 the WBS bespoke online learning environment my.wbs reached its 10 millionth log-in. Over the last year it has been accessed by more than 14,000 students, staff and corporate partners; between them they logged in more than 700,000 times.

Promotion

WBS maintains a solid global presence with a range of below- and above-the-line segmented international marketing. Promotional materials have a contemporary and crisp feel and align WBS closely with the University of Warwick.

WBS uses many creative advertising channels but, ultimately, its highly successful graduates are its best adverts and advocates. They are hugely active within the WBS alumni network, in person and on LinkedIn, and many return for further study at WBS later in their career.

Brand Values

WBS has simple core values: excellence in all it does, an entrepreneurial spirit, encouraging fresh-thinking in staff and students, ensuring a positive impact from the ideas it creates, and continuing to be international and creative in outlook and approach. From these foundations WBS continues to challenge minds, change lives and create tomorrow's leaders.

▶ **www.wbs.ac.uk**

Found under sinks, in garages and in nearly every toolbox in the UK (Source: Synovate Research 2011), the world's number one multi-purpose maintenance product in the blue and yellow can is also one of the world's best-kept secrets, with only a few people party to its formula. It might have taken forty attempts to get it right, but WD-40 Multi-Use Product is now sold in 187 countries worldwide with its current 2,000 known uses being added to daily.

WD-40 ALSO CLEANS!

See what WD-40 Multi-Use Product also cleans at www.WD40.co.uk

PROTECTS | LUBRICATES | PENETRATES | DISPLACES MOISTURE | CLEANS   WD-40 TAKES CARE OF IT

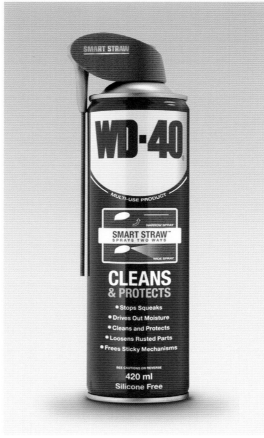

Market

WD-40 Multi-Use Product is distributed and sold across a number of key sectors within retail, trade and industry. The sheer breadth of its market reflects the brand's versatility while its consistently high sales figures – US$336.4 million in its 2010/11 fiscal year – are particularly strong in the current climate. Globally, 100 million cans of WD-40 were sold in 2011.

Product

WD-40 stands for 'water displacement – 40th attempt'. It's a product moniker that is a lasting legacy to the research and patience that went into its creation. Given the tremendous effort that went into perfecting WD-40, it's hardly surprising that it has stuck with its same winning formula since 1953.

WD-40 Multi-Use Product performs five key product functions – lubricating, penetrating, cleaning, protecting and displacing moisture – and is available in a range of sizes to meet the demands of different channels.

Achievements

WD-40's most notable achievement speaks for itself: a product that has not changed its formula for more than 50 years and still delivers. This dependability has fed into its high brand awareness – 92 per cent total UK brand awareness – and popularity, with 84 per cent of active DIY enthusiasts currently using the product (Source: Synovate Research 2011).

Yet despite this 'winning formula', it is not a brand that remains static – as demonstrated by the invention and engineering that has been invested in its recent product launch, the Smart Straw.

Recent Developments

Following customer feedback that they frequently lose the straw that comes with each can of WD-40 Multi-Use Product (for precision application), the brand has developed Smart Straw. This innovation offers a fixed applicator delivery system that enables the user to apply a wide spray for larger areas and a narrow spray for a more precise application.

A further key development, and a first in WD-40 history, is the launch of a new range of high quality, technical solutions that carry the famous WD-40 shield. Launched in January 2012, the WD-40 Specialist range is aimed at

Brand History

▶ **1953:** In San Diego, three employees of the Rocket Chemical Company take 40 attempts to get the right formula for a rust-prevention solvent and degreaser. They name it WD-40, which stands for 'water displacement – 40th attempt'. The product is so effective that employees begin to take it to use around the home.

▶ **1958:** WD-40 Multi-Use Product in an aerosol makes its first appearance on-shelf, following founder Norm Larsen's experiments to make the product available for home use.

▶ **1960:** The company grows in size to seven people, who sell an average of 45 cases per day from the boot of their cars.

▶ **1961:** Rocket Chemical Company employees work extra hours to produce concentrate to send to the victims of Hurricane Carla. Their first ever truckload of WD-40, it will be used to recondition vehicles damaged by the floods and rain.

▶ **1969:** The Rocket Chemical Company is renamed WD-40 Company in honour of its most successful product.

▶ **2005:** WD-40 Company launches Smart Straw, featuring a new dual action system with a permanently attached straw.

▶ **2012:** The WD-40 Specialist range of high quality, technical solutions aimed at industry and trade professionals launches in January.

industry and trade professionals and features a line-up of lubricants, greases and cleaners, all of which have been formulated to deliver outstanding performance across a diverse range of tasks.

Promotion

The WD-40 brand has grown into the household name it is today largely through word-of-mouth promotion. With five primary functions to choose from, new uses for the product are continually being discovered.

Interestingly, research carried out by the company revealed that WD-40's cleaning function is one of the product's least known attributes, yet it is the one that offers the largest volume growth potential because of its effectiveness. Avid WD-40 users have passed the product down through generations, but their children and grandchildren still tend to use it today for similar tasks every time and in a familiar, conventional way – for instance, to resolve a squeaky door hinge or to loosen a nut and bolt. This has prompted WD-40 Company to embark on one of the hardest journeys for a brand: re-educating its end users.

In a time of uncertainty, the WD-40 brand has successfully launched its first ever national above-the-line advertising campaign, which has been designed to address this issue and to encourage more maintenance and repair in today's throwaway culture. The company has also striven to educate consumers on new uses within high areas of relevance, particularly in automotive, cycling, tools and industry, where the product can really help to save time and money.

WD-40 Company has worked with sponsors to contextualise and increase awareness of its product within these targeted areas. Through a brand partnerships initiative, WD-40 is also looking to work with synergistic brands in a mutually beneficial way.

Brand Values

When it comes to brand values WD-40 Company believes, like its product, in keeping it simple. It's all about reliability: getting the job done, doing it well and delivering on promises. Dependability is a key trait that has been integral to the brand's ethos since its inception. For nearly 60 years, and without the help of expensive gimmicks, brand values have been reflected through product performance. Straightforward and trustworthy, WD-40 Multi-Use Product enables its customers to get jobs done – and to do them well.

▶ **www.wd40.co.uk**

Did You Know?

WD-40 Multi-Use Product has five key functions: lubricating, penetrating, cleaning, protecting and displacing moisture.

A bus driver in Asia used it to remove a python that had coiled itself around the undercarriage of his bus.

Police officers once used it to remove a naked burglar trapped in an air conditioning vent.

It can remove chewing gum from a pair of jeans.

WEBER SHANDWICK

Weber Shandwick is a full service global communications agency, building and protecting brand and company reputations. It puts ideas at the heart of its business; ideas that create movements, change attitudes and behaviour, and transform through powerful engagement. Its creative talent, communications expertise and specialist teams work for some of the most innovative brands and biggest organisations in the private, public and not-for-profit sectors.

Market

Despite the continued economic climate of the past 12 months, and against a backdrop of flat budgets, the UK public relations (PR) market continued to grow steadily in size and diversity in 2011.

Many companies and organisations are switching their marketing resources from traditional advertising to other channels that live in today's peer-to-peer and engagement-driven world. Key growth areas for the industry in 2012 will therefore continue to include digital and social communications, consumer and sports marketing, and corporate reputation.

The UK consultancy sector currently supports hundreds of marketing-oriented PR firms, from one-man operations to UK-only agencies and international players.

Product

Internationally, Weber Shandwick maintains the largest PR network in the world. With a core of 85 owned offices in 41 countries and affiliates that expand the network to 129 offices in 81 countries, Weber Shandwick operates in virtually every major media, government and business centre on six continents.

In the UK, Weber Shandwick has a number of specialist practice groups including digital and social media communications, consumer marketing, technology PR, healthcare PR, financial communications, corporate communications and public affairs.

With offices in London, Manchester, Glasgow, Edinburgh, Aberdeen, Inverness, Belfast and Dublin, it also offers a strong regional network. Other specialisms include cross-practice consultancy in multicultural and internal

communications, crisis and issues management, corporate social responsibility, cleantech, strategic planning, over-fifties marketing, broadcast PR, sports PR and market research.

Achievements

Engaging ideas are at the heart of Weber Shandwick's business, for which it frequently receives industry recognition.

On an international level, Weber Shandwick was recently named Best Large Agency to Work For by The Holmes Report, Digital Firm of the Year by PR News, and one of Mashable's Top Four Employers for Social Media Professionals.

Did You Know?

Part of the Interpublic Group of marketing companies, Weber Shandwick works closely with sister companies McCann Erickson (advertising), FutureBrand (branding consultancy), Jack Morton (event management) and Octagon (sports marketing) to deliver truly integrated client campaigns.

Did You Know?

In 2011, European and UK CEO Colin Byrne was named one of GQ's Most Influential Men in Britain for the eighth consecutive year.

In the UK alone, Weber Shandwick won more than 20 industry accolades for client work in 2011 including: Outstanding Public Relations Consultancy at the CIPR PRide Awards (Scotland); Best Sponsorship Campaign at the IPRA Golden World Awards; Best Public Affairs Campaign and Best Broadcast Campaign at the PRCA Awards; and three European SABRE Awards including Best pan-European Programme.

The Holmes Report said the firm "is an industry giant not only in terms of size but also – more importantly – in terms of quality, having consistently outperformed the market over the past five years and established itself as a leader and thought leader around the world".

Brand History

▶ **1974:** Shandwick International is established in London with a single client and a global vision.

▶ **1987:** The Weber Group is founded in Cambridge, Massachusetts as a communications agency for emerging technology companies. In less than a decade it goes on to become a top 10 PR firm.

▶ **1998:** Shandwick International is acquired by the Interpublic Group.

▶ **2000:** Shandwick International merges with The Weber Group and becomes Weber Shandwick.

▶ **2001:** BSMG Worldwide merges with Weber Shandwick.

▶ **2011:** Celebrating its 10th anniversary in the UK, Weber Shandwick continues to win leading industry awards and is recognised for its work internationally.

Recent Developments

To build on its reputation for excellence in traditional PR, Weber Shandwick continues to invest in innovation and thought leadership, setting a new agenda for the future of the PR industry.

In 2011, Weber Shandwick launched Creation @ Weber Shandwick, a brand experience business supported by a full-scale, end-to-end production team. Working across the firm's client base, the specialist team provides live, digital, technology, content and programming solutions to clients' needs. Specific capabilities include: broadcast content creation and editing; creative film and viral production; product placement and TV format creation; motion graphics and animation; web, app and mobile design and build; event management; stage production; and high-impact experiential marketing.

builds stories by identifying audiences, creating content in the right format and picking the best channels through which to drive those stories.

2011 also saw the launch of FireBell, Weber Shandwick's award-winning social media crisis simulator. In an age of real-time information, brands and companies are more at risk than ever to viral attacks from unexpected sources that demand ever-faster responses. FireBell is a software application that simulates PR crisis situations, including viral media attacks across multiple social media platforms.

Brand Values

Weber Shandwick's values are creativity, innovation, passion and commitment.

As one of the world's leading communications agencies, 2011 saw Weber Shandwick continue to grow, invest, innovate and prosper. It has continued to build on its reputation for excellence in traditional PR to set a new agenda for the future of the industry. The past 12 months have seen the company expand its global network, launch new products and services, invest in its people and increase collaboration between its offices.

Did You Know?

Organisations benefiting from Weber Shandwick's Making a Difference programme, which encourages its employees to do pro-bono and community relations work, have included The Moyer Foundation, World Wildlife Fund, Habitat for Humanity, and War Child.

▶ **www.webershandwick.co.uk**

In the run up to the London 2012 Olympic and Paralympic Games an Olympics marketing offering has been added to the UK Sports PR practice, providing organisations and industry bodies with a unique insight into Games marketing and helping them to navigate the surrounding complexities. Specialist consultancy services include strategic communications planning, brand marketing, sponsorship activation, athlete profiling, digital communications, event management and community engagement.

Promotion

Fusions between marketing disciplines, content formats and the very notion of publishing mean that organisations need a new approach to take full advantage. To help navigate this area, Weber Shandwick developed Content Fusion. A proprietary methodology, Content Fusion

A Decent Proposal

By Tim Bourne
CEO
Exposure

Hardly a week goes by, it seems, without an announcement of a new brand collaboration. In fact, the top 500 Global companies have, on average, 60 major strategic alliances each. But perhaps the more pertinent question to ask is, how many of them actually work and how well?

According to previous studies (Dyer, Prashant, Singh), almost 50 per cent of the strategic alliances of Fortune 500 companies fail. But when they do work, they work so well that investors notice average stock price increases of US$54 million upon the announcement of a significant new alliance. When Nike formed its partnership with Apple, sales of the resulting product topped 56 million in 2008 alone.

Such successful brand partnerships do not happen by accident. They are built upon solid strategic foundations, with clear objectives beyond the overall aim to contribute commercial value. In general terms, there appear to be four main strategic themes: creating new distribution channels and reaching new audiences; cost and resource sharing; enhanced performance and/or acquiring new product attributes; and competitive advantage in commoditised categories.

> "Successful brand partnerships do not happen by accident. They are built upon solid strategic foundations, with clear objectives beyond the overall aim to contribute commercial value."

As companies face up to the twin challenges of austerity and increased competition, driven in part by technological convergence, there has perhaps never been a more important time to consider who you can build a strategic alliance with. This article aims to provide some guidance through the cluttered terrain of brand partnerships.

In working towards some core principles for ensuring any proposal to a prospective brand partner is a decent one, let us learn from some of the most interesting examples of strategic alliances from a varied set of categories.

Ambi Pur and National Geographic

The Ambi Pur National Geographic range includes two fragrances: Japan Tatami, inspired by the soothing aroma of Japanese Tatami mats, and Nevada Desert Flower, inspired by a rare flower that only blossoms after heavy winter rain in the Nevada Desert. The emphasis is very much on the natural world: both fragrances are available in a range of formats, including candles made with natural vegetable wax, all packaged in recycled and recyclable materials. These products bring a new experiential element to the home fragrance arena, which could have the potential for a broader customer base. National Geographic may also gain new readership through exposure to a different audience.

National Geographic is a well established and respected publication. Renowned as an expert in the fields of exploration and experience, it is a name

known for transparent, cultural reporting (Source: Mintel 2009). Through the partnership, Ambi Pur has brought some much needed authenticity to the home fragrance market, while also connecting with the current 'natural' trend. National Geographic, meanwhile, will be able to diversify its revenue out of the ever-shrinking print magazine business.

Coca-Cola and Karl Lagerfeld

In 2011 Coca-Cola launched 'Love It Light', a fashion campaign giving consumers the opportunity to build their relationship with fashion in a fun way through unique properties and inspiring and engaging content. The campaign includes TV, out-of-home, designer collaboration and partnership, experiential and sampling as well as a brand new digital and interactive fashion platform. The digital platform gives consumers access to daily fashion features, news and reviews of the latest trends, and video content. It is also available as an app for smartphones.

The campaign builds on the strong fashion heritage of the Coca-Cola Light/Diet Coke brand, which includes associations with Manolo Blahnik, Patricia Field and Helena Christensen. This time, Coca-Cola Light/Diet Coke is collaborating with Karl Lagerfeld, the legendary and iconic designer. Karl Lagerfeld has designed three unique bottles, each based on the distinctive personalities of the Coca-Cola Light/Diet Coke girls – three stylish puppets that have been used by the brand since 2010.

Missoni and Target

For Missoni, the partnership was about generating awareness in the huge and largely untapped North American marketplace. It was a chance to reach an audience 50 times the size of its current one, with minimal marketing spend.

For Target, this was another opportunity to bolster its value message with the kind of design and premium associations that ensure differentiation from arch-rival Walmart. And a rare chance to entice the metropolitan fashionista back into Target and to convince her that this is a place where she can shop for staples and not feel embarrassed.

Nokia and Microsoft

It's a partnership that would, perhaps, have been unthinkable in Nokia's heyday at the start of the millennium. But commentators are now going so far as to suggest that Nokia's agreement to exclusively use Windows Phone 7 as the operating system inside its smartphones is its last chance to turn things around.

What is certain is that Microsoft will give Nokia's new range of high capability handsets a much needed technological advantage by using Microsoft's huge muscle. It will also provide Nokia with the opportunity to reach out to the huge base of consumers who currently use Microsoft Windows 7 in their PCs, offering them an integrated operating system across mobile phone and PC.

AkzoNobel and Ralph Lauren

By introducing its home furnishings and decorating paint in the 1990s, Ralph Lauren was a pioneer in high quality, premium priced paint and faux finishes.

The Ralph Lauren brand name and fashion credentials enabled AkzoNobel to attract a whole new segment of home shoppers and importantly, increase the price premium of an otherwise commodity product. Ralph Lauren benefited from superior technical product knowledge, legal and logistics, manufacturing facilities as well as the distribution network of the multibrand paint and chemicals producer.

What does this all mean?

These are just a handful of the hundreds of alliances brands are currently exploiting; the list and learnings go on. But it's time to make some sense of all these examples. If you are planning to enter into a brand partnership, how do you ensure your alliance is a success and not a waste of valuable financial and human resource?

Principles of partnership planning

▶ Clarify and quantify what you aim to achieve. Define precise measurable targets and methods of objective evaluation.
▶ Ensure you have secured stakeholder buy-in to objectives and partner targets prior to entering into any discussions.
▶ Approach negotiation as a trade of assets and where possible, define the commercial value of those assets.
▶ Identify what assets you have at your disposal to share (and any that will be regarded as off limits – for example, celebrity endorsement contracts often prevent sharing of talent associations with partners).

"As companies face up to the twin challenges of austerity and increased competition, there has perhaps never been a more important time to consider who you can build a strategic alliance with."

▶ Identify what you want from the partner and bring these into the negotiation at an early stage (this will save considerable time).
▶ Recognise that a 'fair exchange' is the only partnership negotiation that is likely to deliver sustained success.
▶ Identify whether the values of your partner are consistent with your own. Corporate ethics, social responsibility and attitude to risk should all be considered.

In practice, we have found that once you enter the negotiation process there are a few key principles that will help to define whether or not you will come out with a happy and sustainable marriage.

Principles of partnership negotiation

▶ Understand your partner's business intimately, including business strategy, production process and lead times, supply chain management, corporate structure, approval systems and measurement methods.
▶ Aim to get out only as much as you put into the relationship.
▶ Plan as far ahead as possible. Negotiation generally takes about twice as long as you expect. Once into production you will be forced to work to the pace of the slowest production process.
▶ Seek a partnership with a company that you admire and with which you share consistent values.

Images courtesy of Coca-Cola and Nokia

Playing the Culture Game

By Jack Horner
Co-Founder & Creative Director
FRUKT

With London gearing up to enjoy the unprecedented arrival of the most iconic and illustrious event in the sporting calendar this summer, you'd be forgiven for assuming that the absolute focus is on the action on the track and field. But you'd be wrong. This is not merely a celebration of athletic achievement on a Herculean scale; this is also a vast opportunity to connect with impassioned fans of entertainment and culture, not just in the UK, but also across the globe.

A universal language

The core foundations of the Olympic Games are rooted in sport in the strict sense; the discipline of human athletic achievement in clearly defined areas. However, the broader Olympic experience has now evolved into an unparalleled global entertainment event that extends well beyond the individual prowess of shot putters and high jumpers. The Olympic authorities and host nations have been steadily increasing the weight of cultural legacy versus sporting legacy with every Games, creating a melting pot of culture that offers unprecedented scope for robust, emotional connections with passionate fans of entertainment. Yes, sport clearly has entertainment value of its own, however it's the use of music, film and art by brands around the Olympics that provides tangible, inclusive value for wider audiences – turning a collection of niche events into an accessible, entertaining whole.

Never before in the history of marketing have brands been so eagerly invited into the cultural spaces coveted by the general public. We conducted some research last year into the relationship between brands and audiences in the UK and found that a resounding 91 per cent are positive about brand involvement in entertainment and culture. This wave of acceptance now offers a plethora of opportunities for brands to engage in broader entertainment marketing – not just because it adds credibility, but also because there is a genuine return on investment to be gained.

We believe that when people are being entertained, they are happy, positive, grateful, more receptive to messages, more inclined to share their experience and more likely to try something new. It's an incredible state of being which, if harnessed and used sensitively, can be exceptionally powerful for brands.

> "Entertainment is universal; it provides a window on the world that everyone can access, that transcends culture, demographic or economic background."

In order to create moments of heightened entertainment opportunity on a wide scale, there needs to be a trigger, an event that inspires and gives focus. These events, such as the World Cup or the Olympics, offer strong foundations, however it is entertainment that provides the inclusive platform. For example, the two-billion-strong audience for the opening ceremony of the Beijing Olympics outstripped every other event because it had a universal appeal beyond other, often polarising, sporting activities. Arguably, it's entertainment here that acts as the social glue, not the event itself.

Driving the world's biggest brands

To put our argument to the test we decided to analyse the companies in the higher echelons of the Consumer Superbrands list to see how entertainment impacted on their status. A sizeable 90 per cent of the top 10 brands have forged a distinct alignment with entertainment in order to reach consumers, with a further 72 per cent of the top 50 brands having utilised entertainment, be it music, film or art, in their marketing efforts.

Images provided by Coca-Cola

Rolex, at the pinnacle of this year's list, has placed cultural support for the arts at the core of its brand, setting in motion the Rolex Mentor and Protégé Arts Initiative in 2002, delivering a year-long programme of creative collaboration between upcoming artists and mentors across dance, film, literature, music, theatre and the visual arts. Overall, the luxury timepiece brand has forged alignments with some 150 varying entertainment platforms, from sponsoring Olympic-standard sailing to supporting concert orchestras, delivering a diverse portfolio of cultural assets.

Closely contesting Rolex for the top spot is Coca-Cola, a brand that was recently name-checked as the most recognised Olympic Games sponsor. So what sets the drinks brand apart so firmly in the minds of consumers? As part of the Coca-Cola team delivering their Olympic activity, as well as broader music and cultural marketing initiatives around the world, I believe the reason for their success lies in their ability to make global events more relevant to a broader, and critically, younger audience. Coca-Cola understood that the last Football World Cup was not as much about football as the engagement with football, and the applauded 'What's Your Celebration?' campaign played this out. The activation's global music release (K'naan's 'Wavin' Flag') and the overriding notion of celebration in many ways became elevated above football

as a unifying theme. Brands like Coca-Cola have grasped naturally the notion that you need to deliver something more, something rooted in the emotion and culture of the once-in-a-lifetime event, yet going beyond the subject matter of an event that can polarise interest.

Coca-Cola's 'Future Flames' campaign – which saw it partner with key British music talent (Dizzee Rascal, Eliza Doolittle, The Wanted and You Me At Six) to promote a search for inspirational young people to carry the Olympic Flame during the London 2012 Olympic Torch Relay – is a case in point, developing an inclusive celebratory event focused on people, not individual sporting activities. Likewise, 'Move to the Beat', which saw producer Mark Ronson working with five global Olympic athletes and singer Katy B on a new music anthem, further leverages accessible entertainment value around the iconic sporting event.

BMW is yet another in the Consumer Superbrands top 10 that has a long and varied association with entertainment, having championed innovative film-makers, sponsored live concerts and pioneered global art experiences. The German auto manufacturer is also no stranger to leveraging entertainment around the Olympic Games, having hosted community celebrations at local dealerships during the run-up to the 1996 Summer Olympics in Atlanta.

And the list goes on across the top 50; from those with a direct affiliation with entertainment, such as the BBC, Apple and Google, to pioneering brands such as Guinness, Nike and Jack Daniel's, each has a foot firmly in the door of entertainment.

Investing in smart entertainment

Entertainment is universal; it provides a window on the world that everyone can access, that transcends culture, demographic or economic background. Where sport can often polarise opinion, entertainment unifies.

Brands now have a vital role to play in nurturing, curating and syndicating the next generation of entertainment for an audience that thrives on being brought closer to areas such as sport, music, art and film. It's no longer about sponsoring from the sidelines and dipping in for a fleeting moment of PR; it's about making a deeper and more visible commitment to culture and the role it actively plays in people's lives.

To put it in its simplest terms, entertainment and culture are good for business. They have the ability to provide that most elusive and sought after return on investment – a long-term emotional connection. To bring it back to the Olympics, entertainment is the spark that fires the flame, a flame that lights a pathway to a more passionate relationship between audiences and brands.

FRUKT

FRUKT helps some of the biggest brands in the world deliver smart entertainment marketing solutions. From conception through to activation, FRUKT creates ideas that deliver against brand and business challenges. Its clients include Coca-Cola, Nokia, Diesel, Carlsberg and Microsoft – for whom it has created award-winning integrated platforms spanning Live, Digital, ATL, In-store and more, across 150 countries.

▶ **www.fruktcomms.com**

Discounting Cut-price Culture

By Emma Wright Managing Director Publicasity PR

Protecting brand equity in a recession is mission critical. But how do we resist the temptation to try to increase sales through discounting?

Price-led promotions are a PR nightmare waiting to happen, although unfortunately a necessary evil for many. While driving short-term sales spikes, they rarely translate into loyal brand advocacy and can genuinely damage reputation in the long term. What happens when things eventually look brighter? Reinstating a premium takes significant investment and is for the medium to long haul – if it can be regained at all, that is. Often expedient discounting is only a one-way fix.

It is a sad reality that marketing budgets often get slashed as a recession deepens, and the temptation to provide value and discount offers increases. However, this is dangerous territory as brands become less visible and consumers become more and more promiscuous in their buying behaviour. Are we not doing what the banking sector did four years ago by sacrificing long-term growth for short-term gain?

The strongest brands know that during tough times, smart investment in better understanding consumer insights and responding with above- and below-the-line communications leads, in turn, to improved market share and return on investment (while competitors are cutting back). Recession can often serve to kill off weaker brands as consumers crave the reassurance and familiarity of a trusted name.

However, at what point does price become the deciding factor when paying for a brand? With commodity prices increasing across the board, as well as inflation running above pay rises (with more redundancies around the corner), is there a tipping point when consumers feel compelled to trade down and ignore the role of brand? With no spare money, how can the average household find cash for the premium goods that are paradoxically needed to spur the recovery?

Economics dictate that there is no one rule for any group of customers; the marketer has to get their marketing and pricing strategy aligned and 'on the money'. It is this 'feel', backed up by research, that provides some brands with the opportunity to eschew pricing promotions

> **"Price-led promotions rarely translate into loyal brand advocacy and can genuinely damage reputation in the long term."**

first and look at the longer game of maintaining or elevating their brands to 'must have' status. Premium brands that have stood the test of time know how to achieve this and resist the pressure to discount from shareholders, retail channels and others who believe that cutting prices is a one-way bet on sales. It isn't. The answer lies instead in offering genuinely valuable and complimentary rewards in return for brand loyalty.

Future-proofing your brand

It's not easy, of course. It takes nerves of steel and an absolute belief in what is the very essence of your brand. Here are some brand management principles that we advocate to help brands secure a foothold in the future:

▶ Continuing to build strong emotional connection and engagement is key; consumers are actively seeking brands that they believe in and want to be part of.

▶ Online marketing and buzz is critical, with a focus on understanding niche markets. More and more programming, content and forums will be experience-focused and will develop around cultural and social trends – watch out for everything from ZUMBA TV to the Cheese Tasting Channel!

clearly differentiating itself from the 'big three' supermarkets, which focus on price. (As this article was being researched, Waitrose had just announced a £1 billion investment in the UK with 100 new stores being rolled out in the North of England despite the deepening financial gloom.)

Clearly these brands have got their marketing right in tough times and are bucking the trend, so imagine what benefits they will reap when the markets eventually start to recover!

In conclusion

The bottom line is that brands must passionately advocate why they are singularly unique and special, and avoid if possible the 'buy one get one free' threat to brand marketing. Establishing a long-lasting reputation and proposition is mission critical if you are to build value into the future, as is a commitment to consistently delivering quality customer service. Do or die, otherwise you will run the risk of not being around for the next economic upturn.

▶ Customer experience and brand entertainment will be one of the main battlegrounds, both for building the customer base and for keeping consumers loyal, as our lives are led on and offline simultaneously.

▶ An internal culture will become more transparent to the outside world. If there is any inconsistency between what a brand promises and what is delivered, this will be exposed with potentially huge consequences for reputation.

▶ The holy grail for brands will be owning the end-to-end customer experience. Customer service can no longer sit separate to customer marketing, and PR continues to be the heartbeat of a brand's reputation.

▶ Integrity and consistency of message will remain key across all communications.

▶ Brands should ensure their architecture is simplified as they evolve, merge and acquire new businesses. Less really is more.

▶ Do or die; brands need to be passionate about what they stand for and stick to it.

▶ Brands must protect themselves from the worldwide threat of counterfeiting. Fakes can

disintegrate a brand overnight, especially if the consumer isn't aware the product is a fake – or starts to believe the price compromise is worth it.

▶ Peer-to-peer pressure will become more important as we strive to hold on to the luxuries that were once seen as an essential part of our everyday lives and defined our social standing.

And the winners are....

I believe there are some obvious brands that are really benefiting from applying some or all of these principles. Clear winners include the likes of:

Costa – its focus has been to never compromise on quality and to offer a flexible retailing format, partnering with many outlets to meet consumers' thirst for convenience and great coffee on the go.

Kia – the car manufacturer offers value but is also uncompromising on quality, reassuring purchasers with a seven-year warranty. In September 2011 it launched the world's most fuel-efficient car, the Rio.

Waitrose – the brand has made a niche out of offering a premium product and service,

Publicasity PR is a brand marketing and communications agency, offering the perfect mix of on and offline PR, social media, experiential, design and brand protection. Its campaigns don't just amplify a brand's activity; they win over hearts and minds to create loyal brand advocates, drive click-through and most importantly, generate sales – all backed by the Publicasity ROI guarantee.

Publicasity's clients encompass such well known names as Heinz, Bacardi Brown-Forman, United Biscuits, Wrigley, South Africa Tourism, Chelsea Football Club, Kia Motors, Rigby & Peller and Travis Perkins.

Proud to be an independent agency, it is ranked 25th in the PR Week Consumer League Table 2011.

▶ **www.publicasity.com**

Random Acts of Creativity

By Charli Matthews
Trainer & Writer
The Writer

Betfair Poker isn't, perhaps, the place you'd look for poetic ramblings and entertaining tidbits, but they say:

@**Betfairpoker** When it's this hot, it reminds me of my childhood as a gang member in New York. It was the 1860s and I was Leonardo di Caprio.

@**Betfairpoker** I stare out of my window. The sun refracts off a raindrop, splitting into tiny rainbows, bathing the office in colour. My sandwich is stale.

The BBC has an 'award-winning travel tweeting service'. They say things like:

@**BBCTravelAlert** Circle line with minor anticlockwise delays, after earlier 'dicky ticker' signals. Crow-barring 'Allo Allo!' phrases in today.

@**BBCTravelAlert** The Underground railway isn't available at Liverpool Street at present whilst the fire alarms reverberate within.

Tim Pinn works for Transport for London at Warwick Avenue tube station. Three years ago he started writing messages on the information board. He's done it every day since.

His messages say things like, 'You've given work enough for the day, the rest of it is yours for the evening.' As a result he won a London Transport Award for his 'excellent rapport with customers'. He's even had a Facebook page set up in his honour.

If only more brands allowed their people to do something creative and individual.

But here lies the problem. How does that sit with brand guidelines, style guides and your tone of voice? Surely it's breaking the rules. Well, yes. Technically. But I think what we think of as 'tone of voice' has moved on somewhat.

It used to be that a brand was monolithic and all about consistency across territories, media, audiences, etc. A brand in the 21st century is more about being a collection of people. Increasingly, brands are recognising the value of things that 'don't fit'.

Getting your people to understand and use guidelines gives you consistency. But the best guidelines will give people the confidence to go

beyond the rules and show flashes of creativity. Sometimes radical. And the best brands out there are giving their people the power to decide when it's right to break the rules. It's like the rules of grammar. It's only when you understand them that you can play with them.

You can start giving people that power. Here are a few ideas on how:

> "A brand in the 21st century is more about being a collection of people. Increasingly, brands are recognising the value of things that 'don't fit'."

Lead by example
Nokia's CEO, Stephen Elop, caused a stir with his brutally honest memo to all staff. In it he talks about how Nokia is seriously lagging behind the likes of Apple and Microsoft. The whole memo is built around a metaphor. There's a man stuck on a burning oil platform. He has a choice: he can stay on the rig and die, or take his chances in the icy waters below. 'We had a series of misses,' Elop writes. 'We haven't been delivering innovation fast enough. We're not collaborating internally. Nokia, our platform is burning.'

He did something different. Something genuinely surprising. And he got the attention not just of the Nokia employees, but the entire world.

He's given people the confidence to talk about Nokia's problems in a radically different way.

Reward personality

When someone does a good job, tell them. In fact tell everyone. At Testway Housing, an association we worked with, they had the Tone Awards. Each month someone was picked out for a good piece of writing they'd done. The award was an Action Man (called Tone) strapped to a bit of wood. It sounds silly, but Tone was coveted and it made people think more about their writing and ways to be unexpected.

Free people from the rules

One of our clients had a company-wide template for their out of office messages. We encouraged them to do away with it. They did and this is the sort of thing their people now say:

I'm in Wales and either:
a) Lost
b) In a field (slightly lost)
c) On a horse (very lost)
d) Bobbing in the sea (exceedingly lost)

Urgent? Come out and find me. Or contact someone from my team. I'm back Monday 15 Aug.

Others have thrown out the usual puffed up job titles and let people write their own. One of our clients at a technology services company has an email signature that signs her off as an 'Internal Comms Bod'.

Get the right people

Your people should reflect your company. So your ads should set the tone. They're your filter. If your applicants 'get' you and your business, it'll show in their language.

For the people you already have, encourage the ones who can bring to life what you're about. And help the ones who can't. That doesn't mean you send people on a mandatory 'how to be unexpected in your words' workshop*. Do something different. Get in a writer, a poet, a stand-up comedian. Anything you can do to get people to think a little harder about the way they express themselves.

Measure success

Lots of our clients have got into the habit of measuring how better writing helps their businesses. For example, they've measured call handling times when they've rewritten their call centre scripts. But few, yet, measure the impact of a bit of unexpected creativity.

We did. Our MD had a slightly bonkers two-page out of office. It was about him being stuck at home with the kids, with nappies and finger paints and the like. It went to a potential client. Then it went viral and was sent on to hundreds of people. Off the back of it, we won a big project. And later, when it came to looking

over our lead generation, we made sure we logged that it was 'Martin's mad out of office' that won us the business. So measure what good writing does. But measure the unusual too.

M&S hit the headlines, nationally, when one of their customer advisors sent out a hand-drawn smiling dinosaur after a customer complained about being overcharged and asked for a hand-drawn smiling dinosaur. I wonder if they recorded what a massive and positive impact that had on their brand? They should have.

Because this is what it comes down to. We're so used to businesses missing the mark, that when one does something different and gets it right, we find it disproportionately charming. So: encourage your people to break your rules. That's the new rule.

*But if you want one, we can run it for you.

> "This is what it comes down to ... Encourage your people to break your rules. That's the new rule."

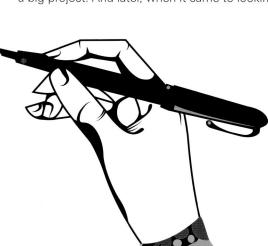

TheWriter™

The Writer does three things:

1. Thinking. It helps people shape messages, stories and brands.

2. Writing. Everything from crisp packets to bids.

3. Training. It helps people become more effective, more confident, engaging writers.

The Writer is on a mission to fight against the lazy, the boring, the ineffective, the expected. To rescue its clients from the tyranny of corporatespeak. In its place, it helps people use words to change how people see them, to make and save them money, and to change how their people feel. And it does it with people like the BBC, Virgin, The Economist and Twinings.

▶ **www.thewriter.com**

From Super Brand to Social Brand

By Adele Gritten
Head of Media & Financial Services
Consulting, YouGov

The next generation of marketing

Since 2008 and the near collapse of global capital markets, brands have had an increasingly tough time. Maintaining cut-through and increasing share is the brand marketer's biggest headache as consumer wallets continue to take a hit, and as the certainty of continuing Western prosperity and long-term economic growth is increasingly under the spotlight both financially and morally.

Despite such immediate woes and long-term risks, the history of brand marketing should be celebrated. Marketers should be pleased how far they came in a century that not only saw the proliferation of product choice due to mass production capabilities and the explosion of technology, but also witnessed the birth of the globally interconnected – and thus socially aware – consumer. It is easy to forget that it is only 70 years since the world's first TV ad was aired, when the watchmaker Bulova paid US$9 for a placement on New York station WNBT before a baseball game between the Brooklyn Dodgers and Philadelphia Phillies on 1st July 1941. Now, consumers are exposed daily to thousands of commercial messages, whether analogue or digital, whether via paid, owned or earned media messaging, and across multiple platforms and devices.

While the media and communications landscape has evolved rapidly, brands have been dissected in various guises. Since the 1950s in particular, marketers have explored brand environment, equity, ethics, evolution, experience, identity, loyalty, personality, positioning, power, psychology, sensory capabilities, strength and value, to name but a few in purely alphabetical order. Brand theorists have looked at corporate brands, challenger brands, people brands, experiential brands and until very recently, the monolithic brands. Google, Facebook and Apple are often cited here.

As we enter uncharted territory beyond capitalism, or at least its next stage, brands face new challenges. The global balance of power is changing, with the rise of the East and decline of the West well documented. In Europe and the US, consumers are increasingly reflecting on their relationship with capitalism and corporatism, making use of social media to exchange thoughts, ideas and plans with other consumers across the globe. We are entering an era in which social media rivals traditional media as the lead communications channel in which brands can talk to consumers, and vice versa.

> "Social Brands are malleable and versatile. They are different things to different people at different points in time and space."

This is the era of the Social Brand. Social Brands are malleable and versatile. They are different things to different people at different points in time and space. They can be accessed via multiple media touch points. They can help both to build communities and to be an integral part of communities. They can entice brand champions and advocates but are equally comfortable in responding to their detractors. Perhaps most importantly, Social Brands are highly sociable and positively responsive.

They value the voices of their supporters but learn from the criticisms of their detractors. They focus on delivering high-impact, high-quality and specifically targeted messages, both personalising and generalising in equal measure, according to the mood of the day or the needs of a campaign. Their true value is distributed amongst their multiple stakeholders and users.

In short, Social Brands are disciplined and high-performing phenomena. Academic theory tells us that brands perform according to three criteria: as cultural performances they are efficacious; as managerial performances they are efficient; and as technological performances they are effective. Harnessing all three modes of high performance turns Super Brands into Super Social Brands.

Today's consumers want to engage with brands on their own terms: when it is convenient for them, whether in the middle of the night or early morning, whether from the office in their lunch hour, from the smartphone on the train on the way home from work, or from the laptop or tablet in bed on a weekend morning. Social Brands fully embrace this shift in the way in which consumers want to engage and transact, to be listened to and treated. Today's consumers are no longer passive; they produce activity and interaction: they are literally 'prosumers'. These consumers are preparing themselves for the emerging 4G world. Some brand categories – media, music and entertainment, for example – are significantly ahead of the curve compared to others, such as financial services, in truly demonstrating that they have fully taken on board what it means to be a Social Brand.

Social Brands achieve cut-through not only by being social per se, but by using social media purposefully, efficiently and creatively in line with their brand mission. They use social and traditional media to both listen to and respond to consumers' voices. They aim for transparency and honesty in terms of customer interaction. They are responsive and show that they value their customers and understand the power of the collective consumer voice, which is increasingly exercising itself online.

Today's Social Brands are in a powerful position. They have more control than ever over the people they can reach, with the ability to

target above and beyond demographics and the opportunity to leverage individual personal interests. They can also harness for their own benefit the content that is shared by people via social media. Crucially, they can deepen and extend their relationship with consumers well beyond exploiting technological prowess. They have strong emotional appeal and invest in their brand for sustainable, competitive advantage.

Tomorrow's Super Social Brands will give back to the consumer and society, not just in terms of corporate social responsibility or other charitable gestures, but by playing a truly valuable social role and giving people useful platforms for activity. They will constantly invent, innovate and launch new services. They will understand the macro global implications of their actions and continue with umbrella-led marketing and advertising communications. However, Social Brands will also focus on the local and the micro: the day-to-day reality of customer experience. Social Brands will have a real-time view of their brand strength, consumer opinion and the forces driving the global economy. They will be loved by consumers and will act as a positive and re-enforcing presence during the coming years of rapid global change.

Illustration, left page: iStockphoto.com © chris_lemmens

Superbrands
Selection Process

The annual Consumer Superbrands and Business Superbrands surveys are independently administered by The Centre for Brand Analysis (TCBA). Brands do not apply or pay to be considered; rather, the selection processes are conducted as follows:

▶ TCBA researchers compile lists of the UK's leading business-to-consumer and business-to-business brands, drawing on a wide range of sources, from sector reports to blogs to public nominations. From the thousands of brands initially considered a final shortlist is created for each survey. For 2012, just over 1,700 brands were shortlisted for Consumer Superbrands and just under 1,500 for Business Superbrands.

▶ Each shortlist is scored by an independent and voluntary Expert Council, which is assembled and chaired by TCBA's chief executive. Each survey has a separate council, refreshed each year. Bearing in mind the definition of a Superbrand, the council members individually award each brand a rating from 1–10. Council members are not allowed to score brands with which they have a direct association or are in competition to, nor do they score brands they are unfamiliar with. The lowest scoring brands (approximately 40 per cent) are eliminated after each council has ratified the collective scores.

▶ The remaining brands are voted on by the consumers of those brands, accessed via a YouGov panel. For Consumer Superbrands, the panel comprises a nationally representative sample of more than 2,000 British consumers aged 18 and above. For Business Superbrands, just over 1,600 individual business professionals – defined as those who have either purchasing or managerial responsibilities within their organisation – are surveyed.

▶ For the Consumer Superbrands survey, the number of consumer votes received by each brand determines its position in the final rankings. For the Business Superbrands survey, the views of the council and the business professionals are taken into equal account when determining each brand's position in the official league table. In both cases, only the top 500 brands are deemed to be Superbrands.

Definition of a Superbrand

All those involved in the voting process bear in mind the following definition:

'A Superbrand has established the finest reputation in its field. It offers customers significant emotional and/or tangible advantages over its competitors, which customers want and recognise.'

In addition, the voters are asked to judge brands against the following three factors:

▶ **Quality**
▶ **Reliability**
▶ **Distinction**

Our Research Partners

The annual Superbrands surveys canvass the opinions of both experts and consumers – and Superbrands is proud to partner with two separate research businesses to facilitate this. As well as managing the overall research process, The Centre for Brand Analysis compiles the initial shortlists and appoints and surveys the Expert Councils. YouGov informs the consumer stage of the voting by surveying the British public (for Consumer Superbrands) and business professionals (for Business Superbrands) through its online panels.

About TCBA

The Centre for Brand Analysis (TCBA) is a specialist brand research consultancy dedicated to understanding the performance of brands. Its services aim to allow people to understand how a brand is performing, either at a point in time or on an ongoing basis, and gain insight into wider market and marketing trends. Services fall into three categories:

Brand analysis – includes measuring brand strength and/or values. This might require surveying the attitudes of customers, opinion formers, employees, investors, suppliers or other stakeholders. The analysis is conducted for a range of purposes from evaluating market performance to competitor benchmarking, as well as part of a wider repositioning or strategic market analysis projects.

Market analysis – includes providing intelligence, trends and examples of best practice from across the globe for benchmarking, encouraging enhanced performance and generating insight and learnings for consideration in brands' strategic and tactical plans.

Marketing analysis – includes reviewing brand activity, such as assessing the impact of marketing campaigns from both a perceptual and return on investment perspective.

TCBA works for brand owners and also provides intelligence to agencies and other organisations. It utilises extensive relationships within the business community and works with third parties where appropriate. TCBA's executives provide insight at company events, conferences and within the international media. The CEO of TCBA acts as an expert witness in major brand disputes in both the UK and international courts.

▶ **www.tcba.co.uk**

About YouGov

YouGov is an international, full service online market research agency offering custom research, omnibus, field and tab services, qualitative research, syndicated products and market intelligence reports.

Founded in the UK in 2000, YouGov is considered the pioneer of online market research. The unique fully integrated online model has a well-documented and published track record of accuracy. YouGov conducts research in all continents and its online model allows clients to get international results faster and more cost-effectively than traditional methods, with no compromise on quality.

YouGov's goal is to understand the world you live in, the sector you operate in, and your brand, providing a live stream of continuous, accurate data and insight into what people are thinking and doing all over the world. Information that not only serves in tackling current issues facing your organisation but also aims to offer a comprehensive understanding of your organisation and its place in the world we live in today.

The group operates an online panel of more than 2.5 million respondents worldwide representing all ages, socio-economic groups and other demographic types, which allows it to create nationally representative samples online and access hard to reach groups, both consumer and professional. YouGov's UK panel has more than 350,000 respondents.

YouGov has offices in the UK, US, Europe and the Middle East.

▶ **www.yougov.co.uk**

Introducing the Experts

The pages that follow give a brief introduction to the members of the Business Superbrands (**B**) and Consumer Superbrands (**C**) Expert Councils.

Business Superbrands Council

Jaakko Alanko, Founder, Alanko Consulting
Richard Bush, Founder & CEO,
Base One Group
Steve Dyer, Managing Director,
Clockwork IMC
James Farmer, Publisher, B2B Marketing
Pamela Fieldhouse, Senior Managing
Director, International Corporate
Communications, FTI Consulting
Clamor Gieske, Founder, Zeitgeist 365 London
Andrew Gorman, Creative Director,
Radley Yeldar

Steve Kemish, Director, Cyance
Vikki Mitchell, Director, BPRI Group
Rob Morrice, Managing Director,
IAS B2B Marketing
Ruth Mortimer, Associate Editor, Marketing Week
Andrew Pinkess, Director of Strategy & Insight,
Lost Boys International (LBi)
Rebecca Price, Managing Director,
Lloyd Northover
Shane Redding, Managing Director, Think Direct
Elizabeth Renski, Business Journalist and Editor,
CLIMATE CHANGE The New Economy

Gareth Richards, CEO, Ogilvy Primary Contact
Ian Ryder, Deputy Chief Executive,
BCS, The Chartered Institute for IT
Matthew Stibbe, CEO, Articulate Marketing
Terry Tyrrell, Worldwide Chairman,
The Brand Union
David Willan, Chairman, Circle Research
Professor Alan Wilson, Professor of Marketing,
University of Strathclyde Business School
Chris Wilson, Managing Director, Earnest
Peter Young, Marketing & Brand
Development Specialist

Consumer Superbrands Council

Niku Banaie, Global Chief Innovation Officer,
Isobar
Nick Blunden, Global Managing Director
& Publisher, The Economist online
Tim Britton, Chief Operating Officer, EMEA,
YouGov
Vicky Bullen, CEO, Coley Porter Bell
Colin Byrne, CEO, EMEA, Weber Shandwick
Nicola Clark, Head of Features, Marketing
Jackie Cooper, Global Vice Chair, Brand
Properties, Edelman
Paul Edwards, CEO Europe, Hall & Partners
Stephen Factor, Brand Engineer
Lee Farrant, Partner, RPM
Cheryl Giovannoni, President, Global Key

Client Relationships, Landor Associates
Paul Hamilton, Managing Director,
Addiction London
Graham Hiscott, Deputy Business Editor,
Daily Mirror
Jack Horner, Co-Founder & Creative Director,
FRUKT
Mike Hughes, Director General, ISBA
Lucy Johnston, Founder, The Neon Birdcage
Paul Kemp-Robertson, Editorial Director &
Co-Founder, Contagious Communications
John Mathers, CEO, Holmes & Marchant Group
Toby Moore, Founding Partner, Mesh Marketing
Richard Moss, Director, Good Relations (part of
the Bell Pottinger Group)

Julian Pullan, President, EMEA,
Jack Morton Worldwide
Crispin Reed, Managing Director, Brandhouse
Nicolas Roope, Founding Partner, Poke London
James Sanderson, CEO, Skive Group
Raoul Shah, Joint CEO, Exposure
Professor Robert Shaw, Honorary Professor,
Cass Business School and Director,
Value Based Marketing Forum
Neil Taylor, Creative Director, The Writer
Darren Thomas, Managing Director,
Quiet Storm
Alan Twigg, Managing Director,
Light Brigade PR
Andrew Walmsley, Digital Pluralist

Stephen Cheliotis
▶ Chairman, Expert Councils
▶ Chief Executive, The Centre for Brand Analysis (TCBA)

Stephen is a leading branding commentator and prominent consultant. Founding TCBA in 2007, his work there includes brand evaluations, brand awareness and perception studies, and market analysis for brand owners. He has also produced detailed branding studies for agencies and media owners. Stephen speaks regularly at conferences, comments on branding issues for the media, and acts as an expert witness in brand disputes.

Jaakko Alanko
▶ Founder
▶ Alanko Consulting

Following 40 years in international advertising, most recently as chairman of McCann Enterprise, Jaakko retired from active service in 2011. He then established boutique consultancy Alanko Consulting, focusing on enterprise brand development and activation in large international organisations. Jaakko enjoys this entrepreneurial status and close collaboration with a small number of UK and European companies. **B**

Niku Banaie
▶ Global Chief Innovation Officer
▶ Isobar

Niku joined Isobar, one of the leading full service digital networks, in June 2008. Prior to this he was the youngest partner at Naked Communications. He has created award-winning work for Nokia, Honda, Orange, E4 and Nike among others. **C**

Nick Blunden
▶ Global Managing Director & Publisher
▶ The Economist online

As managing director and publisher of The Economist online, Nick has responsibility for all commercial aspects of Economist.com globally. Before joining the Economist Group, Nick was UK CEO of Profero – the award-winning full service global digital communications agency. Earlier in his career Nick also enjoyed a successful stint as a management consultant with IBM Consulting and as a client-side marketer. **C**

Tim Britton
▶ Chief Operating Officer, EMEA
▶ YouGov

Tim has almost 20 years' experience working directly and indirectly in the research industry, culminating in his current role as chief operating officer of YouGov for its EMEA region. His experience in research is both on and offline, in areas ranging from financial services through business-to-business research, to work on public policy. **C**

Vicky Bullen
▶ CEO
▶ Coley Porter Bell

With more than 20 years' experience, Vicky has spent her career in the design industry, becoming chief executive of Coley Porter Bell in 2005. There, she leads work for many of the world's largest brand owners, including Unilever, Nestlé, Coca-Cola and Pernod Ricard. Vicky also sits on the Ogilvy UK Group Board. **C**

Richard Bush
▶ Founder & CEO
▶ Base One Group

Richard is the driving force behind the international, multi-disciplined B2B specialist agency, Base One Group. In addition, he is a regular presenter at The Institute of Direct and Digital Marketing, and writes and speaks on occasion for several industry publications and institutions, including B2B Marketing, the Internet Advertising Bureau and the Association of Business-to-Business Agencies. **B**

Colin Byrne
▶ CEO, EMEA
▶ Weber Shandwick

Colin is one of the UK's leading PR practitioners, with 30 years' experience spanning domestic and international communications campaigns, politics, corporate social responsibility, and crisis and issues management. Colin joined Weber Shandwick in 1995 and is now CEO of the global agency's Europe and Africa network as well as a member of its global management team. **C**

Nicola Clark
▶ Head of Features
▶ Marketing

Nicola heads up features content for Marketing magazine and its website, and specialises in fashion, social media, media and branding. She joined the magazine in 2005 from Emap, where she was features reporter on Media & Marketing Europe, a pan-European monthly. Nicola started her journalism career as a financial journalist at Standard & Poor's and has a history degree from Bristol University. **C**

Jackie Cooper
▶ Global Vice Chair, Brand Properties
▶ Edelman

Jackie is one of the pre-eminent voices and influencers in UK brand marketing today. She sold Jackie Cooper PR to Edelman in 2004 and now serves as global vice chair, brand properties. Jackie is responsible for developing new products, concepts and relationships that lie at the critical intersection of brand, content and partnerships. **C**

Steve Dyer
▶ Managing Director
▶ Clockwork IMC

Steve founded Clockwork IMC, a dedicated B2B integrated agency, in 1993. He has over 20 years' B2B agency experience, supporting various industrial, technology and professional service brands. A strategic communications marketer, he has helped to develop a number of industry initiatives while on the DMA's B2B Committee and as a past vice chair of the Association of Business-to-Business Agencies. **B**

Paul Edwards
▶ CEO Europe
▶ Hall & Partners

Paul joined Hall & Partners, the Omnicom-owned advertising research company, in March 2011. Prior to this he was at Research International and became chairman of the UK business following its merger with TNS. Roles as group CEO at Lowe & Partners, and chairman and CEO of The Henley Centre, saw his responsibilities span serving clients' integrated marketing needs and future strategic direction, respectively. **C**

Stephen Factor
▶ Brand Engineer

Stephen has almost 30 years' experience in the areas of consumer insight and brand strategy. He has worked in Paris, Milan, New York and London, and has consulted for FMCG manufacturers in more than 70 countries. For much of his career he has held top management roles in global market research agencies; he blends hands-on corporate management experience with a deep understanding of FMCG markets and brands. **C**

James Farmer
▶ Publisher
▶ B2B Marketing

James held a variety of senior publishing roles at Reed Elsevier before breaking away to co-found B2B Marketing. He was one of the frontrunners in driving the importance of business-to-business marketing worldwide. B2B Marketing's media portfolio encompasses a full range of online and offline services, consumed by the international community and focused on reporting, training and driving innovation in the profession. **B**

Lee Farrant
▶ Partner
▶ RPM

A partner at marketing specialists RPM since 1996, Lee manages the agency's visual content requirements. Lee has spent a career in sport, covering football, rugby and cricket world cups, as well as Formula 1, The Camel Trophy and whitewater rafting. He believes in encouraging participation in, and accessibility to, all levels of sport. He currently advises clients in cricket, rugby, football, cycling and horse racing. **C**

Pamela Fieldhouse
▶ Senior Managing Director, International Corporate Communications
▶ FTI Consulting

Pamela is a senior communications consultant with more than 20 years' experience in corporate reputation, issues and crisis management, brand strategy, change management and business communications. She provides strategic counsel to senior executives from both the public and private sector and currently advises clients across a wide range of industry sectors. **B**

Clamor Gieske
▶ Founder
▶ Zeitgeist 365 London

Clamor is the founder of Zeitgeist 365, an international marketing strategy firm based in London and Berlin. Previously, he managed the UK office of Vivaldi Partners, a global management consultancy. Clamor's international experience spans strategy, innovation, marketing and brand consulting projects. This has seen him advise clients across Europe, as well as in countries as diverse as Saudi Arabia and Russia. **B**

Cheryl Giovannoni
▶ President, Global Key Client Relationships
▶ Landor Associates

As president of Landor's global key client relationships, Cheryl is a leading presence in the branding community and a strong advocate for the transformational power of design in building brands. Having run the London office of Landor, as well as the European network during the last five years, Cheryl has expertise across a diverse portfolio of corporate, service and fast-moving consumer brands. **C**

Andrew Gorman
▶ Creative Director
▶ Radley Yeldar

Andrew is creative director of business-to-business focused creative communications consultancy, Radley Yeldar. He helps maintain the consultancy's longstanding creative reputation through an inherent understanding that creativity is about honest storytelling. And that good honest storytelling is about so much more than design alone. **B**

Paul Hamilton
▶ Managing Director
▶ Addiction London

Paul started his advertising career at D'Arcy before moving on to M&C Saatchi to run the Direct Line, Lucozade Sport, RBS and Trinity Mirror accounts. He later moved to Chick Smith Trott before joining Addiction London as managing director. The agency currently retains Remington, isme and Krispy Kreme accounts amongst others. **C**

Graham Hiscott
▶ Deputy Business Editor
▶ Daily Mirror

Graham was appointed consumer editor of the Daily Express in March 2005, with a string of exclusives earning him the London Press Club's Consumer Journalist of the Year award in 2007. In March 2008 Graham moved to the Daily Mirror as deputy business editor, covering City as well as consumer stories. **C**

Jack Horner
▶ Co-Founder &
Creative Director
▶ FRUKT

Jack founded entertainment, music and lifestyle communications agency FRUKT, which helps consumer brands create entertaining experiences and content that sparks conversation. It works with clients globally, including Coca-Cola, Tuborg, Nokia and Diesel.

C

Mike Hughes
▶ Director General
▶ ISBA

Following a career in marketing and general management at Coca-Cola, Guinness and Bulmer, Mike assumed his current role as director general of ISBA, The Voice of British Advertisers, in 2007. A member of all key UK industry bodies, Mike also sits on the executive committee of the Worldwide Federation of Advertisers.

C

Lucy Johnston
▶ Founder
▶ The Neon Birdcage

Lucy is a curator, writer and strategist, specialising in developing cultural and social projects for leading brands and organisations including Levi's®, Courvoisier, Coca-Cola and London 2012. Through The Neon Birdcage she has also launched a new initiative – Bright Young Brits – a platform to promote young emerging creative talent across the UK, and inject fresh effervescent thinking into British industry.

C

Steve Kemish
▶ Director
▶ Cyance

Steve has over 13 years' experience in digital marketing. He offers considerable hands-on expertise, having worked client-side in B2B and B2C, and is chair of the IDM Digital Marketing Council and a member of the DMA future proofing group. He has worked on digital marketing strategy with global brands including Motorola, ITV, Skype, the BBC, British Airways and Oracle, and is a regular speaker throughout the world.

B

Paul Kemp-Robertson
▶ Editorial Director
& Co-Founder
▶ Contagious
Communications

Paul co-founded Contagious in 2004. This quarterly magazine, online intelligence resource and consultancy service reports on marketing innovation and the impact of new technologies on brands. Paul has written articles for numerous publications, co-edited D&AD's The Commercials Book, appeared on BBC radio and frequently speaks at advertising conferences around the world.

C

John Mathers
▶ CEO
▶ Holmes & Marchant
Group

John is CEO of the H&M Group, overseeing the Holmes & Marchant and Lloyd Northover businesses in the UK. Prior to joining Holmes & Marchant in 2009, he held management roles at The Brand Union, Fitch and Blue Marlin. An active member of the design industry, John was president of the Design Business Association for three years and still works with both the DBA and the Design Council.

C

Vikki Mitchell
▶ Director
▶ BPRI Group

With nearly 15 years' experience, Vikki is a specialist in branding, positioning, reputation and creative development research. Vikki sits on the board of the BIG Group, which represents business-to-business research and market intelligence services, is a frequent speaker at B2B events and has written articles for various business and research magazines.

B

Toby Moore
▶ Founding Partner
▶ Mesh Marketing

Toby is a founding partner of Mesh Marketing. One of the UK's leading and fastest growing shopper marketing agencies, it specialises in helping FMCG and retail brands to convert shoppers into buyers.

C

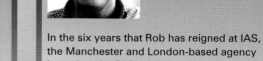

Rob Morrice
▶ Managing Director
▶ IAS B2B Marketing

In the six years that Rob has reigned at IAS, the Manchester and London-based agency has taken the B2B marketing world by storm; its bevy of awards is testament to the team's creative and strategic know-how. Twice crowned UK B2B Agency of the Year, IAS trumped this in 2011 by becoming the first UK agency to claim B2 Agency of the Year at the Business Marketing Awards in the US.

B

Ruth Mortimer
▶ Associate Editor
▶ Marketing Week

Ruth is associate editor for Marketing Week. In addition to her current role, she often appears on CNN, Sky and the BBC as an expert on business issues and is author of four books about marketing effectiveness. She is also a regular speaker at marketing conferences.

B

Richard Moss
▶ Director
▶ Good Relations
(part of the Bell
Pottinger Group)

Richard started his career in FMCG marketing, responsible for brands including Andrex®, Robinsons and Mr Kipling. Since moving into PR he has advised brands as diverse as Smirnoff, Yeo Valley, Nokia and Airbus. He has published a number of pieces of research on how to improve the levels of advocacy achieved by brands and writes a blog, wordofmoss.com.

C

Andrew Pinkess
▶ Director of
Strategy & Insight
▶ Lost Boys
International (LBi)

Andrew has 20 years' experience in brand, advertising, digital and marketing consultancy. His specialisms include brand strategy and development, digital strategy, integrated communications, branded content and social media. His client experience spans business-to-business, business-to-consumer and the public sector.

B

Rebecca Price
▶ Managing Director
▶ Lloyd Northover

Rebecca is a brand strategist and communications specialist with a track record spanning more than 25 years spent both client-side and agency-side. At the helm of Lloyd Northover, a consultancy with a 36-year history, she is a powerful champion of great creativity – firmly understanding that creativity involves so much more than design alone.

B

Julian Pullan
▶ President, EMEA
▶ Jack Morton Worldwide

Julian is president and managing director of brand experience agency Jack Morton Worldwide in EMEA. Rated among the top global brand experience agencies, Jack Morton Worldwide integrates live and online experiences, digital and social media, and branded environments that engage consumers, business partners and employees for leading brands everywhere.

C

Shane Redding
▶ Managing Director
▶ Think Direct

Shane is an independent consultant with more than 20 years' international direct marketing experience. She provides strategic marketing advice and practical training to both end users and DM suppliers. Shane has also been awarded an IDM honorary fellowship and is co-founder of the digital and direct B2B agency, Cyance.

B

Crispin Reed
▶ Managing Director
▶ Brandhouse

Crispin has a rounded perspective on brands, having worked in leading global advertising and design agencies, brand consultancy and client-side in the fragrance and beauty sector. In addition to his current role, Crispin is an associate of Ashridge Management College and sits on the Advisory Boards of the Global Marketing Network and the Branded Content Marketing Association.

C

Elizabeth Renski
▶ Business Journalist
▶ Editor, CLIMATE CHANGE The New Economy

With over 15 years' experience in B2B magazines, Elizabeth has been the driving force behind titles including CEO Today and CLIMATE CHANGE The New Economy, which showcases the latest thinking on low-carbon growth and green technology. She has worked with leading brands such as BT, Siemens, B&Q, Philips and Toyota, all of which have embraced environmental responsibility as a core part of their brand.

B

Gareth Richards
▶ CEO
▶ Ogilvy Primary Contact

Following a PhD in Biochemistry, Gareth has gained more than 20 years' experience in B2B marketing communications with spells on both the agency and client sides of the business. He runs B2B agency Ogilvy Primary Contact and is client service director for UPS, Sage, Syngenta and FM Global.

B

Nicolas Roope
▶ Founding Partner
▶ Poke London

Nicolas is an impassioned digital media visionary. The founder and creative director of Poke London, he also founded and creatively directs the cult electronics brand, Hulger – producer of the world's first designer energy saving light bulb, the Plumen 001.

C

Ian Ryder
▶ Deputy Chief Executive
▶ BCS, The Chartered Institute for IT

A founding director of Medinge Group, a global brand thinktank, Ian is an international speaker, chairman, author and visiting professor on the subjects of brand strategy and customer management. Formerly the director of global brand management for Hewlett-Packard and CEO of Uffindell, he is a specialist reviewer for Harvard Business School, sits on numerous boards, and is a fellow of the CIM, IoD, BCS and RSA.

B

James Sanderson
▶ CEO
▶ Skive Group

James has spent the last 15 years helping some of the world's largest brands navigate the digital communications landscape. He spent seven years co-leading Glue before leaving in 2009 to run Digitas in the UK. He joined the multi-award-winning independent digital agency Skive in 2011 and works with Aviva, Carlsberg, Nestlé and Dunhill.

C

Raoul Shah
▶ Joint CEO
▶ Exposure

Raoul is a visionary thinker with over 20 years' experience in marketing and communications. In 1993 he launched Exposure, a communications agency built on the power of network, great ideas and word-of-mouth. With offices in London, New York, San Francisco and Tokyo, current clients include Coca-Cola, glacéau vitaminwater, Levi's®, Hunter, Nike, Dr. Martens and John Smedley. Raoul is also a trustee of the British Council.

C

Professor Robert Shaw
▶ Honorary Professor, Cass Business School
▶ Director, Value Based Marketing Forum

As a consultant, businessman and best-selling author of Marketing Payback, Database Marketing and Improving Marketing Effectiveness, Robert is a leading authority on value-based marketing and customer relationship management. He is in demand both in the UK and overseas as a conference chairman and keynote speaker and also teaches on in-company executive education programmes.

C

Matthew Stibbe
▶ CEO
▶ Articulate Marketing

Matthew runs Articulate Marketing, a specialist marketing and copywriting agency that helps high-technology companies communicate with customers and employees. Clients include Hewlett-Packard, Microsoft, Symantec, Gemalto and NetJets. He is also CEO of TurbineHQ.com – a web application that simplifies company paperwork – and he writes the popular blog, BadLanguage.net.

B

Neil Taylor
▶ Creative Director
▶ The Writer

Neil is creative director of The Writer, the world's largest language consultancy. He travels the minor airports of the world helping brands and businesses stand out, change their culture, or make and save money through the words they use. He wrote Brilliant Business Writing (and some others) and has a slight Doctor Who obsession.

C

Darren Thomas
▶ Managing Director
▶ Quiet Storm

Darren's career has spanned nearly 20 years' marketing communications experience in both client-side and agency roles. He joined Quiet Storm, a creative communications agency and production company, in 2005 as client services director. Today Darren is managing director of the business, delivering advertising, digital and branded content solutions for its clients.

C

Alan Twigg
▶ Managing Director
▶ Light Brigade PR

A trained journalist, mouthy Scot and award-winning PR, Alan is managing director of Light Brigade PR, the consumer brand and lifestyle agency. With more than 20 years' agency experience, he has worked with many leading brands from M&S, Waterstones and Hamleys to Nintendo, Peroni, Grants and Glenfiddich.

 C

Terry Tyrrell
▶ Worldwide Chairman
▶ The Brand Union

Terry is the worldwide chairman of The Brand Union, the agency he co-founded in 1976 that now employs more than 500 people in 20 offices globally. Terry is responsible for major corporate branding programmes, leading teams across The Brand Union network. Recently these have included UBS, Shell, Canon, Rolls-Royce plc, DP World, Credit Suisse, Abu Dhabi Investment Company, BBVA and Fidelity Investments.

B

Andrew Walmsley
▶ Digital Pluralist

Andrew co-founded digital agency i-level in 1999 and built it to more than £100 million turnover, winning a Queen's Award for Enterprise and achieving Agency of the Year eight times, before selling to a private equity group in 2008. He is now an investor, active non-executive and adviser to a number of companies seeking success in the digital economy.

C

David Willan
▶ Chairman
▶ Circle Research

A co-founder of BPRI (now part of WPP), David has worked in B2B marketing research for more years than he's prepared to admit to. A frequent contributor to the likes of B2B Marketing, David is also a guest speaker at Ashridge Business School. He is currently chairman of B2B marketing research agency Circle Research and works as a practitioner in branding, development and customer relationship management.

B

Professor Alan Wilson
▶ Professor of Marketing
▶ University of Strathclyde Business School

Alan is a professor of marketing at the University of Strathclyde Business School. Before joining the University, he was a senior consultant at a London-based marketing consultancy and prior to that, an associate director of a leading marketing research agency. He has written numerous articles on corporate reputation and branding, and is a fellow of the Chartered Institute of Marketing and the Market Research Society.

B

Chris Wilson
▶ Managing Director
▶ Earnest

Chris has spent 15 years in B2B marketing, working with some of the world's largest brands in the technology, telecommunications and financial sectors. Chris founded the agency Earnest in 2009 to help B2B marketing step out of the shade and stop being a poor cousin to FMCG. Chris also chairs the Association of Business-to-Business Agencies.

B

Peter Young
▶ Marketing & Brand Development Specialist

Peter is chairman of the B2B Marketing Awards as well as a consultant and non-executive director, advising businesses on brand development and marketing. Formerly a member of board-level management teams in Europe-wide communications consultancies, he has helped establish and grow brands in the service and product sectors, from corporate institutions to government information departments.

B

Highlights of the 2012 Results

By Stephen Cheliotis
Chairman, Expert Councils
and Chief Executive,
The Centre for Brand Analysis

CONSUMER SUPERBRANDS

The British public has once again taken part in the annual Consumer Superbrands survey, casting judgment on just under 900 brands (from an original list of more than 1,700 brands, which was whittled down by an independent expert council). Having voted on whether or not each brand is worthy of 'Superbrand' status, UK consumers have chosen their winners. And for the fifth year in a row, the number one brand has changed.

Sitting at the top of the pile in 2012 is a premium brand renowned for its quality, heritage and high profile sponsorship of international sporting events such as Wimbledon. In second place last year, the brand has crept up to take the top berth thanks to a positive vote from 66 per cent of the British public – an increase of three per cent year-on-year. The brand receives almost the same level of support from both men and women, and from those in the ABC1 and C2DE socio-economic groups – although its results by age of respondent do vary. The brand, of course, is the iconic watchmaker Rolex.

Last year's winner, Mercedes-Benz, slips down to fourth place but retains its top 10 placing for the sixth year in a row. In fact, seven of last year's top 10 retain their position in the elite grouping. Among them, Coca-Cola moves up from fourth place to second, showing its best performance since the 2007/08 survey in which it also secured second place. Votes for the soft drink giant decreased, however, from 60 per cent in 2011 to just over 56 per cent in 2012.

The BBC not only retains its place in the top 10 but claims its sixth year in the top five. During the six years that The Centre for Brand Analysis (TCBA) has overseen the Superbrands research process, the BBC has performed incredibly well; its placing over the period reads second, fourth, fourth, fifth, third and fifth (in 2012), which is an extremely strong and consistent showing. More than 50 per cent of the British public voted the BBC a Superbrand, with equal support from men and women. Interestingly, it secures the highest percentage of support from 18–24 year-olds, while its regional vote varies, with the east of England showing the highest degree of support for the BBC.

Google moves up to third from fifth, reclaiming its 2009/10 position. The brand took the top spot in 2008/09 but has since failed to outperform all the other brands considered. In 2012 it was voted a Superbrand by just over 56 per cent of the public.

Two other brands also retain their top 10 status, namely car manufacturers BMW and Jaguar. The former climbs one place to sixth, while the latter moves up from 10th to ninth.

Falling out of the top 10 this year are Microsoft, British Airways and Apple. Software giant Microsoft falls from sixth in 2011 to a lowly 45th this year; having claimed the top spot in 2006/07, 2007/08 and 2009/10, this is a big fall from grace. The percentage of consumers voting it a Superbrand has dropped from 58 per cent last year to 35 per cent this year. British Airways falls from eighth to 33rd,

although the research was conducted prior to its significant repositioning campaign, which reiterates its heritage and promise 'to serve'. Apple, despite its ongoing success and the continued popularity of the iPhone, falls from ninth to 18th, with its votes dropping from 55 per cent last year to 42 per cent this year. As one might imagine, votes for Apple vary considerably. For instance, while 60 per cent of 18–24 year-olds deem Apple to be a Superbrand, this falls to just 31 per cent of those aged 55 and above. Equally, while 55 per cent of voters from London see Apple as a Superbrand, other regions show varying support; its lowest level of support (33 per cent) comes from Wales.

Entering the top 10 this year are Duracell®, Dulux and Royal Doulton. Duracell climbs from 14th last year. The battery giant, owned by Procter & Gamble, is in its highest position in the six years that TCBA has been overseeing the research. That said, the brand has been a consistently strong performer throughout the period; in the three years prior to 2012 the brand placed 12th, 12th and 14th. Its last appearance in the top 10 was in 2006/07 when it reached ninth.

Dulux has risen five places year-on-year, moving from 13th to eighth. In 2007/08 the brand placed 57th, in 2008/09 it climbed to 22nd, and in 2009/10 it finished in 15th. Dulux has thus shown steady improvement over a five-year period as its iconic brand regains momentum and support among the British population.

The annual Consumer Superbrands and Business Superbrands surveys aim to identify the UK's strongest business-to-consumer and business-to-business brands, respectively, from a wide variety of sectors and industries. Both processes are subjective and take into account the views of a relevant council of experts, together with those of consumers and potential consumers of those brands. The research is commissioned by Superbrands (UK) Ltd and for the past six years, has been independently managed by The Centre for Brand Analysis.

For full details of the selection process, see page 158.

To many, Royal Doulton may seem a surprise entry in the top 10. Yet, it is no stranger to this group, missing out by just two places last year. It last featured in the top 10 in 2008/09; in sixth place, it was the brand's highest ever position.

Just missing out on the top 10 this year are Wedgwood (11th), the Royal Albert Hall (12th) and John Lewis (13th), showing that heritage really assists in the survey. The top 20 also includes innovative appliance manufacturer Dyson, retail giant Marks & Spencer, and famous stout Guinness – the brand behind many of the most famous advertising campaigns of all time.

Sitting in the 500th slot, snack brand Pringles is the last brand to achieve Superbrand status this year. Falling just under the qualifying mark are brands such as laundry detergent Surf, takeaway brands Subway and Pizza Hut, Swedish vodka Absolut, high street bank Natwest, and soft drink Tango.

In terms of the many categories that we explore, the most represented in the top 500 is Food – General, which has 52 brands in the top 500. This was also the most popular category last year when 55 of its brands made the grade. Kellogg's tops this highly competitive category, as it did last year. As per last year's survey, Toiletries & Cosmetics is the second most popular category, with 41 brands represented in the top 500 compared to 42 last year. The category is topped by Chanel, which is just ahead of last year's category winner Gillette.

A big gulf then divides the second and third most popular categories. With just 28 brands, Retail – General sits in third and is led by John Lewis, which overtakes last year's most popular retail brand, Marks & Spencer. The smallest category in the top 500 is Travel – Airlines, which features only Virgin Atlantic and British Airways. Three categories have just three entries in the top 500: Media – Radio, with Capital FM, Heart and Classic FM (which are all owned by Global Radio); Travel – Bus & Rail Operators, which features Eurostar, Virgin Trains and National Express; and Leisure & Entertainment – Gambling, which features The National Lottery, Ladbrokes and William Hill. Overall, 43 different sectors have representation in the top 500.

CONSUMER SUPERBRANDS 2012 – OFFICIAL TOP 20

Rank	Brand	Category	Year-on-year change
1	Rolex	Watches & Accessories	↑ 1
2	Coca-Cola	Drinks – Carbonated Soft Drinks	↑ 2
3	Google	Internet – General	↑ 2
4	Mercedes-Benz	Automotive – Vehicle Manufacturer	↓ 3
5	BBC	Media – TV Stations	↓ 2
6	BMW	Automotive – Vehicle Manufacturer	↑ 1
7	Duracell®	Household – General Consumables	↑ 7
8	Dulux	Household – General Consumables	↑ 5
9	Jaguar	Automotive – Vehicle Manufacturer	↑ 1
10	Royal Doulton	Household – General	↑ 2
11	Wedgwood	Household – General	↑ 11
12	Royal Albert Hall	Leisure & Entertainment – Destinations	↑ 6
13	John Lewis	Retail – General	↑ 8
14	Michelin	Automotive – General	↑ 11
15	Hilton	Travel – Hotels & Resorts	↑ 12
16	Dyson	Household – Appliances	↑ 15
17	Marks & Spencer	Retail – General	↓ 6
18	Apple	Technology – Computer Hardware & Software	↓ 9
19	Guinness	Drinks – Beer & Cider	—
20	Bang & Olufsen	Technology – General	↑ 20

BUSINESS SUPERBRANDS

Unlike Consumer Superbrands, the Business Superbrands final rankings take into account both the views of the independent expert council, assembled for the business-to-business survey, and the views of just over 1,600 UK business professionals. And unlike Consumer Superbrands, the Business Superbrands rankings do not see a change in leadership, as UK engineer Rolls-Royce Group maintains its number one position. Despite a high profile engine incident on a Qantas flight in late 2010, the brand continues to be rated highly by experts and professionals alike. At the time of writing, its share price and business performance have also continued to improve and as the debate around rebalancing the economy towards manufacturing continues, this UK engineer has established itself as a world-leading provider of power systems and services for use on land, at sea and in the air. It is no surprise, therefore, that this local champion has overcome the short-term PR

CONSUMER SUPERBRANDS 2012 – TOP 20 CATEGORIES REPRESENTED IN THE TOP 500

Category	Number of brands in the top 500	Category leader	Category leader's rank
Food – General	52	Kellogg's	34
Toiletries & Cosmetics	41	Chanel	103
Retail – General	28	John Lewis	13
Pharmaceutical	25	Nurofen	76
Clothing & Footwear	20	Levi's®	61
Drinks – Spirits	20	Glenfiddich	23
Household – Cleaning Products	19	Fairy	36
Leisure & Entertainment – Games & Toys	17	LEGO®	31
Technology – General	17	Bang & Olufsen	20
Household – General	16	Royal Doulton	10
Automotive – Vehicle Manufacturer	14	Mercedes-Benz	4
Drinks – Beer & Cider	14	Guinness	19
Food – Chocolate & Confectionery	14	Cadbury	38
Household – Appliances	13	Dyson	16
Drinks – General	12	Robinsons	43
Financial	11	Visa	146
Leisure & Entertainment – Destinations	11	Royal Albert Hall	12
Automotive – General	10	Michelin	14
Travel – Hotels & Resorts	10	Hilton	15
Drinks – Coffee & Tea	9	Twinings	25

difficulties surrounding the Qantas incident to maintain its brand leadership. The brand was in second place for the two years prior to last year's survey and has been in the top 10 every year since 2007.

Like Consumer Superbrands, the Business Superbrands top 10 has remained reasonably consistent year-on-year, with eight brands remaining in the top group (compared to seven in Consumer Superbrands).

Google moves up two places to take second place from BlackBerry, which falls out of the top 10 altogether to sit in 23rd place. The other brand falling out of the top 10 is software giant Microsoft. That said, the brand only misses out on the top 10 by one place – although this still represents Microsoft's worst position in the Business Superbrands survey since TCBA has been overseeing the research. The brand had been in the top five in the

previous five surveys undertaken under the existing methodology.

The two brands entering the Business Superbrands top 10 are both UK airlines, namely British Airways and Virgin Atlantic. The former just pips its fierce rival to the last of the top five places. Last year the two airlines were in 48th and 14th, respectively, so while both have improved their performance it is British Airways that has experienced the more dramatic improvement, eclipsing its rival. Interestingly, both airlines were in the top 10 two years ago, so having both lost ground they have regained it in unison.

Brands retaining their top 10 position year-on-year are Rolls-Royce Group, Google, GlaxoSmithKline, Apple, the London Stock Exchange, Bosch, Visa, and the audit, accountancy and management consultancy giant PricewaterhouseCoopers (now known just as PwC).

As mentioned, the official Business Superbrands rankings are based on the combination of views from the expert council and UK business professionals. Looking at the top 10 for each audience, only the official number one brand overall, Rolls-Royce Group, features in both; it is placed third by the expert council and first by the business professionals.

Google takes the top spot with the experts but manages only 13th with the professionals. Placing second with the council is Apple,

which comes in 20th with the professionals. Other brands to feature in the experts' top 10 (with the professionals' ranking shown in brackets) are London Business School (192nd), McKinsey & Company (265th), Bosch (12th), BlackBerry (36th), Microsoft (14th), FTSE (148th) and FedEx (18th).

Conversely, brands in the professionals' top 10 but not in that of the experts (whose ranking is shown in brackets) are British Airways (41st), GlaxoSmithKline (13th), BAE Systems (92nd), the London Stock Exchange (21st), Virgin Atlantic (11th), PricewaterhouseCoopers (27th), Visa (23rd), BP (182nd) and BT (96th).

Clearly this shows the difference of opinion between the two groups and the fact that many of the brands featured in the research polarise the opinions of the two audiences. The overall winners are those that are most successful in impressing both the buyers of business services and the experts who are, perhaps, more in tune with each brand's marketing activity, positioning and differentiation vis-a-vis rivals. Size, heritage and market leadership appear to be heavier influences on the professionals.

While Consumer Superbrands has representation in the top 500 from 43 different categories, the Business Superbrands rankings have representation from 55 different sectors. This shows that there is more diversity in the list and more sectors with just a few leading brands making the grade. As was the case last year, the most represented sector is Technology – Hardware & Equipment, which has 36 brands in the top 500, nine more than it had last year. The leading brand in the category is Apple, as it was last year. The second most represented category is Support Services – Associations & Accreditations; it is led by BSI (British Standards Institution), which overtakes last year's category winner, the Law Society. Last year the category had 22 brands in the top 500, while this year it contains 27. The third most represented category is Industrial Engineering – General, meaning that the top three categories are exactly the same as last year. Siemens is the leading brand in this category, as it was last year.

BUSINESS SUPERBRANDS 2012 – OFFICIAL TOP 20

Rank	Brand	Category	Year-on-year change
1	Rolls-Royce Group	Aerospace & Defence	—
2	Google	Media – Marketing Services – Advertising Solutions	↑ 2
3	GlaxoSmithKline	Pharmaceuticals & Biotech	↑ 5
4	Apple	Technology – Hardware & Equipment	↑ 1
5	British Airways	Travel & Leisure – Airlines	↑ 43
6	Virgin Atlantic	Travel & Leisure – Airlines	↑ 8
7	London Stock Exchange	Financial – Exchanges & Markets	↓ 1
8	Bosch	Construction & Materials – Tools / Equipment	↑ 2
9	Visa	Financial – Credit Cards & Payment Solutions	—
10	PricewaterhouseCoopers	Support Services – Accountancy & Business Services	↓ 3
11	Microsoft	Software & Computer Services	↓ 8
12	FedEx	Industrial Transportation – B2B Delivery Services	—
13	BAE Systems	Aerospace & Defence	↑ 21
14	Boeing	Aerospace & Defence	↑ 4
15	Eddie Stobart	Industrial Transportation – Logistics / Distribution / Freight Services	↑ 12
16	DHL	Industrial Transportation – B2B Delivery Services	↑ 1
17	BT	Telecommunications – General	↑ 9
18	Shell	Oil & Gas	↓ 7
19	Ernst & Young	Support Services – Accountancy & Business Services	↓ 3
20	Vodafone	Telecommunications – Mobile & Online	↓ 5

BUSINESS SUPERBRANDS 2012 – TOP 20 CATEGORIES REPRESENTED IN THE TOP 500

Category	Number of brands in the top 500	Category leader	Category leader's rank
Technology – Hardware & Equipment	36	Apple	4
Support Services – Associations & Accreditations	27	BSI (British Standards Institution)	42
Industrial Engineering – General	25	Siemens	21
Support Services – General	18	AA	52
Financial – Banks	17	HSBC	80
Retailers – Office Equipment & Supplies	17	Staples	161
Construction & Materials	16	Pilkington	44
Support Services – Consultancies	15	McKinsey & Company	116
Travel & Leisure – Business Hotels	15	Hilton	39
Aerospace & Defence	14	Rolls-Royce Group	1
Construction & Materials – Tools / Equipment	14	Bosch	8
Executive Education, Training & Development	14	London School of Economics and Political Science	49
Insurance & Risk Management	14	Lloyd's of London	33
Software & Computer Services	14	Microsoft	11
Support Services – Information Providers	13	Bloomberg	72
Pharmaceuticals & Biotech	12	GlaxoSmithKline	3
Support Services – Recruitment	11	Reed	201
Media – Marketing Services – Advertising Solutions	9	Google	2
Media – Marketing Services – Market Research	9	Ipsos MORI	84
Media – Trade Publications	9	Jane's	140

CONCLUSION

Both the Consumer Superbrands and Business Superbrands surveys are a snap shot of the UK's brand landscape across many diverse sectors. They are not meant to offer detailed brand equity insights but they provide an overview of a brand's performance and reputation in the UK generally, taking into account a wide audience of consumers or business buyers. They therefore may not reflect a given brand's reputation among its specific stakeholders or customers.

Congratulations to Rolex on taking the top spot in the Consumer Superbrands survey

for the first time and to Rolls-Royce Group for retaining its top place in the Business Superbrands rankings. In both surveys the many brands that retained their top 10 berths from the previous year should also be congratulated. More widely, all of the brands featuring in the top 500s should be applauded for achieving Superbrands status. As ever, the UK brandscape is particularly competitive with even those brands below the 500 mark being significant players, often enjoying considerable awareness, high levels of marketing spend and a strong heritage.

The 1,000-odd brands not to make the grade in Consumer Superbrands range from Sprite to Cosmopolitan, from KFC to Expedia, and from Avon to Pizza Express. In Business Superbrands, the brands failing to make the top 500 include a significant proportion of the FTSE 100 companies, such as Xstrata, Bunzl and Inmarsat, as well as brands ranging from Scottish & Southern Energy to Datamonitor. This shows that achieving a place in the top 500, let alone a high placing in that ranking, is as difficult as ever.

stephen.cheliotis@tcba.co.uk

Qualifying Business Superbrands

3663
3I
3M
AA
ABB
ABI (ASSOCIATION OF
    BRITISH INSURERS)
ABTA
ACCA (ASSOCIATION OF CHARTERED
    CERTIFIED ACCOUNTANTS)
ACCENTURE
ACCOUNTANCY AGE
ACER
ADDISON LEE
ADECCO
ADOBE
ADT
ACAS (ADVISORY, CONCILIATION &
    ARBITRATION SERVICE)
AEGON
AIM
AIRBUS
AKQA
AKZONOBEL
ALAMO
ALCATEL-LUCENT
ALLEN & OVERY
ALLIANCE HEALTHCARE
ALLIANZ INSURANCE
ALSTOM
AMD
AMEC
AMERICAN EXPRESS
AMERICAN EXPRESS BUSINESS TRAVEL
AMEY
ANGLO AMERICAN
AON
APPLE
ARCHITECTS' JOURNAL
ARM HOLDINGS
ARRIVA
ARUP
ASHRIDGE BUSINESS SCHOOL
ASSOCIATED BRITISH PORTS
ASTRAZENECA
AUTOCAD
AVAYA
AVERY
AVIS
AVIVA
AXA
AXA PPP HEALTHCARE
BABCOCK
BAE SYSTEMS
BAIN & COMPANY
BALFOUR BEATTY
BARCLAYCARD
BARCLAYS
BARCLAYS CORPORATE
BASF
BASILDON BOND
BAXI
BAYER
BBH
BDO
BELL POTTINGER
BEST WESTERN
BG GROUP
BHP BILLITON
BIFFA
BLACK & DECKER
BLACKBERRY
BLOOMBERG
BLUE ARROW
BMA (BRITISH MEDICAL ASSOCIATION)
BMI
BNP PARIBAS
BOC GASES
BOEING
BOMBARDIER
BOOKER
BOOZ & COMPANY
BOSCH
BOSTON CONSULTING GROUP
BP
BRISTOL-MYERS SQUIBB
BRITISH AIRWAYS
BRITISH CHAMBERS OF COMMERCE
BRITISH COUNCIL
BRITISH DENTAL ASSOCIATION
BRITISH GAS BUSINESS
BRITISH GYPSUM
BRITISH LAND
BRITISH RETAIL CONSORTIUM
BROOK STREET
BROTHER
BRUNSWICK
BSI (BRITISH STANDARDS INSTITUTION)
BT
BUDGET
BUPA
BURSON-MARSTELLER
BUSINESS DESIGN CENTRE

CABLE & WIRELESS WORLDWIDE
CALOR
CAMBRIDGE JUDGE BUSINESS SCHOOL
CANARY WHARF GROUP
CANON
CAPGEMINI
CAPITA
CARAT
CARBON TRUST
CARILLION
CARPHONE WAREHOUSE
CASIO
CASS BUSINESS SCHOOL
CASTROL
CATERPILLAR
CB RICHARD ELLIS
CBI (CONFEDERATION OF
    BRITISH INDUSTRY)
CHARTERED MANAGEMENT INSTITUTE
CHUBB
CIMA (CHARTERED INSTITUTE OF
    MANAGEMENT ACCOUNTANTS)
CIPD (CHARTERED INSTITUTE OF
    PERSONNEL & DEVELOPMENT)
CISCO
CITI
CITRIX
CITY & GUILDS
CITY LINK
CLEAR CHANNEL
CLIFFORD CHANCE
COMPARETHEMARKET.COM
COMPASS GROUP
CONFUSED.COM
CONQUEROR
COSTAIN
COSTCO
COSWORTH
CRANFIELD SCHOOL OF MANAGEMENT
CREDIT SUISSE
CROWN TRADE PAINTS
CROWNE PLAZA
D&B
DE LA RUE
DE VERE VENUES
DELL
DELOITTE
DEUTSCHE BANK
DEWALT
DHL
DOW CHEMICALS
DOW CORNING
DRAPER
DRAPERS
DULUX TRADE
DUPONT
DURHAM BUSINESS SCHOOL
E.ON UK
EADS
EALING STUDIOS
EASYJET
EBAY
EDDIE STOBART
EDF ENERGY
EGON ZEHNDER INTERNATIONAL
ELI LILLY
ELSTREE STUDIOS
ENTERPRISE
EPSON
EQUIFAX
ERICSSON
ERNST & YOUNG
EUROPCAR
EUROSTAR
EUROTUNNEL
EVERSHEDS
EXCEL LONDON
EXPERIAN
EXXON MOBIL
FEDERATION OF SMALL BUSINESSES
FEDEX
FIDELITY
FIRST
FLIGHT INTERNATIONAL
FLYBE
FRESHFIELDS BRUCKHAUS DERINGER
FTSE
FUJITSU
FUJITSU TECHNOLOGY SOLUTIONS
G4S
GALLUP
GARMIN
GATWICK AIRPORT
GATWICK EXPRESS
GE
GENERAL DYNAMICS UK
GETTY IMAGES
GFK NOP
GKN
GLAXOSMITHKLINE
GLENCORE INTERNATIONAL
GOCOMPARE.COM
GOLDMAN SACHS

GOOGLE
GRANT THORNTON
GREAT PORTLAND ESTATES
GREEN FLAG
GROSVENOR
GULFSTREAM
HANSON
HAPAG-LLOYD
HARGREAVES LANSDOWN
HARRIS
HARRIS INTERACTIVE
HARROGATE INTERNATIONAL CENTRE
HAWKER SIDDELEY SWITCHGEAR
HAY GROUP
HAYMARKET NETWORK
HAYS
HEATHROW AIRPORT
HEATHROW EXPRESS
HENLEY BUSINESS SCHOOL
HERBERT SMITH
HERTZ
HILL & KNOWLTON
HILTI
HILTON
HISCOX
HITACHI
HOLIDAY INN
HONEYWELL
HOOVER'S
HOTELS.COM
HOWDEN
HOWDENS JOINERY
HP
HRG (HOGG ROBINSON GROUP)
HSBC
HSS HIRE
IBIS
IBM GLOBAL BUSINESS SERVICES
ICAEW (THE INSTITUTE OF CHARTERED
    ACCOUNTANTS IN ENGLAND
    & WALES)
ICM RESEARCH
IMPERIAL COLLEGE BUSINESS SCHOOL
INFOSYS
INGERSOLL RAND
INITIAL
INTEL
INTERBRAND
INTERLINK EXPRESS
INVENSYS
INVESTEC
INVESTORS IN PEOPLE
IOD (INSTITUTE OF DIRECTORS)
IPSOS MORI
J.P. MORGAN
JANE'S
JC DECAUX
JCB
JEWSON
JIFFY
JOHN LAING
JOHNSON & JOHNSON
JOHNSON MATTHEY
JOHNSTONE'S TRADE PAINTS
JONES LANG LASALLE
JUPITER
JWT LONDON
KALL KWIK
KIER GROUP
KIMBERLEY-CLARK PROFESSIONAL
KITEMARK
KNIGHT FRANK
KOMATSU UK
KONICA MINOLTA
KPMG
KUEHNE + NAGEL
LAFARGE
LAND SECURITIES
LATEROOMS.COM
LENOVO
LETTS
LEXISNEXIS
LEXMARK
LEYLAND TRADE PAINTS
LG
LIFFE
LINKEDIN
LINKLATERS
LLOYDS
LLOYD'S OF LONDON
LOCKHEED MARTIN
LOGICA
LOGITECH
LONDON BUSINESS SCHOOL
LONDON CITY AIRPORT
LONDON METAL EXCHANGE
LONDON SCHOOL OF ECONOMICS
    AND POLITICAL SCIENCE
LONDON STOCK EXCHANGE
M&C SAATCHI
MAERSK LINE
MAKITA
MAKRO

MALMAISON
MANCHESTER BUSINESS SCHOOL
MANPOWER
MARKETING WEEK
MARRIOTT
MARSHALLS
MASSEY FERGUSON
MASTERCARD
MCAFEE
MCCANN-LONDON
MCKINSEY & COMPANY
MEDIACOM
MERCER
MERCK
MERRILL LYNCH
MICHAEL PAGE INTERNATIONAL
MICROSOFT
MICROSOFT ADVERTISING
MILLENNIUM & COPTHORNE
MILLWARD BROWN
MINTEL
MITSUBISHI ELECTRICS
MONEYSUPERMARKET.COM
MONSTER
MOODY'S
MORGAN STANLEY
MOTOROLA
NATIONAL
NATIONAL EXPRESS
NATIONAL FARMERS UNION (NFU)
NATIONAL GRID
NATWEST
NEC
NETGEAR
NETJETS
NICEDAY
NIELSEN
NOKIA
NORTHROP GRUMMAN
NORTON
NOVARTIS
NOVOTEL
NPOWER
O2
OFFICE ANGELS
OFFICE DEPOT
OGILVY & MATHER
OLYMPUS
ORACLE
ORANGE
OXFORD BLACK N' RED
PA CONSULTING
PANASONIC
PARCELFORCE WORLDWIDE
PARK PLAZA
PAYPAL
PC WORLD BUSINESS
PEARL & DEAN
PFIZER
PHILIPS HEALTHCARE
PILKINGTON
PINEWOOD STUDIOS GROUP
PITNEY BOWES
PORTAKABIN
POWWOW
PRATT & WHITNEY
PREMIER INN
PRESS ASSOCIATION
PRICEWATERHOUSECOOPERS
PRIMELOCATION.COM
PRONTAPRINT
PRUDENTIAL
PUBLICIS LONDON
QINETIQ
RAC
RACKSPACE
RADISSON EDWARDIAN
RAYTHEON SYSTEMS
REDWOOD PUBLISHING
REED
REED ELSEVIER
REGUS
RENTOKIL
REXEL
RIBA (ROYAL INSTITUTE OF
    BRITISH ARCHITECTS)
RICOH
RICS (ROYAL INSTITUTION OF
    CHARTERED SURVEYORS)
RIGHTMOVE.COM
RIO TINTO
ROCHE
ROLLS-ROYCE GROUP
ROTHSCHILD
ROYAL MAIL
RS COMPONENTS
RSA
RYMAN
SAATCHI & SAATCHI
SAGE
SAID BUSINESS SCHOOL,
    UNIVERSITY OF OXFORD
SAINT-GOBAIN

SALESFORCE.COM
SAMSUNG
SANDISK
SANTANDER
SAP
SAVILLS
SCHRODERS
SCOTTISH POWER
SCREWFIX
SEAGATE TECHNOLOGY
SECURITAS
SERCO
SHARP
SHELL
SIEMENS
SIR ROBERT MCALPINE
SITA
SKANDIA
SKANSKA
SKYPE
SLAUGHTER & MAY
SMITH & NEPHEW
SMITHS
SMURFIT KAPPA
SNAP-ON
SOCIETY OF MOTOR MANUFACTURERS
    AND TRADERS (SMMT)
SODEXO
SOIL ASSOCIATION
SONY PROFESSIONAL
STABILO
STAEDTLER
STAGECOACH
STANDARD & POOR'S
STANLEY
STAPLES
STRUTT & PARKER
SWISS RE
SYMANTEC
TALKTALK BUSINESS
TARMAC
TATA STEEL EUROPE
TETRA PAK
THALES
THAMES WATER
THE BANKER
THE CO-OPERATIVE BANK
THE FAIRTRADE FOUNDATION
THE GROCER
THE ICC BIRMINGHAM
THE LAW SOCIETY
THE LAWYER
THE MET OFFICE
THE NEC BIRMINGHAM
THE OPEN UNIVERSITY
    BUSINESS SCHOOL
THE QUEEN ELIZABETH II
    CONFERENCE CENTRE
THOMSON LOCAL
THOMSON REUTERS
THYSSENKRUPP
T-MOBILE
TNS RESEARCH INTERNATIONAL
TNT
TOMTOM
TOSHIBA
TOTAL
TOTALJOBS.COM
TRAVELEX
TRAVELODGE
TRAVIS PERKINS
UBS
UNIPART
UNISYS
UNIX
UPS
USWITCH
VENT-AXIA
VEOLIA ENVIRONMENTAL SERVICES
VIKING
VIRGIN ATLANTIC
VIRGIN MEDIA BUSINESS
VIRGIN TRAINS
VISA
VODAFONE
VOLVO CONSTUCTION EQUIPMENT
WALES MILLENNIUM CENTRE
WARWICK BUSINESS SCHOOL
WEBER SHANDWICK
WEIR
WESTFIELD
WICKES
WINCANTON
WOLFF OLINS
WOLSELEY
WOOLMARK
WUNDERMAN
XEROX
YAHOO! ADVERTISING SOLUTIONS
YALE
YELLOW PAGES
ZENITHOPTIMEDIA
ZURICH

Please note that some brand names have been changed since the research was conducted. These lists reflect the brands as they are generally marketed (at the time of going to press) and may differ slightly from the name analysed in the survey.

Qualifying Consumer Superbrands

AA
ADIDAS
AEG
AFTER EIGHT
AGA
AIRFIX
ALFA ROMEO
ALKA-SELTZER
ALTON TOWERS
AMAZON.CO.UK
AMBRE SOLAIRE
AMBROSIA
AMERICAN EXPRESS
ANADIN
ANCHOR
ANDREX
APPLE
ARGOS
ARIEL
ARSENAL FC
ASDA
AUDI
AUNT BESSIE'S
AUSTIN REED
AUTOGLASS
A-Z MAPS
B&Q
BACARDI
BAILEYS
BANG & OLUFSEN
BARBIE
BARCLAYCARD
BARCLAYS
BBC
BECK'S
BEECHAMS
BEN & JERRY'S
BENADRYL
BENYLIN
BERGHAUS
BIRDS EYE
BIRKENSTOCK
BISTO
BLACK & DECKER
BLACKBERRY
BLAUPUNKT
BMW
BOLD
BOMBAY SAPPHIRE
BONJELA
BOOTS
BOSCH
BOSE
BP
BRABANTIA
BRANSTON
BRAUN
BRIDGESTONE
BRITA
BRITAX
BRITISH AIRWAYS
BRITISH GAS
BRITVIC
BT
BUDWEISER
BULMERS
BUPA
BUXTON
CADBURY
CALPOL
CALVIN KLEIN
CAMBRIDGE UNIVERSITY PRESS
CAMPBELL'S
CANON
CAPITAL FM
CARLING
CARLSBERG
CARTE D'OR
CARTE NOIRE
CASTROL
CATHEDRAL CITY
CENTER PARCS
CESAR
CHAMPNEYS
CHANEL
CHANNEL 4
CHELSEA FC
CHIVAS REGAL
CIF
CLARINS
CLARKS
CLASSIC FM
CLINIQUE
CNN
COCA-COLA
COLGATE
COLLINS
COLMAN'S
COMFORT
CONTINENTAL TYRES

COSTA
COURVOISIER
COW & GATE
CRABTREE & EVELYN
CRAYOLA
CROWN PAINTS
CROWNE PLAZA
CUNARD
DAIRYLEA
DAZ
DE VERE
DEBENHAMS
DEEP HEAT
DELL
DETTOL
DIESEL
DIOR
DISCOVERY
DISNEY
DISNEY CHANNEL
DKNY
DOMESTOS
DOUWE EGBERTS
DOVE
DR MARTENS
DUCATI
DULUX
DUNLOP
DURACELL
DUREX
DYSON
EA GAMES
EARLY LEARNING CENTRE
EBAY
EDEN PROJECT
EDF ENERGY LONDON EYE
ELASTOPLAST
ELECTROLUX
ELIZABETH ARDEN
ENCYCLOPÆDIA BRITANNICA
ESTÉE LAUDER
EUROSTAR
EVIAN
FACEBOOK
FAIRTRADE
FAIRY
FAMOUS GROUSE
FANTA
FEBREZE
FELIX
FERRERO ROCHER
FINANCIAL TIMES
FINISH
FISHER-PRICE
FLASH
FLORA
FLYMO
FORD
FOSTER'S
FOX'S
FREEVIEW
FRENCH CONNECTION
GALAXY
GAP
GARNIER
GAVISCON
GHD
GILLETTE
GLENFIDDICH
GLENMORANGIE
GOODYEAR
GOOGLE
GORDON'S
GREEN & BLACK'S
GROLSCH
GUINNESS
HÄAGEN-DAZS
HALFORDS
HALIFAX
HAMLEYS
HARD ROCK CAFE
HARDYS
HARPIC
HARVEY NICHOLS
HEAD & SHOULDERS
HEART
HEINEKEN
HEINZ
HELLMANN'S
HELLY HANSEN
HENNESSY
HIGHLAND SPRING
HILTON
HOLIDAY INN
HOMEPRIDE
HONDA
HOOVER
HORLICKS
HORNBY
HOTEL CHOCOLAT

HOUSE OF FRASER
HOVIS
HP
HP (SAUCE)
HSBC
HUGGIES
HUGO BOSS
IAMS
IKEA
IMODIUM
IMPERIAL LEATHER
INNOCENT
INTERFLORA
ITV
J2O
JACK DANIEL'S
JACOB'S
JACOB'S CREEK
JAEGER
JAFFA CAKES
JAGUAR
JAMESON
JCB
JEAN PAUL GAULTIER PERFUMES
JOHN LEWIS
JOHN SMITH'S
JOHN WEST
JOHNNIE WALKER
JOHNSON'S
KAREN MILLEN
KELLOGG'S
KENCO
KENWOOD (KITCHEN APPLIANCES)
KETTLE CHIPS
KINGSMILL
KIT KAT
KLEENEX
KODAK
KRONENBOURG 1664
KUONI
KWIK-FIT
LADBROKES
LADYBIRD
LANCÔME
LAND ROVER
LE CREUSET
LEA & PERRINS
LEGO
LEGOLAND
LEMSIP
LENOR
LEVI'S
LEXUS
LG
LINDEMANS
LINDT
LIVERPOOL FC
LLOYDS
LONELY PLANET
LONGLEAT
L'ORÉAL PARIS
LURPAK
LYLE'S GOLDEN SYRUP
LYNX
MACLAREN
MACLEANS
MADAME TUSSAUDS
MAGNERS IRISH CIDER
MAGNUM
MALTESERS
MAMAS & PAPAS
MANCHESTER UNITED
MARIGOLD
MARKS & SPENCER
MARMITE
MARRIOTT
MARS
MARTINI
MASTERCARD
MAX FACTOR
MB GAMES
MCCAIN
MCDONALD'S
MCVITIE'S
MERCEDES-BENZ
MICHELIN
MICHELIN TRAVEL GUIDES & MAPS
MICROSOFT
MIELE
MINI
MIRACLE-GRO
MOLTON BROWN
MONOPOLY
MONSOON
MORRISONS
MOTHERCARE
MR KIPLING
MR MUSCLE
MR SHEEN
MSN

MÜLLER
NATIONAL EXPRESS
NATIONAL GEOGRAPHIC
NATIONWIDE
NEFF
NESCAFÉ
NEUTROGENA
NEW COVENT GARDEN FOOD CO.
NEXT
NICORETTE
NIGHT NURSE
NIKE
NIKON
NINTENDO
NIVEA
NOKIA
NUROFEN
O2
ODEON
OLAY
OLD SPECKLED HEN
OLYMPUS
OMEGA
OPTREX
ORAL-B
ORANGE
OXFORD UNIVERSITY PRESS
OXO
P&O CRUISES
P&O FERRIES
PAMPERS
PANADOL
PANASONIC
PAUL SMITH
PAYPAL
PC WORLD
PEDIGREE
PEPSI
PERNOD
PERRIER
PERSIL
PG TIPS
PHILADELPHIA
PHILIPS
PIMM'S
PIRELLI
PIRITON
PLAY-DOH
PLAYSTATION
PLEDGE
POST OFFICE
PREMIER INN
PRET A MANGER
PRINGLE
PRINGLES
PUMA
PURINA
QUAKER OATS
RAC
RADIO TIMES
RADISSON EDWARDIAN
RADOX
RALEIGH
RALPH LAUREN
RAY-BAN
RED BULL
REEBOK
RÉMY MARTIN
REVLON
RIBENA
RIMMEL LONDON
ROBINSONS
ROLEX
ROTARY
ROUGH GUIDES
ROWNTREE'S
ROYAL ALBERT HALL
ROYAL CARIBBEAN INTERNATIONAL
ROYAL DOULTON
RYVITA
SAINSBURY'S
SAMSONITE
SAMSUNG
SANDALS
SANTANDER
SAVLON
SCALEXTRIC
SCHOLL
SCHWARZKOPF
SCHWEPPES
SEGA
SEIKO
SELFRIDGES
SENSODYNE
SEVEN SEAS
SHEBA
SHELL
SHREDDED WHEAT
SIEMENS
SILENTNIGHT BEDS

SILVER CROSS
SILVER SPOON
SINGER
SKY
SLUMBERLAND
SMEG
SMIRNOFF
SONY
SONY ERICSSON
SOUTHERN COMFORT
SPECSAVERS
STANLEY
STANNAH STAIRLIFTS
STARBUCKS
STELLA ARTOIS
STREPSILS
SUDAFED
SUDOCREM
SURE
SWATCH
TAG HEUER
TAMPAX
TATE & LYLE CANE SUGAR
TATE
TCP
TED BAKER
TEFAL
TERRY'S
TESCO
TETLEY
TEXACO
THE BODY SHOP
THE CO-OPERATIVE
THE DAILY TELEGRAPH
THE ECONOMIST
THE GLENLIVET
THE GUARDIAN
THE INDEPENDENT
THE NATIONAL LOTTERY
THE NORTH FACE
THE O2
THE TIMES
THOMAS COOK
THOMSON HOLIDAYS
THORPE PARK
TIMBERLAND
T-MOBILE
TOBLERONE
TOMMEE TIPPEE
TOMTOM
TOMY
TONI&GUY
TOYOTA
TROPICANA
TUPPERWARE
TWININGS
TWITTER
UMBRO
UNCLE BEN'S
VANISH
VASELINE
VICKS
VIDAL SASSOON
VIRGIN ATLANTIC
VIRGIN HOLIDAYS
VIRGIN MEDIA
VIRGIN TRAINS
VISA
VODAFONE
VOLKSWAGEN
VOLVIC
VOLVO
WAITROSE
WALKERS
WALL'S
WALL'S ICE CREAM
WARBURTONS
WATERFORD
WATERSTONES
WD-40
WEDGWOOD
WEETABIX
WERTHER'S ORIGINAL
WHIRLPOOL
WHISKAS
WHITTARD OF CHELSEA
WHSMITH
WIKIPEDIA
WILKINSON SWORD
WILLIAM HILL
WINALOT
WOLF BLASS
WONDERBRA
WRANGLER
XBOX
YAHOO!
YELLOW PAGES
YORKSHIRE TEA
YOUTUBE
ZANUSSI